ELLIOT B. GOSE, JR is a member of the Department of English at the University of British Columbia.

James Joyce gave a life to *Ulysses* which is still felt today, after the shock of its realism and the dislocation of its techniques have been absorbed into the traditions they helped to establish. This study demonstrates the sources of that life, how Joyce's characters go through the conflicts he himself experienced and how Joyce was concerned not only with the grotesque potential of life but also with its comic dimension, attempting to transmit that 'feeling of joy' which he adopted early as his artistic commitment.

Joyce's belief in the malleability and resilience of man's physical and spiritual nature attracted him to the transformation process as a technique for fiction and as an expression of his belief that we need to be linked with both our higher and lower natures, that the soul is transformed by its immersion in the life of the body. Integrating the views of Giordano Bruno and Sigmund Freud into his thought and art, Joyce balanced the grotesque and the comic, the realistic and the idealistic, the psychological and the spiritual.

Professor Gose traces in detail the development of the two important transformation processes in which Joyce involved Stephen Dedalus and Leopold Bloom. He also demonstrates Joyce's conception of the artist as necessarily involved in such a process himself. Joyce understood the psychopathology of everyday life; he also came to value and make a central concern of his art mankind's residence in the matrix of the bodily functions.

Grotesque physical transformations are an important part of *Ulysses*. In the Nighttown episode Joyce combined the grotesque with the comic to purge Bloom's emotions, and the reader's. Essential as purging was to Joyce, however, he used it only as a preparation for the joyful affirmation of the last two episodes. Joyce reconciles his reader to the comedy of life by providing a cosmic view of our connection with the stars and our own corpuscles, with an eternal process in which our spirits naturally progress through all the forms of the universe. Elliott Gose offers a brilliant interpretation of this high and humane vision, and the transformation processes through which it is expressed.

ELLIOTT B. GOSE, JR

The Transformation Process in Joyce's Ulysses

UNIVERSITY OF TORONTO PRESS
Toronto Buffalo London

Toronto Buffalo London
Printed in Canada

Canadian Cataloguing in Publication Data

Gose, Elliott B., 1926-
The transformation process in Joyce's *Ulysses*

Includes index.
ISBN 0-8020-5492-7

1. Joyce, James, 1882-1941. *Ulysses*. I. Title.

PR6019.09U6532 823'.912 C79-094900-8

Contents

Preface vii
Prologue xi

PART 1: INTRODUCTION 3
1 Joyce and Bruno 8
2 Material Universe and Spiritual Activity 20
3 The Round of Nature 38
4 Roads Parallel and Roads Contrary 50
5 Transformations of the Creator 61
6 The Comic Vision and the Grotesque 77

PART 2: INTRODUCTION 95
7 Conditioned Ego and Observing Self 102
8 The Image of the Artist: Destruction, Perversion, Creation 116
9 Comedy in 'Circe' 137
10 The Grotesque in 'Circe' 153
11 'Ithaca': Reduction and Sublimation 167
12 A Great Joker at the Universe 186

Notes 199
Index 220

Preface

In writing *Ulysses*, James Joyce aimed to include as much of the human body and the human spirit as his art and his insight would allow. He was attracted to what I call the transformation process because of his belief in the malleability and resilience of man's physical and spiritual nature. That process offered him not only a technique for creating a fiction but also a vehicle for his belief that man needs to be linked with both his higher and his lower nature. In fact, once the two poles are connected the valuation implied by 'high' and 'low' tends to blur.

The images associated with these poles of man's nature are god and animal. As a youth in Dublin, Joyce was stimulated by reading Giordano Bruno, the Renaissance philosopher who spoke of animal qualities in human 'voices, gestures, affects, and inclinations.' Bruno also traced 'the mutation of various affects that Jove, the soul, and man incur, finding themselves in this fluctuating matter' (*The Expulsion of the Triumphant Beast*). The fluctuations of matter, an ebb and flow through the forms of nature, fall into patterns such as birth, struggle, spasm, and death; these patterns are accompanied by mutations of feeling and vision, moods of exaltation, and despair. Such artistically patterned mutations became the transformation processes I shall be tracing in *Ulysses*.

Sigmund Freud was also fascinated with process, with those distortions (as he saw them) by which unconscious impulse and desire are transformed so that they may make their appearance in consciousness through dreams, jokes, and slips of the tongue. In Trieste and Zürich, Joyce gained a knowledge of these transformations which he then used in constructing *Ulysses*. Freud was more thorough and circumstantial than Bruno in tracing man's roots to his animal nature. Focussing on the pathology of the psyche, Freud believed it was right for society to divert those lower impulses to more civilized ends. Joyce the religious iconoclast would have approved Freud's hostility towards established religion, but Joyce the former Catholic retained a spiritual concern which could find its model in Bruno's heterodox affirmations of the divine. At the risk of excommunication, Bruno in Switzerland, France, England, and Germany developed his belief in the individual soul as containing God, in any individual being a potentially enlightened exemplar of divine intelligence and power.

Integrating the views of Bruno and Freud into his thought and art, Joyce had to balance the realistic and the idealistic, the psychological and the spiritual, the grotesque and the comic. Man's connection with the animal on the one hand grounds him on earth, while on the other it exposes him to the risk of grotesque devolution. Joyce's own strong sense of the animal in man encouraged him to adopt Bruno's and Freud's concern with it for both thematic and technical ends. Grotesque transformations are therefore an important part of the art of *Ulysses*.

But the grotesque is only one pole; Joyce created *Ulysses* as a comedy according to his early notion of that form: 'the feeling which is proper to the comic art is the feeling of joy' ('The Paris Notebook,' 1903). Now that the initial outrage at the 'filthiness' of the book has been succeeded by the relaxed acceptance of a more permissive age, now that the solemnity of Freudian symptom-hunting has lost its cachet, I believe it is time for a fuller look at *Ulysses* as joyful comedy. As suggested, Joyce received from Freud an insight into the sources of the comic. Perhaps more important, he inferred from Freud a rationale for joking that was compatible with Aristotle: the notion of purging which I see him using in the Nighttown scene – the dramatic and comic climax of the book. (If it be objected that Aristotle discussed purging as characteristic of tragedy rather than comedy, it may be replied that Joyce in his early note on the *Poetics* concluded that 'tragedy is the imperfect manner and comedy the perfect manner of art.')

Important though purging was to Joyce's art, it consists only in eliminating what is not wanted. Bruno served as a corrective to Freud, providing a prospective for affirming what is wanted. His view was comic in the sense that the *Divine Comedy* was: at their best his dialogues reconcile us to our part in the comedy of this world by giving us a cosmic view of man's connection with the stars, with an eternal process in which man's spirit progresses naturally through all the forms of the universe. If we have a bestial side, that is cause not for pessimism but for optimism: Since the bestial is only one point on the continuum of experience we can be confident also of experiencing godhead, when each soul shall shine forth like a star. A Freudian purging dominates the transformation process that Stephen and Bloom experience in Nighttown, but a Brunian reduction and sublimation dominate the question and answer mode of describing their later arrival at Bloom's house. Just as Joyce's concept of man encompassed both the animal and the divine, so his idea of the comic included both purging and affirmation, both the reductive and the sublime.

It is this breadth of vision which has made *Ulysses* last after the shock of its realism and the dislocation of its techniques have been absorbed into the continuity of the traditions they helped establish. This humane vision, along with the transformation processes in which it is embodied, constitute the basis on which I have tried to build this study.

ACKNOWLEDGEMENTS

I owe thanks to the library of the University of British Columbia for obtaining several books and theses for me. I have appreciated the co-operativeness and friendliness of the staff there over a number of years. To my typist, Mrs Doreen Todhunter, I also owe a debt, not only for efficient work, cheerfully performed, but for her helpful knowledge of scholarly forms (including spelling). My greatest personal debt is once again to my wife, Kathleen, who helped me recast early versions of these chapters. Her faith in the worth of the book lighted its path and lightened mine.

I must also express my appreciation to the Canada Council for two travel grants to visit Ireland. Although the results of my research in Dublin are visible mainly in notes, they added an important dimension both to me and to this work. I am also grateful to the Canada Council for a Senior Fellowship in 1971-2. This, combined with a year's study leave granted by the University of British Columbia, enabled me to write the first draft of the book. This book has been published with the assistance of grants from the Canadian Federation for the Humanities, using funds provided by the Canada Council, and from the Publications Fund of the University of Toronto Press.

For material quoted in this book, I am indebted as follows: From *Ulysses* by James Joyce. Copyright 1914, 1918 by Margaret Caroline Anderson and renewed 1942, 1946 by Nora Joseph Joyce. Reprinted by permission of Random House, Inc. and The Bodley Head. From *The Critical Writings of James Joyce* (ed. by Ellsworth Mason and Richard Ellmann). By permission of Viking Penguin Inc., Faber and Faber, Ltd., and The Society of Authors as the literary representative of the Estate of James Joyce. From *James Joyce* by Richard Ellmann. Permission granted by Oxford University Press.

Prologue

In 1914, as James Joyce prepared himself for the writing of *Ulysses*, he bought a number of literary works, Flaubert's *Tentation de Saint Antoine*, for instance, a book which influenced both the dramatic structure of the Nighttown section and its reliance on phantasmagoric transformations. He also bought a non-literary book which provided him with more general principles for shaping the great work on which he embarked.[1] First published in 1907, Henri Bergson's *L'Evolution créatrice* attempted to reverse the deterministic direction of science by adding a spiritual and psychological dimension to the concept of evolution. It also undercut logical positivism by connecting progress with flux and individual choice. Equally important, Bergson attempted to demonstrate the inadequacy of traditional metaphysics, arguing, for instance, that Aristotle's concept of form is finally as rigid as Plato's Eternal Idea.

This latter point would have struck Joyce most forcibly, since he had been a champion of Aristotle, and a foe of Plato. During his stay in Paris in 1903, he studied Aristotle and wrote a brief aesthetic based on the *Poetics*.[2] Stephen Dedalus as we meet him in *Ulysses* in 1904 is also an admirer of Aristotle, but the Joyce who began writing *Ulysses* in 1914 had learned to temper that admiration. The plan for the novel which Joyce later gave his friends Herbert Gorman (his first biographer) and Stuart Gilbert (author of the first 'authorized' study of *Ulysses*) lists Aristotle as the rock and Plato as the whirlpool of the Scylla and Charybdis episode, each a threat to the hard-pressed mariner. Bloom as Ulysses is easily able to repel the claims of philosophy, as he does the particular qualities which Joyce associates with these two philosophers: dogma with Aristotle and mysticism with Plato. Stephen, another mariner, also rejects mysticism in the form of theosophy. Although he has broken with the dogma of the church establishment, he has more difficulty with the dogmatic Aristotle and his medieval successor Aquinas, both of whom he would like to make applicable to the twentieth century. In this scholastic aim, as in other characteristics, Stephen resembles the young Joyce. But Bergson's analysis would have made evident to the later Joyce why his early aesthetic position would produce a limited art.[3]

Before developing Bergson's views, I must say a few words about Joyce and how influences worked on him. We know that he claimed not to have an energetic imagination (envying Emily Brontë and W.B. Yeats for their imaginative power; *J.J.* 673). He prided himself, however, on his ability to develop the insights and techniques of others. As he once said to his friend, Frank Budgen, 'When you get an idea, have you ever noticed what I can make of it?'[4] In addition, he liked to champion unknown writers. His debt to Giambattista Vico and to Giordano Bruno for the structural principles of *Finnegans Wake* is by now well established. Both were little known in the English-speaking world of the 1920s. On the other hand, Joyce was less likely to acknowledge popular writers, even if their influence on him was strong. Although Bergson was still popular before World War I, Joyce clearly found himself sympathetic with the ideas advanced in *Creative Evolution*. I am not claiming that those ideas are germinal for *Ulysses*, but they did help Joyce develop his mature views about the intellect, about life as a process of transformation, about nothingness, about man's place in the universe, and about the importance of creativity and art.

In his criticism of Aristotle and Plato, Bergson is led to a contrast which expresses a key theme in his book: 'Ancient philosophy proceeds as the intellect does. It installs itself in the immutable, it posits only Ideas. Yet becoming exists: it is a fact. ... He who installs himself in becoming sees in duration the very life of things, the fundamental reality.'[5] In *Ulysses*, when Stephen Dedalus tests the world with his senses while walking on the strand (Proteus episode), he is attempting to leave the world of Ideas in order to experience the sensory flux of a more immediate given world. Later, in the library (Scylla and Charybdis episode), Stephen comes close to the idea of duration: 'Hold to the now, the here, through which all future plunges to the past' (p 186). Applied to the individual and his experience, Bergson's emphasis on becoming leads to an attenuation of personality reminiscent of Pater's famous conclusion to *The Renaissance*:

> Consciousness cannot go through the same state twice. The circumstances may still be the same, but they will act no longer on the same person, since they find him at a new moment of his history. Our personality, which is being built up each instant with its accumulated experience, changes without ceasing. By changing, it prevents any state, although superficially identical with another, from ever repeating it in its very depth. (p 8)

Stephen makes a similar point in the library: 'The mole on my right breast is where it was when I was born though all my body has been woven of new stuff time after time. ... So in the future ... I may see myself as I sit here now but by reflection from that which I shall be' (p 194). Obviously the two authors share a concern with change and its influence on the evanescence of experience and the relativity of identity.

Despite the fine phrases which Bergson and Joyce employ to describe the changing states of the individual, the notion itself is potentially a threat. If all is change, what is dependable? Stephen attacks this problem with a resounding paradox. In the library, he praises the church he has left, claiming it is 'founded irremovably because founded, like the world, macro- and micro-cosm, upon the void' (p 207). Later, in Bloom's house, Stephen restates this proposition, in the language of scholastic philosophy, making it an article of his own creed: 'He affirmed his significance as a conscious rational animal proceeding syllogistically from the known to the unknown and a conscious rational reagent between a micro- and a macrocosm ineluctably constructed upon the incertitude of the void' (p 697). Since Stephen's conscious rationality has not served him very well on 16 June 1904, this particular 'affirmation' invites doubt. That doubt is confirmed by a long analysis in *Creative Evolution*. At the beginning of the fourth chapter, Bergson probes the concept of the void or nothingness (*vide* or *néant*) and concludes that 'the idea of the absolute nought, in the sense of the annihilation of everything, is a self-destructive idea, a pseudo-idea, a mere word' (p 308). But this conclusion follows a thorough attempt to understand the likely origins of the idea. Of half a dozen versions of the concept that Bergson puts forward before discarding them, this one is close to Stephen's:

> If something has always existed, nothing must always have served as its substratum or receptacle, and is therefore eternally prior. A glass may have always been full, but the liquid it contains nevertheless fills a void. In the same way, being may have always been there, but the nought which is filled, and, as it were, stopped up by it, pre-exists for it none the less, if not in fact at least in right. In short, I cannot get rid of the idea that the full is an embroidery on the canvas of the void, that being is superimposed on nothing, and that in the idea of 'nothing' there is *less* than in that of 'something.' Hence all the mystery. (p 300)

Needless to say, Bergson is neither charmed nor satisfied with this mystery.

To penetrate it, he closes his eyes and cuts off all his other senses. But try as he will, he cannot extinguish the consciousness which observes this annihilation of the outer (or the inner) world. He concludes not only that there is always something left (an observer), but also that the sense of void is a dis-ease of consciousness when it has fallen between observation of the outer and the inner worlds. 'The void of which I speak, therefore, is, at bottom, only the absence of some definite object, which was here at first, is now elsewhere and, in so far as it is no longer in its former place, leaves behind it, so to speak, the void of itself' (p 306). I would argue that Bergson's test with closed eyes is one of the determinants of Stephen's comparable test in the Proteus episode. As he walks on the strand, Stephen closes his eyes and then wonders, 'Has all vanished'? He opens them and reassures himself, 'There all the time without you.'[6] Joyce also believed in the reality of the world our senses inform us of; despite his commitment to the fullness of the universe, however, he knew well Bergson's sense of the void.[7] But I believe he would have agreed with Bergson's conclusion that

> the full always succeeds the full, and ... an intelligence that ... had neither regret nor desire, whose movement was governed by the movement of its object, could not even conceive an absence or a void. The conception of a void arises here when consciousness, lagging behind itself, remains attached to the recollection of an old state when another state is already present. (p 307)

In other words, the intellect attempts to fix our consciousness of things. Since things are not themselves fixed, when they change the intellect feels deprived and frightens us with the idea of annihilation or the void. In reality our inner and outer worlds are always as full as they ever were, though each is constantly changing. Hence Bergson's distrust of the intellect and its metaphysical system; hence his emphasis on change in the world, on becoming in the mind.

We can now appreciate why Joyce after reading Bergson would have felt all the more convinced that Bloom rather than Stephen should be the hero of his novel. Stephen, as Joyce complained to his friend Frank Budgen, 'has a shape that can't be changed' (p 105). As an artistic creation, Stephen had been developed from childhood in *A Portrait of the Artist as a Young Man* into the disillusioned young adult of the beginning of *Ulysses*. When Joyce made this statement to Budgen, he had just finished the episode in which Bloom has lunch (Lestrygonians) and was developing other facets of his hero in the Ormond Bar (Sirens episode), at Barney Kiernan's (Cyclops), and on the strand (Nausicaa). But I believe Joyce's comment can be taken in another sense too. Because Stephen is only in his early twenties, he can be expected to change as he matures. On the other hand, Bloom, in his late thirties, cannot be expected to alter much as he moves into middle age. Yet the sense we have of the two is that Stephen's is a much more rigid personality than Bloom's. As an intellectual, Stephen is more at home in ideas than in everyday realities, more comfortable with the dialectical process than the process of becoming. Bloom, in contrast, is weak on dialectic and theory, although possessed of curiosity and a large (though undependable) number of facts. Like Ulysses, Bloom is resourceful, inventive, adaptable.

In developing his conception of Bloom's prototype, Joyce insisted that Ulysses was the only 'complete all-round character presented by any writer' (Budgen 15). This conception appears in *Ulysses* as one of the few sympathetic remarks that a Dubliner makes about Bloom: '– He's a cultured allroundman, Bloom is' (p 235). But his culture is actually as flawed as his science. He worries about both, off and on during the day, unclear about *voglio* and *parallax*, about the mathematical analysis of the musical scale or the law of falling bodies. His strength is his allroundness, what Budgen calls his plasticity, his flexibility, his ability to change to meet different circumstances. In Bergson's opposition, Bloom has installed himself in becoming, while Stephen has installed himself in the immutable. As we have seen, Stephen is trying to step out of the intellect, and in learning to appreciate Bloom may be moving in that direction. But he has far to go.

Bergson's attempt to dethrone the Idea as the final cause and goal of the universe grew from his desire to make change as respectable as the Eternal had been for so long in Western thought. As he summed it up, '*a self-sufficient reality*' may be found in '*duration*' (p 324). Practically, he believed, 'we must accustom ourselves to think being directly,' without letting metaphysics interpose 'the phantom of the nought' between ourselves and reality. 'Then the Absolute is revealed very near us and, in a certain measure, in us. It is of psychological and not of mathematical nor logical essence. It lives with us. Like us, but in certain aspects infinitely more concentrated and more gathered up in itself, it *endures*' (p 324). Bergson's position here would have appealed to Joyce for at least two reasons. First, the assertion that 'the Absolute is revealed very near us and, in a certain measure, in us' is almost a paraphrase of Giordano Bruno, whose philosophy had influenced Joyce profoundly in his youth. Second, Bergson's conception links the individual and the absolute, in a way Joyce as artist was committed to.

In fact, Bergson himself frequently drew a parallel between his theory of creative evolution and the creativity of the artist. Here, for instance, is how he builds on the connection between the Absolute and the notion of duration.

> The future is not altogether determined at the present moment[;] ... if it has for the consciousness that is installed in it absolute value and reality, it is because there is unceasingly being created in it ... something unforeseeable and new. ... *The duration of the universe must therefore be one with the latitude of creation which can find place in it.* (p 369)

He then offers this illustration:

> To the artist who creates a picture by drawing it from the depths of his soul, time is no longer an accessory; it is not an interval that may be lengthened or shortened without the content being altered. The duration of his work is part and parcel of his work. To con-

tract or to dilate it would be to modify both the psychical evolution that fills it and the invention which is its goal. The time taken up by the invention is one with the invention itself. It is the progress of a thought which is changing in the degree and measure that it is taking form. It is a vital process, something like the ripening of an idea. (p 370)

Bergson's emphasis on duration as a key to creation harmonizes with Joyce's success in creating *Ulysses*. By concentrating so many words on only one day, Joyce enforces on his reader the sense that 'the time taken up by the invention is one with the invention itself,' that the reader lives through that day, enduring all the mundane details which inform it. The reader is introduced to this sense of duration and becoming by experiencing the mind flow first of Stephen and then of Bloom, but as the novel progresses the 'vital process' intensifies until in the lying-in hospital (Oxen of the Sun episode), the reader goes through a recapitulation of what Joyce called 'faunal evolution,'[8] and in Nighttown (Circe episode) he follows Bloom through transformations to which Bergson's term, 'psychical evolution,' might well be applied.

The novel ends, of course, with the most famous of its streams of consciousness, the amorphous monologue of Molly Bloom, through which the reader swims in a flow of words somewhat lacking in form. A clue to Joyce's rationale for this episode (Penelope) may also be found in Bergson. The description of creation in the following passage may be taken as a description of Joyce's achievement through most of *Ulysses*, while the lapse of attention Bergson mentions could be applied to the effect not only of Molly's disjointed soliloquy but also of the drunken exit from the lying-in hospital, the fagged out perceptions in the cabman's shelter (Eumaeus episode), and Bloom's drifting off to sleep (at the end of the Ithaca episode):

We seize from within, we live at every instant, a creation of form, and it is just in those cases in which the form is pure, and in which the creative current is momentarily interrupted, that there is a creation of matter. Consider the letters of the alphabet that enter into the composition of everything that has ever been written: we do not conceive that new letters spring up and come to join themselves to the others in order to make a new poem. But that the poet creates the poem and that human thought is thereby made richer, we understand very well: this creation is a simple act of the mind, and action has only to make a pause, instead of continuing into a new creation, in order that, of itself, it may break up into words which dissociate themselves into letters which are added to all the letters there are already in the world. (pp 261-2)

Form is creation during which 'we put back our being into our will' (p 261). But if will relaxes, then attention lapses, and words lose meaning and form; in the analogy Bergson was developing, when life loses focus, 'there is a creation of matter' instead of form.

Joyce's conception of Molly Bloom perfectly exemplifies this distinction. As he wrote Frank Budgen after finishing Penelope, the episode 'seems to me to be perfectly sane full amoral fertilisable untrustworthy engaging shrewd limited prudent indifferent *Weib. Ich bin das Fleisch das stets bejaht*' (*Letters* I, 170). His deliberate description of the episode as a woman parallels the reader's experience of it; form and content coalesce in duration, but the result is less form than content or matter, as Joyce insists with his reference to 'das Fleisch.' The consciousness is limited and amoral because it lacks will; the reader experiences this limitation as a lack of focus most obviously in the unformed 'sentences' he encounters, but even in such particulars as the unclear references of male pronouns (men tend to be interchangeable to this shrewd fertilizable *Weib*). Yet the episode successfully endures. It is a triumph for Joyce, who managed to hold the balance between informed language and what Bergson calls a 'mere assemblage of materials' (p 261). It is also a triumph for the consciousness portrayed, for it does assert its will finally, in the *yeses* that end the book and in its conscious commitment to one male (Bloom) of all those that have flowed through it.

These two achievements are perfectly consonant with Bergson's theory of the use of words. They are mobile, he claimed, and that has allowed them 'to pass from one thing to another, has enabled them to be extended from things to ideas.'

> An intelligence which reflects is one that originally had a surplus of energy to spend, over and above practically useful efforts. It is a consciousness that has virtually reconquered itself. But still the virtual has to become actual. Without language, intelligence would probably have remained riveted to the material objects which it was interested in considering. It would have lived in a state of somnambulism, outside itself, hypnotized on its own work. Language has greatly contributed to its liberation. (p 175)

Language thus can aid the process of becoming, although it can also be used to describe a fixed philosophy of static forms.

Molly's consciousness is more concerned with the past than with the future. In this she resembles her creator, who spent much of his self-imposed exile from Dublin dwelling on the memory of his native city. Joyce would have found justification for this obsessive concern in *Creative Evolution*.

> Our duration is not merely one instant replacing another; if it were, there would never be anything but the present – no prolonging of the past into the actual, no evolution, no concrete duration. Duration is the continuous progress of the past which gnaws into the

future and which swells as it advances. And as the past grows without ceasing, so also there is no limit to its preservation. (pp 6-7)

Though preserved, the past is not readily available; memory presses upon consciousness, but it has difficulty finding entry.

All that we have felt, thought and willed from our earliest infancy is there, leaning over the present which is about to join it, pressing against the portals of consciousness that would fain leave it outside. The cerebral mechanism is arranged just so as to drive back into the unconscious almost the whole of this past, and admit beyond the threshold only that which can cast light on the present situation or further the action now being prepared – in short, only that which can give *useful* work. At the most, a few superfluous recollections may succeed in smuggling themselves through the half-open door. These memories, messengers from the unconscious, remind us of what we are dragging behind us unawares. (p 7)

This difficulty the past has in entering consciousness does not, however, mean that it is powerless to affect the present. 'Doubtless we think with only a small part of our past, but it is with our entire past, including the original bent of our soul, that we desire, will and act' (p 8). This power of the past is exemplified in the inability of Stephen Dedalus to escape the memory of his dead mother or the Catholic God, both of which he has consciously repudiated.

Bergson's evocation of the dynamics of conscious and unconscious thought condenses some of the insights being developed contemporaneously by Sigmund Freud. *Psychopathology of Everyday Life* (1904), for instance, rests on the assumption that the past is active in the mind, that unconscious desires determine much of what an individual does. (Specifically, this book, which was in Joyce's library, analyses what we now call the Freudian slip as an unconscious desire forcing its way through a door that consciousness has tried to keep closed.) This brief parallel between Bergson and Freud provides an opportunity to step back and look at the reason I have chosen to introduce a book concerned primarily with James Joyce by investigating a book he may be presumed to have read in 1914.

The answer lies in the complexity of Joyce's mind. Given a classic education, he retained a commitment to Aristotle and Aquinas. Possessed of an inquiring disposition, he explored both previous heresies and contemporary sceptical systems of thought. At the age of eighteen he delivered an impressive paper on 'Drama and Life' in which he made both hard-headed statements ('drama is strife, evolution, movement in whatever way unfolded; it exists, before it takes form, independently; it is conditioned but not controlled by its scene') and poetic suggestions ('I believe further that drama arises spontaneously out of life and is coeval with it').[9] The first excerpt blends Darwin with Ibsen. The second is an affirmation in a spirit which anticipates Bergson, who also attempted by a lyric rationality to reconcile the Darwinian and the spiritual. Freud, in his more hard-headed manner, tried to reconcile the scientific with the irrational. By generalizing in this fashion, I am trying to give a sense of the climate in which Joyce's literary ambitions took shape.

But my case for understanding Joyce and *Ulysses* is more particular, based on habits of mind and qualities of writing which are best understood through a consideration of Bruno as an early and acknowledged influence and of Freud as a later half-repudiated influence. Bergson contains elements of both, especially in his insistence on freeing the mind from bondage, a motif even more pronounced in the writings of Bruno and Freud (not to mention those of Joyce). Bergson's emphasis on change as the locus of reality, his insistence on inner and outer process as more vital than fixed forms, and his putting will 'into the impulsion it prolongs' all suggest 'that reality is a perpetual growth, a creation pursued without end' (p 261). Whether optimistically affirmed by Bruno, or more guardedly advocated by Freud, this insistence became the thoroughly worked-through premise of Joyce's later fiction.

Part 1

Introduction

In the first six chapters of this study, my aim is to demonstrate the importance to Joyce of a mode of vision which finds its epitome in the Renaissance philosopher, Giordano Bruno. This mode – seeing nature as the divine in a process of transformation – has its roots in a number of other thinkers with whom Joyce was also familiar, notably Ovid in his *Metamorphoses* and the early Christian mystic, Dionysius. What Bruno's exposition added was comprehensiveness of view and a style by turns colloquial and lyric, down to earth and exalted – a presentation which would have appealed greatly to Joyce when he read Bruno's Italian dialogues while at university.[1] Furthermore, it is clear that there was something about the personality and career of the former Dominican which attracted Joyce's sympathy.

Joyce's championing of Bruno has sometimes been taken as more show than substance. By referring to the philosopher as 'The Nolan,' Joyce was able to mystify his acquaintances at University College.[2] By praising a monk-turned-cosmologist who had been burned as a heresiarch, he could sustain his reputation for intellectual daring. But Bruno appealed to much deeper parts of Joyce's nature than this. As we shall see in Chapter 1, the young Joyce, like Bruno, desired to enlighten those who had been blinded by conventional authority. Like Bruno, he chose to become an exile from his native country rather than conform to its narrow religious and social norms. Also like Bruno, he then lived in several other countries; but unlike the nomadic Italian, Joyce finally settled in the last of these countries. Where Bruno returned to the land of his birth knowing that the Inquisition was still active there, Joyce refused to move back to Ireland, even when it had ceased to present any obvious threat to him. The grounds for his refusal are so irrational that they suggest another reason for emphasizing the importance of Bruno to him. Bruno was denounced to the Inquisition by his Venetian 'patron' and held in prison for seven years before being burned. Joyce always feared betrayal by a friend; his refusal to return to Ireland was based on fear of such treachery, of mutilation or death.[3] Joyce's brooding over a martyr's fate is clearly suggested in the biography that Herbert Gorman wrote under the active scrutiny of its subject. He records that Joyce's failure to have *Dubliners* published in his native city 'had intensified the bitterness he felt towards that city and its inhabitants. He was convinced that a conspiracy to crush him completely existed amongst his former companions in that lively centre of mingled religiosity and ruthlessness.'[4] Joyce's tendency towards paranoia was undoubtedly helped along by the small-mindedness of the Dublin publishers and printers, but it may have been augmented too by the fate of one of his models, Giordano Bruno.

Bruno had many qualities of mind that would have appealed to Joyce. Some of these are mentioned by W.Y. Tindall: 'A relapsed Dominican, who retained an affection for ritual while rejecting dogma, could not but appeal to the relapsed, ritualistic Jesuit, who felt himself martyred by the world. Like Bruno, Joyce was the coincidence of Catholic and heretic. ... *The Triumphant Beast*, in which Bruno attacks the Church's tyranny over mind and speech, expressed Joyce's own rebellion against authority, and a quotation from Bruno in *The Day of the Rabblement* (1901) supports Joyce's individualism.'[5] Bruno was, like Joyce, a good hater, as indicated by the paraphrase with which Joyce began the 'Rabblement' essay: 'No man, said the Nolan, can be a lover of the true or the good unless he abhors the multitude.'[6] A more elevated group that Bruno disliked were the scholastic grammarians of Oxford, whom he saw as 'slaves of definite and determined sounds and words.'[7] Like Joyce, Bruno prided himself on giving 'the appropriate name to him to whom Nature gives an appropriate being. He [the Nolan] does not call shameful that which Nature makes worthy' (*Expulsion* 71). Reading such sentiments in Bruno would clearly have encouraged Joyce in his early determination to embody earthy truth in new forms.

I shall emphasize throughout the book how Joyce's breakthrough in *Ulysses* is a matter of the interpenetration of truth and form, of content and shape. Truth for Joyce was not, of course, the received dogma of Catholicism. Nor did he substitute for it the absolute ideas of any Platonic system. The kind of truth that appealed to Joyce may be found in one of Bruno's favourite quotations from Ovid's *Metamorphoses*: 'all things change but nothing perishes.' Mutability ceases to be a Platonic defect; instead it allows truth to exist in all phases of life equally. From this view comes Bruno's emphasis on the transformation process with its broader relation to the universe than can be found in most doctrines, whether ego-centred, man-centred, or heaven-centred.

In Bruno's work, the dialogue form implies that truth evolves, grows out of opposition and questioning. In *The Expulsion of the Triumphant Beast*, for instance, different classical gods offer differing views on the problems involved in restructuring the heavens. The revision of old forms (such as the zodiac) is Bruno's *subject*, and the various views which culminate in a decision by the pantheon constitute Bruno's *form*. The result is a process, in which gods and readers have their preconceptions changed as they move through the dialogue.

In *Ulysses* this mode is greatly varied and intensified. Each chapter has a form 'appropriate' to its subject, and the reader must go through the process which Joyce with insistent thoroughness has embodied in his writing. The result may be that English syntax is distorted towards 'musical' form, as in the Ormond Bar scene (Sirens episode), or that the style turns towards sentimental ladies' literature to register the consciousness of a conventional, self-deceiving young woman, as in the evening scene on the strand (Nausicaa episode).

Equally important, there are a number of what might be called natural transformation cycles which Ovid and Bruno sketched in and which Joyce adapted to shadow forth the actual and desirable psychic evolution of a character.[8] Chapter 2 will trace in detail an important cycle connected with Stephen Dedalus. Chapter 3, after outlining two of Bruno's cycles and comparing one of them to a similar cycle created by Joyce, will conclude with a cycle that is central to the life of Leopold Bloom. Since the word 'cycle' and the phrase 'transformation process' are only abstractions at this point, I propose to conclude this introduction by considering two examples taken from Shakespeare, who was a contemporary of Bruno's.

In the graveyard scene at the opening of Act V of *Hamlet*, there is the following well-known exchange:

HAMLET: To what base uses we may return, Horatio! Why may not imagination trace the noble dust of Alexander, till he find it stopping a bung-hole?
HORATIO: 'Twere to consider too curiously, to consider so.
HAMLET: No, faith, not a jot; but to follow him thither with modesty enough, and likelihood to lead it; as thus: Alexander died, Alexander was buried, Alexander returneth into dust; the dust is earth; of earth we make loam, and why of that loam, whereto he was converted, might they not stop a beer-barrel?

Imperious Caesar, dead and turn'd to clay,
Might stop a hole to keep the wind away:
O! that that earth, which kept the world in awe,
Should patch a wall to expel the winter's flaw.

We have here a transformation process but not a cycle. The metaphor in the final couplet by which 'earth' can be used for 'flesh' is similar to the earth cycle in which we shall see Joyce involve Bloom later, but he gives it a positive twist by adding two other elements, water and fire. On the other hand, Bloom does get depressed during the day; one of the transformation processes that occurs to him in such a mood is therefore as dead as Hamlet's. 'Gasballs spinning about, crossing each other, passing. Same old dingdong always. Gas, then solid, then world, then cold, then dead shell drifting around, frozen rock like that pineapple rock. The moon. Must be a new moon, she said. I believe there is.'[9] But even in this lifeless landscape there is a hint of optimism, because pineapple rock gives nourishment (cf. *Ulysses* 151). Thus Bloom's mind inadvertently gives life to the dead 'frozen rock'; similarly, almost in spite of himself, he remembers the moon and Molly's comment 'must be a new moon.' The emphasis is even more clearly on rebirth here. The moon, in fact, like the movement of the seasons, provides a good example of a process which is also a cycle, that is a process which starts anew at its end.

The other transformation process which Hamlet traces is equally well-known and equally reductive:

KING: Now, Hamlet, where's Polonius?

HAMLET: At supper.

KING: At supper! Where!

HAMLET: Not where he eats, but where he is eaten: a certain convocation of politic worms are e'en at him. Your worm is your only emperor for diet: we fat all creatures else to fat us, and we fat ourselves for maggots: your fat king and lean beggar is but variable service; two dishes, but to one table: that's the end.

KING: Alas, alas!

HAMLET: A man may fish with the worm that hath eat of a king, and eat of the fish that hath fed of that worm.

KING: What does thou mean by this?

HAMLET: Nothing, but to show you how a king may go a progress through the guts of a beggar. (IV, 3)

Having killed Polonius half hoping he was the king, Hamlet is intentionally insulting in reducing a king to food in a beggar's intestines. Yet the underlying premise – that all life shares a common base and is thus interchangeable – can be taken optimistically, as it was by that proud but democratic philosopher, Giordano Bruno. Hamlet's filling out the process with fish as food in the sea parallels the cycle which comes into Stephen's mind when he too thinks of a dead man (cf. Chapter 2).

Also impressive in this scene from *Hamlet* is the way language and vision come together and lend one another vitality: 'A king may go a progress through the guts of a beggar.' Just as king and beggar are contrasted at either end of the clause, so the two nouns between them, 'progress' and 'guts,' are opposed in sound, appearance, and meaning. The progress, or king's 'journey of state' through his kingdom, is of course bounded by buildings on the streets, trees on the roads. But the transformation of these welcome channels into the walls of the intestines suddenly twists our eyesight out of its accustomed rut. My point is that the magic metamorphosis by which conventional eyesight becomes penetrating vision depends on exactly such curious considering as Horatio complained of. But in Hamlet's case, it is pathological vision because it can see only the reduction of a king to fodder or earth, and not the creation of life from loam and plants. In Shakespeare and Joyce, reduction is always present since destruction of the stereotypes is a necessary first step in the creation which is the artist's aim. But beyond that, we shall discover in *Ulysses* the constructive, a vision that relishes the sublime absurdities of life and the resilient spirit of man, a creative refusal to be dragged down by the natural shocks that flesh is heir to.

Ulysses has sometimes been taken as a reductive work, Homer's hero reduced to a modern ad canvasser, a mock king progressing through the guts of a beggarly city. I shall look at Joyce's image of Dublin as a human body in Chapter 3. But beyond this physical base it is important to be aware of other dimensions of *Ulysses*, its revelation of the heroic qualities possible in the everyday. As Richard Ellmann argues, 'Bloom can demonstrate the qualities of man by word of mouth as effectively as Ulysses by thrust of spear.' Furthermore, 'Bloom *is* Ulysses in an important sense.' Like Homer's hero confronting the Cyclops, Bloom, as Ellmann suggests, 'is a nobody ... yet there is god in him.'[10] We could therefore apply Hamlet's process in reverse, seeing Bloom's peregrinations through Dublin as a royal progress, watching him transformed into a king in the Nighttown scene, but also seeing him reduced to an animal there (since it corresponds to Homer's Circe episode). King or animal, like all other men, he has the potential within him to become the highest and the lowest, everything and nothing. A king may make no name for himself; a beggar may master the universe in imagination. Vision, will, and feeling are the qualities that determine the outcome in the life of a common man as in the work of an artist. These three qualities are therefore central in any attempt at understanding Joyce and his characters.

1 Joyce and Bruno

George Bernard Shaw saw the roots of his reformism, and of Charles Dickens's, in their being born into financially failing middle-class families. The same might be said of James Joyce, although his desire for social reform was more pronounced before his literary success than after. Like Shaw, Joyce had a father who drank and evaded work. Like Dickens, he grew up in a large family which lived in a series of increasingly shabby homes. Like both he was reserved and egocentric, though able to exercise a dramatic flair; his pride, like Dickens's, owed quite a bit to his consciousness of the penury and lack of social standing to which his father had brought the family. Set apart from other boys, when he first entered a boarding school, by his youth, delicacy, and lack of social standing, Joyce early determined to remain set apart, but by excelling. By the time he entered university, the pattern was set, but the stakes were higher, the competition keener.

He found himself among a lively-minded group of classmates. His temperament still sought ways of standing out, such as reading a paper to the Literary and Historical Society, a paper on drama which discussed Ibsen, who was at that time not read in Dublin though he was nevertheless condemned as immoral. Joyce's characteristically unpalatable choice of topic forced him to demonstrate an equally characteristic tenacity of purpose when the President of the College at first refused to let him read the paper. Joyce met this attempt at censorship by confronting the president and citing Aquinas against the objection that his paper lacked concern with 'the ethical content of drama' (*J.J.* 73). He was successful, but his paper was attacked from the floor by a number of students in the audience. These criticisms merely enabled Joyce to show his agile intellect and memory at the end of the evening, as he stood to answer each of his critics in a half-hour rebuttal delivered without notes.

Recognized by the more independent-minded students as a person worth cultivating, Joyce usually addressed these few peers with more humanity than he did his literary elders, the established writers of Dublin. His pride turned cold in the presence of Yeats, A.E., Moore, and Lady Gregory. Although the first two treated Joyce sympathetically, it is clear he deserved the judgment Yeats is supposed to have delivered on him: 'Never have I seen so much pretension with so little to show for it' (*J.J.* 105). Since Joyce admired Yeats as the greatest living Irish writer, his arrogant patronizing of the older poet can be seen as a defensive attempt to turn the tables on someone whose influence threatened to be too great. (He told Yeats at the end of a long talk, 'We have met too late. You are too old for me to have any effect on you.' *J.J.* 106). Yeats, at this point in his career, still carried an aura of the celtic twilight. Although he himself had begun to condemn myth and mysticism as escapes, any reader with a romantic bent would need a strong defence against the appeal of both his poetry and his prose. Joyce had such a bent, as is apparent in his own poetry. His Stephen Hero knows by heart every word of Yeats's occult story, 'The Tables of the Law.'[1] Part of Joyce's subsequent defence against this side of himself was to determine to write realistic prose – hence his admiration for Ibsen.

But at that point in his life, the determination was not matched by a clear sense of subject and form. His unequivocal manifesto was cast in verse. In 'The Holy Office' (1904), he attacked all forms of escapism, offering his earthiness as a necessary task, a holy office.

> But all these men of whom I speak
> Make me the sewer of their clique.
> That they may dream their dreamy dreams
> I carry off their filthy streams. (*Critical Writings* 151)

Earlier in the same year, Joyce had written a prose manifesto, less polemic, more lyric. This quasi-biographical essay was entitled 'A Portrait of the Artist' and served as the basis for both *Stephen Hero* (a long fragment of a novel published after Joyce's death) and its successor, *A Portrait of the Artist as a Young Man* (1914).

This early essay not only states themes that are important in Joyce's later work, it also provides a valuable insight into the mind that Joyce kept hidden from almost everyone around him. In the essay, Joyce says that this 'enigma of manner was put up at all comers to protect' the youth during a religious crisis which came to a head as he entered university.[2] Showing an admirable objectivity about the self of six years before, Joyce suggested that the youth's reserve 'was not without a satisfactory flavour of the heroic. It was part of that ineradicable egoism which he was afterwards to call redeemer that he imagined converging to him the deeds and thoughts of the microcosm' (p 61). This convergence brings us to the heart of

Joyce's early nature. A sensitive, spiritual boy of sixteen when he entered university, he was put off by the Church because it was too worldly. Preferring the 'poorer humbler orders' (p 60), he was attracted to St Francis and finally left the Church 'through the gates of Assisi' (p 63). But at the importuning of the imagination's microcosm, he then found the 'simple history' of St Francis also insufficient and turned to the mystic and the magus. Particularly Joachim of Floris and Giordano Bruno, among other 'hierarchs of initiation cast their spells upon him' (p 63). Under their guidance, the youth saw himself as becoming a spiritual leader of men. 'A thousand eternities were to be reaffirmed, divine knowledge was to be re-established. Alas for fatuity! as easily might he have summoned a regiment of the winds' (p 64). For his friends proved impervious to his vision. Although they complained of the rigidities of their church and society, they accepted bondage; 'their treasons were venial only' (p 64).

Turning from men, he found solace in solitude, in nature, and in women (the three seem synonymous or confused in this part of the document; pp 64-6). Solitary by the sea he awoke to what is outside. 'sceptically, cynically, mystically, he had sought for an absolute satisfaction and now little by little he began to be conscious of the beauty of mortal conditions' (p 65). In abandoning the inhuman search for the absolute, the youth as philosopher, mystic, and magus gave up that autonomous isolation by which he mistakenly emulated the gods. The implication is that that search had grown out of a recognition of the inadequacy of conditioned life, immediate experience, the perceptual world. By becoming 'conscious of the beauty of mortal conditions,' the youth ceased contemplating the absolute and returned to the world; this return gave him something to celebrate, something to which he could relate, a release for his feelings. He acquired the motive for becoming an artist.

We are now in a position to appreciate what Bruno would have meant to the Joyce who read his work as a university student. Occasionally in the Italian dialogues Bruno allows the voice of the magus to speak. 'Behold now, standing before you, the man who has pierced the air and penetrated the sky, wended his way amongst the stars and overpassed the margins of the world, who has broken down those imaginary divisions between the spheres.'[3] This appeal to a desire for absolute freedom is usually balanced in Bruno by the social criticism which supports it. He wished to aid any aspirant whose 'wings were clipped, so that he might not soar upwards through the cloudy veil to see what really lies beyond it and liberate himself from the foolish imaginations of those who ... have with many kinds of deceit imposed brutal follies and vices upon the world in the guise of virtues of divinity and discipline' (Yates 236-7). That influence is apparent in the high aspiration of Stephen Dedalus to fly out of Ireland. Stephen claims that, 'When the soul of a man is born in this country there are nets flung at it to hold it back from flight. You talk to me of nationality, language, religion. I shall try to fly by those nets.' (*Portrait* 203). Stephen differs from Bruno in desiring freedom for himself alone. As I have suggested, it appears to have been Joyce's failure in the role of magus which determined him to become an artist. Unlike the magus, who wants disciples for initiation, the artist speaks to humanity indirectly, through his works. Unlike the philosopher he refrains from teaching, preaching, or arguing directly; instead he creates a world where the laws of the cosmologist or the hidden reality of the mystic function unobtrusively, 'naturally.' Although Joyce abandoned Bruno's method of direct appeal, he was heavily influenced by his philosophy and spiritual views, as also by his belief in the heroic role of the truth-loving soul.[4]

Briefly, I believe that Bruno influenced Joyce in three key areas of Joyce's own genius: his ability to embody in his fiction a sense of the happenings of nature as interconnected, of the everyday as containing the eternal, of mind as microcosmos. In Bruno's dialogue, *Cause, Principle and Unity*, the well-intentioned seeker is urged to absorb the 'grandeur' of the divine first principle 'as far as is possible by wandering with the eyes of their well-regulated minds among those magnificent stars and luminous bodies which are so many habitable worlds, great animals, and most excellent deities, and which both seem and are innumerable worlds not much unlike that which contains us.'[5] The stars thus function spiritually and materially, literally and metaphorically. Bruno refuses to accept limitation: philosophy does not belong to the mere logician, religion to the idealist, science to the materialist, or cosmology to the geo-centrist.

From a lay point of view, the most obvious thing about the stars is not that they are worlds like our own.[6] We discern rather their pattern, as constellations on which we have projected the forms and the names of gods and beasts. The connection between animals and deities is made the subject of a dialogue by Bruno entitled *The Expulsion of the Triumphant Beast*, published in 1584, the same year as *Cause, Principle and Unity*. In the *Expulsion*, Jove has undertaken the task of purging heaven of the zodiac figures who have ruled it too long, and of setting in their place the prime virtues, Truth, Prudence, Judgment, and so on.[7] He is doing so because he realizes that he is aging and that the Great Year (of 36,000 years) is soon to end. But the action of Jove is not based on any neo-Platonic snobbery that abstractions are more virtuous than animals. On the contrary, the argument of Momus (the clear-thinking conscience of the gods) is that those who worship animals are more in touch with the nature of the universe than those who set their gods on Olympus. Momus says the Egyptians were right to 'honor live images of beasts,' to which a sympathetic listener responds, 'Natura est deus in rebus' (Nature is god in the form of a thing or puzzle). Momus continues his case:

Think thus, of the Sun in the Crocus, in the narcissus, in the heliotrope, in the rooster, in the lion; you must think thus of each of the gods for each of the species under various genera of the entity. Because just as Divinity descends in a certain manner, to the extent that one communicates with Nature, so one ascends to Divinity through Nature, just as by means of a life resplendent in natural things one rises to the life that presides over them.[8] (p 236)

In developing this Hermetic position, Bruno shows himself more Aristotelian than Platonic. Isis, who is in general agreement with Momus, interrupts him to point out that 'fate has ordained the vicissitude of shadows and light' but that 'the shadows would not be shadows' once they were properly known by the worshippers. Then 'these wise men' would know 'God to be in things, and Divinity to be latent in Nature, working and glowing differently in different subjects and succeeding through diverse physical forms, in certain arrangements, in making them participants in her, I say, in her being, in her life and intellect' (pp 236-7). Plato argued in the *Republic* that the shadows of the material world were to be spurned for the light of higher ideals. Aristotle opposed him in the *Metaphysica*, arguing that nothing is gained 'even if we suppose eternal substances, as the believers in Forms do, unless there is to be in them some principle which can cause change. ... There must then be such a principle whose very essence is actuality.'[9] If Aristotle in his last sentence sounds very much like an existentialist, Bruno on occasion sounds even more like one. In another dialogue, *The Heroic Frenzies*, one character asks another what Aristotle means in *The Physics* 'when he says that eternity is an instant and the whole of time is nothing but an instant.' The reply is 'if there were not the instant, there would not be time, for time in essence and substance is nothing more but an instant' (p 175). Elsewhere, Bruno is even more explicit: 'Nowhere is essence apart from existence; – nature is nothing but the virtue that is immanent (insita) in things.'[10] Holding this view, Bruno can insist that the stars are suns around which inhabited worlds spin, but that the figures those stars make are also true; he can be a literalist and a fabulist, can do justice to flesh and spirit, matter and form.

This brings us to the theory for which Bruno is best known among Joyce scholars, his belief in the coincidence of contraries.

It is a profound magic to know how to draw out the contrary after having found the point of union. To this end, poor Aristotle was tending in his thought when he posited privation, with which is united a certain disposition, as progenitor, parent, and mother of form; but he could not attain to it. He failed to arrive because he halted at the genus of opposition and remained shackled by it; he thus did not go down to the species of contrariety,

did not break through and set his eyes on the goal. Instead, he strayed wholly from the way by stating that contraries cannot actually come together in the same subject.
(*Cause* 149)

But, Bruno insisted, contraries do coincide, 'so that there is one primal foundation both of origin and of end. From this coincidence of contraries we deduce that ultimately it is divinely right to say and to hold that contraries are within contraries, wherefore it is not difficult to compass the knowledge that each thing is within every other' (*Infinite Universe* 369). For Bruno then, this paradoxical conclusion rests securely on the spiritual centre of his philosophy, the 'primal foundation' which makes it 'divinely right' to throw off the shackles of Aristotle's halting logic.

The implications of this position are perhaps best developed in *Cause, Principle and Unity*, where Bruno affirms that 'the universe is one, infinite, indivisible.'

And if in the infinite is found no differentiation, as of part from whole and as of one thing from another, certainly the infinite is one. In the comprehension of the infinite, no part is greater and no part is lesser, since any part however large conforms no more to the infinite's proportion than does any other part however small. In infinite duration hour does not differ from day, day from year, year from century, century from moment, since the moments and the hours are not more than the centuries, and the former have no less proportion than the latter to eternity. (p 136)

This approach brings him back implicitly to the coincidence of contraries and explicitly to the axiom on which that doctrine rests, the ultimate unity of material and spiritual, phenomena and divinity.

Here then we see how it is not impossible, but is necessary, for the best, the greatest, the maximum, the incomprehensible, to be all, because, as simple and indivisible, it can be all, is everywhere, is in all. And thus it has not been vainly said that Jove fills all things, inhabits all parts of the universe, is the centre of all that has being – one in all and that through which one is all. Which, being all things and comprising all being in itself, brings about that everything is in everything. (p 137)

Bruno is voicing here what must be acknowledged as a grand theme. The urge which can be found in most religions, to affirm the unity and connection of all things, is still present among cosmologists and scientific theorists in the twentieth century; scientific evidence is beginning to credit mankind with many responses to cosmic processes.[11] Bruno voiced the same intuition or drive at a time when religion could no longer silence science but before science had rationalized or denigrated religion. For this reason, his synthesis can appeal today not only to a scholar who sees it in terms of occult hermetism but to one who believes Bruno's philosophy is compatible with dialectical materialism.[12]

Having stated one of his noble themes, Bruno is about to launch on another, and one that also came to have great importance to Joyce.

> But you will say to me: Why then do things change? Why does particular matter constrain itself to other forms?
>
> I reply that there is not a change which seeks another being, but a change which seeks another mode of being. And this is what makes the difference between the universe and the things of the universe. The former comprises all being and all modes of being. Through the latter each thing has all being but not all the modes of being ... Every production of any sort whatever is an alteration, with the substance remaining always the same; for there is only one substance, one being divine and immortal.
>
> Pythagoras, who did not dread death, but looked for a transformation, was able to understand all this. All philosophers, vulgarly called physicists, have been able to understand it; for they say that, as far as substance is concerned, nothing is engendered or corrupted – unless we wish to define in this way the changes that go on. (pp 137-8)

Bruno's mystical plea for unity under the appearance of diversity takes on scientific overtones as he argues the law of the conservation of matter to support his insistence (and Pythagoras') that transformation of form makes all being one. His source for the views of Pythagoras appears to have been the last book of Ovid's *Metamorphoses*. Earlier in the *Cause*, he had quoted several lines from this book, concluding 'Souls cannot die, they leave their previous dwelling and live in new homes, which they forever inhabit. All things change, but nothing perishes' (p 90). According to Frances Yates, Bruno had at least two other sources for this belief, the writings attributed to Hermes Trismegistus and the work of Cornelius Agrippa.[13] But where Pythagoras uses the idea of transformation to enforce a cautious piety, the Hermetic writings and Agrippa use it to leave behind earthly limitations.

Hermes, for instance, insists that the intellect 'is drawn from the very substance of God. In men, this intellect is God; and so some men are gods and their humanity is near to the divinity' (Yates 33). This also is Bruno's position, 'that God is near, that each one has Him with him and within himself more than he himself can be within himself, for God is the soul of souls' (*Heroic Frenzies* 193). So Joyce wrote in the notesheets he used for *Ulysses*, 'Gods are in us.'[14] But how can one get in touch with the god within? Not, in Bruno's opinion, by pedantic and logical philosophic inquiry. Rather by a proper humility, a curbing of the hubris of even the creative philosopher, whose penetrating mind may think it can pierce the divine in a frontal assault. Rather, Bruno believed, the philosopher's knowledge, while it might indicate the nature of the cosmos, could not be a substitute for experiencing the divinity which informs the universe. To achieve such experience the inquiring mind must be silenced, the probing eye closed. He advocated, in short, the negative way outlined in *Of Learned Ignorance* by Nicholas of Cusa, who obtained the doctrine from the early Christian writer, Dionysius the Areopagite (whom Bruno also often credited when he developed this doctrine).

Bruno made extensive use of the negative way in *The Heroic Frenzies* (1585). Because this is the one work of Bruno's which we know Joyce to have had in his library (*The Consciousness of Joyce* 103), and because I believe several ideas and techniques in it were important to Joyce, I shall be citing this dialogue frequently in this chapter and those that follow. At the end of the fourth dialogue, one of Bruno's spokesmen suggests that blindness may be an appropriate image for the advanced condition of a certain kind of wise man who

> curbs his eyes from seeing what he most would desire and enjoy, as he holds his tongue from speaking to whom he most longs to speak, for fear that some defect of his glance or of his word might debase him, or in some way cause him disgrace. And this is what happens when the excellence of the object is so far superior to the power of apprehension. For this reason the more profound and divine theologians say God is honored and adored more by silence than by words, and that to see him better one must close one's eyes to the species represented than open them. This is why the negative theology of Pythagoras and Dionysius is so highly renowned above the demonstrative theology of Aristotle and the schoolmen. (p 257)

This emphasis on silence as the negative way, in opposition to logic as the positive way of apprehending god, clarifies Bruno's objection to Aristotle who seeks, as it were, to imprison god within his logic, or to use his intellect as a hunter to track down god, his quarry.

I use the metaphor of the hunter because of an allegory upon which Bruno puts great weight in Part 2 of *The Heroic Frenzies*. He discovers unexpected meaning in the myth of Diana and Acteon.

> I say very few are the Actaeons to whom destiny gives the power to contemplate Diana naked, and the power to become so enamoured of the beautiful harmony of the body of nature, so fallen beneath the gaze of those two lights of the dual splendor of goodness and beauty, that they are transformed into deer, inasmuch as they are no longer the hunters but the hunted. For the ultimate and last end of this chase is the capture of a fugitive and

wild prey, through which the hunter becomes the hunted, the pillager becomes the pillaged. Because in all the other species of the chase undertaken for particular things, it is the hunter who seeks to capture those things for himself, absorbing them through the mouth of his particular intelligence; but in that divine and universal chase he comes to apprehend that it is himself who necessarily remains captured, absorbed, and united. Therefore, from the vulgar ... civil and ordinary man he was, he becomes as free as a deer, and an inhabitant of the wilderness; he lives like a god under the protection of the woods in the unpretentious rooms of the cavernous mountains, where he contemplates the sources of the great rivers, vigorous as a plant, intact and pure, free of ordinary lusts, and converses most freely with the divinity. (p 225)

But even in these heights of almost mystical union, Bruno's hermetism stops short of pretending to obtain godhead: 'If he does not see it in its own essence and absolute light, he sees it in its germination which is similar to it and is its image: for from the monad, the divinity, proceeds this monad nature [Diana], the universe, the world' (p 226). Bruno's piety may not be orthodox, but it is a real check on the danger of ego-inflation to which the magus is subject.

Earlier in this chapter, we saw the youth in Joyce's 'Portrait' essay faced with a similar temptation, being carried almost completely out of touch with his fellow men by his ego-centred desire for the absolute. In his case, too, the return to an appreciation of 'the beauty of mortal conditions' is connected with a vision in which nature and woman are hardly distinguishable. This similarity is intensified in the later *Portrait of the Artist as a Young Man* when Stephen Dedalus, in a similar scene, views a girl in the water of the strand and reacts to her as if to Bruno's Diana; she inspires him to a state 'intact and pure, free of ordinary lusts.' She becomes to him what Diana was to Bruno, 'this monad nature ... the world.' Thus Stephen feels that 'the earth that had borne him, had taken him to her breast ... His eyelids trembled as if they felt the vast cyclic movement of the earth and her watchers ... His soul was swooning into some new world' (pp 172-3). Stephen loses himself in what Bruno called 'the beautiful harmony of the body of nature.'

Not only does Joyce use an image like Bruno's Diana for woman and the world, he also attaches to the youthful seeker Bruno's image of Acteon. In the 'Portrait' essay, Joyce portrays the young artist (prototype of Stephen, autotype of Joyce himself)[15] eluding his enemies: 'Let the pack of enmities come tumbling and sniffing to the highlands after their game; there was his ground: and he flung them disdain from flashing antlers' (*Workshop* 61). He later thought enough of this sentence to include it almost verbatim in *Stephen Hero* (pp 34-5). It also appears in 'The Holy Office,' where the poet pictures himself 'Unfellowed, friendless and alone ... Firm as the mountain-ridges where / I flash my antlers in the air' (*Critical Writings* 152). But these defensive-aggressive uses of the stag image show the artist's fear and pride; though hunted, he has not arrived at Bruno's realization that 'in that divine and universal chase he [must] come to apprehend that it is himself who necessarily remains captured, absorbed, and united.'

The Stephen of *Ulysses* has not arrived at this state either, but he is at once more passive and more down to earth. When he sees the dog on the strand running toward him, Stephen thinks, 'Dog of my enemy. I just simply stood pale, silent, bayed about' (p 45). More cautious, Stephen no longer expects ecstacy, but he would like to see nature naked again. As pointed out in Chapter 2, he is reduced to learning from a dog, but a protean dog that can transform itself into a deer. 'On a field tenney, a buck, trippant, proper, unattired' (p 46). This is a heraldic description; the phrase 'attired' means 'horned,' but a dog has no horns, hence 'unattired.' As William Schutte has argued, Stephen is able to identify with the dog.[16] Stephen is thus the deer too, as we would expect. But whereas in Joyce's earlier evocation of the artist he has flashing antlers with which to defy his enemies in the mountain, now he is defenceless on the strand. Such a shift could be the prelude to a Brunian reconciliation with nature, but it does not work out so for Stephen in *Ulysses*.

One complicating factor is the deer's horns. Stephen gets them back later in the novel, when he sees himself as Shakespeare in the mirror of Bella Cohen's brothel. By then they are a cuckold's horns, for Bloom and for Shakespeare. Stephen seems headed in the same direction. But even in this equivocal use of horns, Joyce is following Bruno. Using the Vulgate Old Testament, Bruno celebrated Moses 'coming down from Mount Sinai with the great tablets ... with a great pair of horns that branched out from his forehead' (*Expulsion of the Triumphant Beast* 245). He also quoted in Italian the Old Testament assertion that 'the horns of the righteous must be exalted' (p 246). Similarly, Stephen, while Shakespeare is still on stage in 'Circe,' watches as 'the face of Martin Cunningham, bearded, refeatures Shakespeare's beardless face' (p 568); then he sees the unfaithful wife of Cunningham and says '*Et exaltabuntar cornua iusti*. Queens lay with prize bulls' (p 569). The Latin means 'The horns of the righteous shall be exalted.' If Joyce has understood Bruno's point, that one may be exalted and yet disdained by the ignorant, Stephen has not. Having voiced the spiritual exaltation, Stephen immediately lowers it to the bestial level, forcing his listeners to picture the bull mounted on the false cow which conceals Pasiphae, his horns thus raised on high.

Obviously Stephen has fallen away from his high spiritual state in *A Portrait of the Artist as a Young Man*. Obsessed by death and sensuality, he is blocked from seeing 'the beauty in mortal conditions' which Joyce in 1904 had been able to appreciate as a saving grace for the artist. In the Circe episode, Stephen has a chance to purge himself, but is unable to do so for reasons investigated in Chapter 8.

If Diana as the 'monad nature' interested Bruno, Circe as corruptor of nature fascinated both him and Joyce. At the very end of *The Heroic Frenzies*, Bruno introduced an allegory in which both goddesses play important roles, the story of the nine blind men. As Circe is first invoked, early in Bruno's prefatory Argument and in Part 1 of the book itself, she appears in her conventional guise, as a demeanour of man.

> Circe ... represents the generative matter of all things. She is called the daughter of the sun, because from the father of forms she has inherited the possession of all those forms which, by a sprinkling of the waters – that is to say by the act of generation and by the power of enchantment – that is by reason of a secret harmony – she transforms all being, making those who see become blind. For generation and corruption are causes of oblivion and of blindness, as the ancients explain by the figure of souls who bathe and inebriate themselves in the waters of Lethe. (p 75)

At the end of the book, however, the nine men who early opted for limited modes of apprehension regain their sight, through the help of Circe. Leading them a rough journey over the physical earth, she finally offers them a vessel of hope which, it is true, she cannot open (nor can they). It is finally opened by Diana, and its contents sprinkled on them; then they regain their vision. They praise not only Diana but also Circe, as their benefactress through 'glorious afflictions' (p 263). The theme is still that the divine may be found in nature; in the vein of Dionysius, Bruno has made blindness comparable to silence (as in the quotation on page 15). Rather than probing arrogantly with their eyes, as Aristotle with his words, these men learn humility through experience and come to appreciate god in this way.

As indicated earlier, Bruno did not see beasts as necessarily bestial. Here again we encounter that change of form which is a necessity and virtue in Bruno's active, coherent universe. However much man might wish to be a pure spirit in free union with the absolute, he must acknowledge that his senses are part of him. Only working through their demands can he purge himself. But as Bruno's remarks on corruption and blindness indicate, this doctrine is the opposite of libertinism. Only if the soul uses darkness as a chastisement of pride can enlightenment follow. In fact, like Ulysses with the Sirens and with Circe, the soul must take steps beforehand not to become the slave of the senses. Then their appeal and the soul's involvement become a source of purging rather than of corruption.

Some such insight was in Joyce's mind as he placed his Ulysses, Leopold Bloom, in the two scenes that correspond to Homer's Sirens and Circe episodes. Bloom leaves the Ormond bar purged of sentimentality by Simon Dedalus' rendition of a love song from *Martha* and by Ben Dollard's singing of the pathetic 'Croppy Boy.' More important, Bloom emerges from the Nighttown section purged by his devastating encounter with a local Circe, Madame Cohen, who helps liberate some of the hidden fantasies which have kept Bloom's soul enslaved to vicarious sensual pleasures. That Bruno's allegorical use of Circe was in Joyce's mind as he wrote this section is indicated by an allusion to it.[17] That he was adapting Bruno's images for his own use is indicated by his substituting for Diana his own pure Nymph, who tries to seduce Bloom from sensuality but who is finally revealed as a sham.

Stepping back, we can remind ourselves that in Bruno, Joyce found not only a mode of rendering the changing universe, but also in Diana and Circe two important images for the relation of man to nature, for embodying one of the oldest philosophic and artistic themes. In Chapters 2 and 3, I shall develop the transformation theme in more detail as it concerns the two protagonists of *Ulysses*. But to begin the next chapter we need to consider two other influences on Joyce, Aristotle and Dionysius, who offered him respectively a hard-headed and a soft-eyed version of man's place in the universe. With his usual daring, Joyce incorporated both in his search for meaningful vision.

2 Material universe and spiritual activity

Because Stephen Dedalus is easily taken as a portrait of the young Joyce, it is worth developing further the ways in which they are similar and different. In the first half of this chapter I shall be looking at their views (and the view of the mature Joyce) towards Aristotle and the Christian Dionysius, while in the second half I shall turn to Stephen's experience in the first three episodes of *Ulysses*. In the mind of Stephen Dedalus, Aristotle has the same high place as he did for Dante: 'master of those who know' (*Ulysses* 37).[1] The notebook Joyce filled in Paris in 1903 testifies to his preoccupation with Aristotle at that time; Gorman printed some of Joyce's translations from Aristotle and his aesthetic comments developed from the philosopher. His biography emphasizes Joyce's commitment: Joyce 'with his worship of Ibsen and his scorn for the empty twilight of the Irish theatre, naturally found in Aristotle a firmer base from which to spring than the quicksand of Romanticism left by the backwash of the nineties' (p 95). In this admiration Joyce is seemingly at odds not only with Bergson but with Bruno, who also disliked Aristotle, mainly because the latter had used a limited logic to refute the early Greek cosmologists whom Bruno tended to adapt for his own purposes. Bruno was angered that Aristotle had become an authority whose dicta were accepted unthinkingly by the respectable. But despite these reservations, Bruno actually looked upon the Greek philosopher as one of 'earth's heroes' (*Infinite Universe* 325).

Almost for the reasons that Bruno disliked Aristotle, the young Joyce admired him. As Gorman put it, 'Aristotle still represented to him Dogma, a Rock set against the turbid tides of inchoate metaphysics. He was System, co-ordination, rationalization. He was the reverse of Plato and Plato's beautiful and ineffectual mysticism' (p 95). Gorman's categorizing clearly draws on Stephen's allegiance in *Ulysses*, being filled out with terms from Joyce's outline chart for the episodes of that novel. As already indicated, for the Scylla and Charybdis episode, Aristotle is identified with Scylla and connected with the rock and dogma. But knowledge of the context in which the mature Joyce put this characterization of Aristotle indicates some diminution of his earlier high regard.[2] Though Gorman indicated a mistrust of mysticism in the young Joyce, we have seen evidence of Joyce's positive attitude towards it. I would say that the mature Joyce was more interested in reconciling Aristotle and Plato than in opposing them as opposites. In this approach he was aided by Bruno, as shown in Chapter 1.

Gorman inadvertently provides evidence of a modified view of Aristotle even in the young Joyce; he reproduces a series of sentences that Joyce 'copied down in his notebook' in 1903 'from the various works of the Stagirite':

> 'Only when it is separate from all things is the intellect really itself and this intellect separate from all things is immortal and divine.'
>
> 'The intellectual soul is the form of forms.'
>
> 'God is the eternal perfect animal.'
>
> 'Nature, it seems, is not a collection of unconnected episodes, like a bad dream (or drama?).' (pp 95-6)

Gorman admits that these quotations are 'perhaps not in the exact words of Aristotle from the *Psychology* and the *Metaphysica* (p 96). The first two are, however, remarkably close to sentences in the translation of *De Anima* by J.A. Smith: 'When mind is set free from its present conditions it appears as just what it is and nothing more: this alone is immortal and eternal.' 'The mind is the form of forms.'[3] But I cannot find in the *Metaphysica* (translated by W.D. Ross, same edition) any statement corresponding as closely to the last two sentences by Joyce. In Chapter 10, Aristotle did affirm that 'the world is not such that one thing has nothing to do with another, but they are all connected' (p 886), a postulate that would also have struck Bruno. Joyce gives this a literary turn: 'Nature, it seems, is not a collection of unconnected episodes, like a bad dream (or drama?).' The result of this distortion is a conception with a great deal of vitality to it. Amplified, with the negatives removed, Joyce is saying, 'Happenings in nature are interconnected, as coherent as the development of good drama or as full of unsuspected meaning as a good dream.' The implication would be that when literature imitates the actions of nature it renders truth, which is naturally dramatic and compelling. As I suggested in the introduction to Part 1, Bruno cast his philosophy in such a form. Joyce was attempting something of the sort with the short stories in *Dubliners*, though he gave himself the difficult task of dramatizing the paralysis of a city.

With the fourth of the quotations I have chosen, we enter the strange world of primitive cosmology: 'God is the eternal perfect animal.' In Chapter 7 of the

Metaphysica, Aristotle insists that 'God is a living being, eternal, most good' (p 880), presumably the basis for Joyce's statement. But a being is different from an animal. In Chapter 8, Aristotle goes on to conclude that the stars cause all movement on earth and to refer to the old Greek tradition that the stars 'are gods and that the divine encloses the whole of nature.' He then adds a later tradition (which he seems to hold less valid) that 'these gods are in the form of men or like some of the other animals' (p 884). Joyce, however, was moving towards animism, not away from it. In the Pola notebook (1904), he wrote, 'Signs of the Zodiac. Earth a living being' (Gorman 136). The ideas behind both these notebook entries were used by Joyce in *Ulysses*. He characterized Molly as earth at the end of the Ithaca episode when she reclines 'in the attitude of Gea-Tellus, fulfilled, recumbent, big with seed' (p 737). Joyce made this conception clear in a letter to Frank Budgen; her soliloquy 'turns like the huge earth ball slowly surely and evenly, round and round spinning, its 4 cardinal points being the female breasts, arse, womb, and cunt' (*J.J.* 516). This sentence can almost stand as a paradigm of that ability Joyce shared with Bruno (and Shakespeare, of course) to combine a conception of high beauty with down-to-earth details.

Thus while not denigrating the importance of Aristotle in Joyce's aesthetic development, I think we must acknowledge a tendency to shift that philosopher's doctrines in a dramatic, hermetic, Brunian direction. For instance, taking the celebrated question of imitation in art, Joyce contends that Aristotle 'says only, "Art imitates Nature" and means that the artistic process is like the natural process' (*Critical Writings* 145). While this is at least a helpful interpretation of Aristotle, I would emphasize that the notion of natural process allows Aristotle's dicta to become consonant with Bergson's view of reality as a perpetual becoming and with Bruno's system of transformation.

This adaptation of Joyce's led him to a conception of art which is very much in harmony with Bruno's philosophy. 'It is false to say that sculpture, for instance, is an art of repose if by that be meant that sculpture is unassociated with movement. Sculpture is associated with movement in as much as it is rhythmic' (p 145). As Jackson Cope has shown, the concept of rhythm is one that Joyce developed fruitfully over the years and used effectively in constructing *Ulysses*. In 1904, it appeared as the preamble to his 'Portrait' essay, where it is linked with nature, though in a manner as reminiscent of Pater as of Aristotle. 'The past assuredly implies a fluid succession of presents, the development of an entity of which our actual present is a phase only.' The artist therefore seeks 'to liberate from the personalised lumps of matter that which is their individuating rhythm, the first or formal relation of their parts' (*Workshop* 60).[4] This emphasis on the connection between change in man and artistic rhythm appears again in Stephen's words in *Ulysses*.

> – As we, or mother Dana, weave and unweave our bodies, Stephen said, from day to day, their molecules shuttled to and fro, so does the artist weave and unweave his image. ... In the intense instant of imagination, when the mind, Shelley says, is a fading coal, that which I was is that which I am and that which in possibility I may come to be. (p 194)

Stephen begins here with a realization of the process of life, a continual transformation in which new matter takes on old form to create identity through time. Again we may see Bruno behind this conception. He claimed that the

> soul and intelligence persist while the body is ever changing and renewed part by part. ... We have not in youth the same flesh as in childhood, nor in old age the same as in youth; for we suffer perpetual transmutation, whereby we receive a perpetual flow of fresh atoms, and those that we have received previously are ever leaving us.
> (*Infinite Universe* 285)

While Bruno's development of physical transformation is compatible with Aristotle's conception of form and content, another side of his philosophy is not at all compatible with Aristotle. This is his emphasis on the spiritual and religious dimension, an important aspect of Bruno which still meant a lot to Joyce when in 1903 he wrote a review of a contemporary book on Bruno and his philosophy.

In his review of McIntyre's *Giordano Bruno*, Joyce made a point which was a harbinger of doctrines to come. 'That idea of an ultimate principle, spiritual, indifferent, universal, related to any soul or to any material thing, as the Materia Prima of Aquinas is related to any material thing, unwarranted as it may seem in the view of critical philosophy, has yet a distinct value for the historian of religious ecstasies' (*Critical Writings* 134). As we might suspect, Joyce by no means looks down on historians of religious ecstasy. In fact, his seriousness here is indicated by his insisting on the word 'indifferent' as a quality of the 'ultimate principle' Stephen Dedalus later uses the same adjective to characterize the artist as god. 'The artist, like the God of creation, remains within or behind or beyond or above his handiwork, invisible, refined out of existence, indifferent, paring his fingernails' (*A Portrait of the Artist* 215). The four adverbs that appear here are less puzzling if we remember Bruno's insistence that the divine is *within* nature, *behind* it as cause, *beyond* it as comprising all totally, and *above* it because ultimately the purified will must look up from nature to see the divine. Like Bruno, Joyce insisted on having it both ways: that the divine is *within* nature, and that the creator is *above* nature.

If the quality of god-like removal seems dominant in the mind of Stephen, Joyce in his review of McIntyre's book on Bruno made it clear that the natural process is also important. '*Inwards* from the material universe, which, however, did not seem to him, as to the Neoplatonists the kingdom of the soul's malady, or as to the Christians a place of probation, but rather his opportunity for spiritual activity, he passes, and from heroic enthusiasm to enthusiasm to unite himself with God' (p 134, my italics). Although he is putting Bruno's case here, we can appreciate what the Italian philosopher must have meant to someone who had opted out of the Church and could not accept the spiritualist theosophy of the respectable literary establishment as an alternative to Catholicism. Never a mere atheist, Joyce could respect even a Christian neo-Platonist like Dionysius, if he represented an unconventional insistence that man can come close to God in this life.

In his 1912 lecture on Blake, Joyce evoked sympathetically the approach of that early Christian mystic. 'Dionysius the pseudo-Areopagite, in his book *De Divinis Nominibus*, arrives at the throne of God by denying and overcoming every moral and metaphysical attribute, and falling into ecstasy and prostrating himself before the divine obscurity, before that unutterable immensity which precedes and encompasses the supreme knowledge in the eternal order' (*Critical Writings* 222). The key phrases are 'divine obscurity' and 'unutterable immensity.' As Joyce states, at the very end of *The Divine Names*, Dionysius not only humbly prostrates himself before God but insists, more strongly and overtly than in earlier chapters, that reason is inadequate to a comprehension of the Divine.

> We have given our preference to the Negative method, because this lifts the soul above all things cognate with its finite nature, and, guiding it onward through all the conceptions of God's Being which are transcended by that Being exceeding all Name, Reason, and Knowledge, reaches beyond the farthest limits of the world and there joins unto God Himself, in so far as the power of union with Him is possessed even by men.[5]

Like Bruno, Dionysius seems both sure and tentative about the possibility of entering into the divine.

When Joyce referred to the concept of an '*unutterable* immensity,' he might have been remembering Dionysius' reference to the '*ineffable* Nature' of the Divine (p 188, my italics). For Joyce's phrase 'divine *obscurity*' the closest I can find at the end of *The Divine Names* is 'the mystery.' Since Dionysius is approved by both Bruno and Aquinas, and since his Plotinian speculations have an occult, mystic tendency, it seems likely Joyce would also have read his *De Mystica Theologia*. In that short work we can find a likely source for Joyce's focus on 'obscurity' and his reference immediately following to the '*dark* ocean of God' (*Critical Writings* 222, my italics). In evocative paradoxes, Dionysius insists that 'unchangeable mysteries of heavenly Truth lie hidden in the dazzling obscurity of the secret Silence, outshining all brilliance with the intensity of their darkness' (p 191). Or again, Dionysius ends Chapter 2 with the possibility that by following the negative way 'we may begin to see that super-essential Darkness which is hidden by all the light that is in existent things' (p 196). Presumably Dionysius' authority for this conception is Genesis, where God gives light to the material universe, after having created it from the void, a nothingness which may be connected with the darkness.[6]

In the *Divine Names* Dionysius' neo-Platonism leads him to deny the anthropomorphic nature of God: 'The Very Existence underlying the existence of all things is not some Divine or Angelic Being...' (p 179). Despite this insistence, however, Dionysius spends most of the book trying to explain how various epithets of God are justly applied to Him in the light of our limited awareness. Several of these explanations presumably influenced Bruno, including a concern with transformation that emerges during Dionysius' discussion of God as 'Omnipotent': 'He is that All-Powerful Foundation of all things which maintains and embraces the Universe, founding and establishing and compacting it; knitting the whole together in Himself without a rift, producing the Universe out of Himself as out of an all-powerful Root, and attracting all things back into Himself as unto an all-powerful Receptable' (p 169). Similarly, Dionysius says of god as 'Ancient of Days' that 'He goes forth from the Beginning through the entire process of the world unto the End' (p 170). It is to such a transformation process that I believe Joyce as creator committed himself. But in order to see how he applied these insights of spiritual and physical process, we must now take a preliminary look at cycles in *Ulysses*.

First we should note that in June 1904, the fictional Stephen has not yet reached the realization we have already seen that Joyce himself actually recorded in January 1904: 'Sceptically, cynically, mystically, he had sought for an absolute satisfaction and now little by little he began to be conscious of the beauty of mortal conditions.' Mysticism would ordinarily seem incompatible with scepticism and cynicism, but if we remember how in *A Portrait of the Artist* scepticism and mysticism are both strong in Stephen, we can understand how they are possible in someone searching for an 'absolute satisfaction.'[7] Not reaching that goal, Stephen becomes cynical, as is emphasized in the Aelous episode of *Ulysses*. Professor McHugh addresses Stephen:

> – You remind me of Antisthenes, the professor said, a disciple of Gorgias, the sophist. It is said of him that none could tell if he were bitterer against others or against himself. He was the son of a noble and a bondwoman. And he wrote a book in which he took away the palm of beauty from Argive Helen and handed it to poor Penelope. (pp 148-9)

Disregarding the several parallels with Stephen, we might note that the aim of Antisthenes' book indicates the idealism behind his cynicism: he wants to elevate the faithful Penelope and lower the world's opinion of faithless Helen. Joyce himself was doing something similar in choosing a modern Ulysses as his hero. He insisted that the un-warlike Ulysses was the only 'complete man' in literature.[8] In any case, the Joyce who wrote *Ulysses* is far removed from the would-be creator Stephen. Joyce was able to celebrate 'the beauty of mortal conditions,' while Stephen is stuck in a life-denying, self-denying cynicism.

Yet Stephen wants to free himself, though we don't see him becoming free in *Ulysses*, as I think we do Bloom; we do, however, see signs of a shift from Aristotelian intellect to an appreciation of everyday experience and feeling. Stephen updates Aristotle in urging himself during the library scene to 'hold to the now, the here, through which all future plunges to the past' (p 186). Although this existential insistence augurs well for his escaping the hold of the past, in fact he is in the mind's bondage all through the scene, spouting a theory which cannot free him: '– A father, Stephen said, battling against hopelessness, is a necessary evil' (p 207).

Yet after Stephen has been through the purgatory of the Circe episode, there is a minimal indication during the exhaustion of the Eumaeus episode that he is prepared to become 'conscious of the beauty of mortal conditions.' What Stephen does is to see Bloom as an avatar of Christ. '– *Ex quibus*, Stephen mumbled in a noncommittal accent, their two or four eyes conversing, *Christus* or Bloom his name is, or, after all, any other, *secundum carnem*' (p 643). As Thornton points out, the Latin words are from the Vulgate New Testament, spoken by Paul of the Jews, 'of their race, according to the flesh, is the Christ.' But Joyce has Stephen give this observation a twist, equating Bloom as Jew with Christ, a heretical suggestion he shares with Bruno. In *The Expulsion of the Triumphant Beast*, Bruno argues that

> the eternal gods (without placing any inconvenience against that which is true of divine substance) have temporal names, some in some times and nations, others in others. As you can see from revealing stories, Paul of Tarsus was named Mercury and Barnabas, the Galilean, was named Jove, not because they were believed to be those gods themselves, but because men believed that that divine virtue that was found in Mercury and in Jove in other times then found itself present in these. (p 238)

Bruno's case for Bloom would thus be not that Bloom is Christ, but that all the divine virtue which Christ had two thousand years ago is present in Bloom when he helps Stephen. I believe that this is essentially Joyce's case, and that Stephen's focussing on the names is part of a pattern in this episode which relies on Bruno's notion of transformation.

Earlier in the episode, Stephen had said, 'Sounds are impostures ... Like names, Cicero, Podmore, Napoleon, Mr Goodbody, Jesus, Mr Doyle. Shakespeares were as common as Murphies. What's in a name?' (p 622). Taking this last question as a challenge, Robert Adams has shown that there is something in each of these names, that they are connected by transformation. 'Cicero as a name comes from Latin *cicera*, chickpea, and might well be something like Podmore in English; Napoleon=Buonaparte=Goodbody; and Jesus=Christ=Anointed=oiled=Doyle.'[9] In addition we might observe that the common Irish name Murphy is soon (p 624) attached to the loquacious sailor in the cabman's shelter with Bloom and Stephen. Later the drowsy narrator slips by referring to someone as 'wrapped in the arms of Murphy, as the adage has it' (p 660). But since the adage had already appeared correctly as 'in the arms of Morpheus' (p 639), we know that Joyce has purposefully given an example of Stephen's earlier point.[10] Different sounds do impose on our understanding: at one level the names that separate us can be transformed into one. Murphy can become like Shakespeare because it is like Morpheus, the Greek god of changing forms. In the arms of Morpheus, in sleep and dreams, all is transformed, the contraries coincide, and being becomes one, as Joyce painstakingly demonstrated in *Finnegans Wake*. But the philosophic and artistic discoveries upon which *Finnegans Wake* is built were made while Joyce was working on *Ulysses* and are embodied in it too, though in a less thoroughgoing fashion.

The connection of high divine and low physical is frequently suggested in *Ulysses*. As already indicated, the writings of Dionysius provide a source, but this connection has an equally strong tradition in the idea and practice of devil worship, which would have had an appeal for Joyce as a renegade Catholic.[11] In the Black Mass at the end of the Circe episode, for instance, the chant which reverses 'Dog' into 'God' (p 600) may be taken in this way. But Joyce's use of the Black Mass is actually more complicated than this. As artist he was the indifferent creator at this point, watching Stephen's mind from above, suggesting also that there was a dialectical relation between Dublin's piety with its many churches and Dublin's iniquity with its large red-light district. Certainly the dog is an appropriate emblem for the un-moral animal appetite which looms so large in Circe. In addition, a dog had already played an important symbolic role in the Proteus episode.

Speaking to his friend, Frank Budgen, in Zürich during the writing of the first half of the book, Joyce indicated a number of his intentions. When Stephen is walking on the strand, he meets a dog because Joyce wanted an animal to embody the theme of transformation with which Proteus is associated. '"Did you see the point of that bit about the dog?" said Joyce. "He is the mummer among beasts – the Protean animal"' (Budgen 53). To get this point across to the reader, Joyce characterized the dog in terms of a number of other animals, including finally a panther (pp 46-7). Of this animal, Joyce said, 'There he is ... Panther: all animals' (Budgen 54). Presumably Joyce had in mind the possible Greek Etymology, *Pan* meaning 'all,' and *theria* meaning 'wild beasts.' But I suspect this insight was put in his head by a figure popular in occult literature, Pantomorphus. As utilized by Bruno, it appears as a shadow to Momus in *The Expulsion of the Triumphant Beast*. After staring at it, Momus addresses another god:

> 'Oh, Mercury, that which I told you seemed to me to be like a shadow, I now see as so many beasts herded together; for I see it as being canine, porcine, ram-like, monkey-like, ursine, aquiline, deer-like, falcon-like, leonine, asinine and as all the "ines" and "likes" that ever were. So many beasts, and yet there is but one body. It certainly appears to me to be the pantomorphosis of brute animals.' 'Better say,' retorted Mercury, 'that it is a multiform beast. It seems one and is one; but it is not uniform, since it is the nature of vices to have many forms, so that they are shapeless and in contrast to virtues, have no faces of their own.' (p 166)

Bruno's use of the figure not only parallels Joyce's comment on 'panther' but ties in with the Circe episode where so many vices appear, often in animal shape. The panther is referred to again there, this time as a man who (in an anti-Christian anecdote, cf. Thornton) is supposed to have made Mary pregnant with Jesus. Virag says, 'Panther, the Roman centurion, polluted her with his genitories' (p 521). Bruno's connection of beast and god can thus be added to the other themes of metamorphosis we have seen in *Ulysses*.

In the remainder of this chapter, I propose to investigate Joyce's use of the transformation process in the first three episodes of the novel. The classical god traditionally associated with shape-changing is Proteus, whose name Joyce gave to his third episode and whose qualities he used to embody and inform the episode. Other classical figures associated with metamorphosis were Morpheus, Hermes, Glaucus, and the Demiurge. I have already mentioned Morpheus, and will be considering Hermes and Glaucus in Chapters 4 and 5, respectively. The special place of the Demiurge demands our immediate attention.

Another writer who represents an area of thought that influenced Joyce is Valentine, as Stephen names him in 'Telemachus' (p 21, cf. Thornton). Valentine was a Gnostic whose philosophy was not available, for hundreds of years, except through the refutation of him by Ireneous, his contemporary Christian opponent. But Joyce had access to at least three views that were more positive towards Gnosticism, in books owned by the National Library of Ireland at the time he was a student there.[12] That Joyce was interested in Gnosticism is clear from phrases in Gorman's biography (pp 4, 168, 242); it is also indicated by an observation in Stephen's mind at the beginning of the Proteus episode. With his eyes closed he taps the ground. 'Sounds solid: made by the mallet of *Los Demiurgos*' (p 37).[13] Taken as Spanish, this phrase suggests that the world was made by 'the demiurges.' These deities were in classical times thought to be subordinate to the main gods and were given the task of making earth. The Demiurge figures importantly in Gnostic philosophy. It was adopted from that philosophy by the late nineteenth-century theosophist, Helene Blavatsky. Joyce came to her two major works, *Isis Unveiled* and *The Secret Doctrine*, through the Dublin theosophists, led by A.E. (George Russell).[14] Mistrusting their fuzzy mysticism, he did not respond to her as positively as to Dionysius or Bruno, partly because she was pretentious and popular. But he found in her work much that coincides with Bruno (whom she praised highly and quoted at some length in *Isis Unveiled* I, Chapter 4). As a result, though in *Ulysses* Joyce makes fun of her followers and their language, he also makes use of some of her insights.[15] As Ellmann insists, Joyce 'was genuinely interested in such Theosophical themes as cycles, reincarnation, the succession of gods, and the eternal mother-faith that underlies all transitory religions' (*J.J.* 103).

At the beginning of the Proteus episode, Stephen is trying to determine the nature of the world in which he finds himself and the nature of the force that shaped it. Knowledge of both is essential to his aim of becoming the artist as interpreter and creator. Briefly he concludes that though we cannot trust all sense perceptions, nature does contain a reality which it is the artist's duty to attempt to embody.[16] As his awareness continues, the animism of nature becomes evident: 'wavenoise, herds of seamorse' (p 46); 'these heavy sands are language tide and wind have silted here' (p 44). The problem of language and communication occurs to Stephen as common to nature and the artist. 'Who ever anywhere will read these written words? Signs on a white field. ... You find my words dark. Darkness is in our souls, do you not think?' (p 48). The 'signs on a white field' are the words Stephen has just written on white paper. They are 'dark' words in two senses, first because that is the literal mark left by pencil on page, second because they come from a dark unknowable somewhere.[17] Like nature, the mind speaks a 'seamorse,' sends up mysterious shapes, phrases to be scanned. The artist therefore faces the task of interpreting the dark mystery from both within and without.

But to this double task must be added a third, the problem of understanding the secrets of language itself. Earlier in the classroom, Stephen had looked at an arithmetic book:

> Across the page the symbols moved in grave morrice, in the mummery of their letters, wearing quaint caps of squares and cubes. Give hands, traverse, bow to partner: so: imps of fancy of the Moors. Gone too from the world, Averroes and Moses Maimonides, dark men in mien and movement, flashing in their mocking mirrors the obscure soul of the world, a darkness shining in brightness which brightness could not comprehend. (p 28)

Stephen takes the side of a dark Jew here, and a few pages later he defends the Jews when Deasy says 'you can see the darkness in their eyes' (p 34).[18] Stephen's phrase, 'obscure soul of the world,' recalls Joyce's reference to Dionysius' 'divine obscurity,' and the rest of Stephen's picture seems influenced by Dionysius' image of 'super-essential Darkness which is hidden by all the light that is in existent things' (*Mystical Theology* 194, cf. Thornton). Light, that is, blinds one to the divine darkness which is its source.

Because the Arabic numbers mime their meaning, they can be understood by Western man even though he may not know the names given them by the Arabs who brought them to him. To particular individuals, their miming may not be clear, as it is not to Stephen's pupil, Sargeant. Stephen tries to explain the meaning behind a problem in arithmetic, but Sargeant wants only the answer, not the universal principle which it exemplifies. Similarly, Stephen would like to recover the principles of those condemned or ignored by the church which, having a monopoly on light, considered the understanding of Jews, Gnostics, and heresiarchs such as Bruno to be darkened. Joyce seems to have accepted Augustine's doctrine that all human beings have dark natures (*Workshop* 65; *Ulysses* 141), but to agree with John of the Cross (cf. *Workshop* 63) and Dionysius that darkness was the most likely place to look for the divine. From some such premise Stephen too seems able to draw the conclusion that the artist and the philosopher must uncover what lies in darkness and expose it in dark letters. Since mankind lives in a world where much is hidden, it behooves him to admit the difficulty of knowing himself or the truth.

Intellectually, then, Stephen has moved a long way towards the philosophic-aesthetic which I sketched as Joyce's. He has begun to turn his attention to the dark mysteries around him, giving up his previous aim of flying to eternity. He has begun to question intellect and the pride that links him not only with Daedalus but with Lucifer.

When Stephen had earlier admitted to Mulligan what he held against him, it turned out to be the phrase 'beastly dead' applied to Stephen's mother. I suggest we accept Stephen's explanation that he takes it as an insult to *him* rather than her. If his mother is dead like any animal, Stephen can also suffer the same fate, is in fact being dragged down from the God-like heights towards which he had flown. In the Proteus episode, for the first time, he actually tries out what it would be like to experience that animal world: he tries to project himself into the consciousness of a dog (pp 46-7). This is the same dog discussed earlier that Joyce intended to portray as 'the mummer among beasts – the Protean animal.' We saw that Stephen has already shown an awareness of the protean nature of the sea and sand, inanimate examples of nature's shifting forms that the artist must learn to interpret. In the dog, Joyce presented an animate example of this same nature.

Stephen is afraid of dogs, but if he can keep his senses focused on the Proteus-like changes of this one (cf. p 46), he will profit from Menelaus' parable in the *Odyssey* and finally break through to the truth of the dog's nature. In doing so, he will live up to an aim of the young Joyce who, in his 1901 letter to Ibsen, praised the master's 'wilful resolution to wrest the secret from life' (*Letters* I, 52). As we have seen, in the Black Mass at the end of the Circe episode (pp 599-600), dog is revealed as the opposite of God. But Joyce, who was not a satanist, learned from Aristotle that 'God is the eternal perfect animal' and from Bruno that Dog is only an earthy *rebus* for God. In the notesheets for *Ulysses*, Joyce wrote, 'Jūpītēr īs ānīmāl,' and 'incarnation, descent of man to dog' (pp 268, 287).

The artistic truth that Joyce seems to have embodied in the dog is connected with the word 'mummer.' Mulligan had earlier called Stephen 'the loveliest mummer of them all,' evidently in allusion to Stephen's ability to play a role. As we have noted, Stephen himself had admired in the book of arithmetic, 'the symbols' moving 'in grave morrice, in the *mummery* of their letters.' 'Mummery' is a good term not only for the silence of print, but for the miming of dance ('morrice' equalling Morris, originally Moorish dancing in which performers impersonate various characters in English folklore); the algebraic symbols, like the mummers, disguise their real value. Similarly the dog silently mimes animals, taking on different disguises. We know also that the young Joyce was a good actor, an excellent mimic (*Workshop* 173).

I would suggest that mumming became Joyce's artistic mode, as witness the colloquial accuracy of his literary dialogue and the constant mimicry of his different styles in *Ulysses*. The model of Proteus becomes radically clear when we look ahead to *Finnegans Wake*, where the language itself changes under our eyes into shapes we must wrestle with long and hard before they reveal their truth to us. But, as I have already suggested, the principles upon which *Finnegans Wake* was constructed were originally worked out by Joyce in *Ulysses*. Most notably, the protean principle informs the Circe episode with its dream shifts and distortions, its seemingly shapeless movement which disguises some of the important revelations of the novel. As Joyce suggested to Budgen, '*The Circe* is a costume episode. Disguises. Bloom changes clothes half a dozen times. And of course it's an animal episode, full of animal allusions, animal mannerisms' (Budgen 228). The odd jump from costume to animal becomes understandable when we remember that disguise and mummery found their focus in the dog of the Proteus episode.

As shape-changer and deceiver, Proteus is a trickster who takes on different disguises in the hope that man will not find out his truth. Since in Greek his name is allied with the words for 'primary' and 'first,' Proteus is a peer of the Demiurge, below the high gods, intermediary to man. Madame Blavatsky put the two on a par in *The Secret Doctrine*, referring to 'the Demiurge of *Logos*, regarded as the CREATOR' on page 380 (Vol. I), having already suggested on page 349 that 'the Logos or Creative diety ... has to be traced to its ultimate source and Essence. In India, it is a Proteus of 1,008 divine names and aspects.' In an early essay, Joyce had generalized a similar insight in wording which shows the possible influence of Madame Blavatsky: 'The ancient gods, who are visions of the divine names, die and come to life many times, and, though there is dusk about their feet and darkness in their indifferent eyes, the miracle of light is renewed eternally in the imaginative soul' (*Critical Writings* 82-3). The fact that he takes the gods as 'visions of divine names' indicates the primacy of word over substance, a point of connection between Joyce's Christian background and his aesthetic future. The imaginative soul cannot take light for granted but must discover its own.

In 1914, Joyce's conception of *Ulysses* had matured enough for him to see that it was not only the story of the Wandering Jew, Hunter, as Odysseus, but also the continuing story of an expatriate son, Stephen Dedalus as Telemachus.[19] This realization caused him to hold back some of the material which he had originally intended to include in *A Portrait of the Artist as a Young Man*.[20] I have already suggested that Joyce intended Stephen's Aristotelian stance to be a limitation on his artistic potential. What such intellectual categories fail to encompass is indicated by Stephen himself in his aesthetic discussion with Lynch. 'So far as this side of aesthetic philosophy extends Aquinas will carry me all along the line. When we come to the phenomena of artistic conception, artistic gestation and artistic reproduction I require a new terminology and a new personal experience' (*A Portrait* 209). I shall investigate the importance to *Ulysses* of 'artistic gestation' in Chapter 6. For now, I would underline the final phrase in the quotation, finding in it a hint to the reader from Joyce that Stephen has not yet had his new experience. Certainly we do not meet the new terminology in *A Portrait*. Stephen carries on with Aquinas on beauty, emphasizing *stasis*, a concept directly opposed to the dynamic notions of 'artistic conception, artistic gestation and artistic reproduction.'

Since the metaphor is biological creation, the new experience the author needs is clearly a wife he can impregnate, whose pregnancy he can share, and whose child he can recognize as his offspring. Ellmann records Joyce's positive reaction to the birth of his first child: 'The event staggered and delighted him; a few years later he said to his sister Eva, "The most important thing that can happen to a man is the birth of a child"' (*J.J.* 212). And in a frank letter he wrote Stanislaus just before the birth, he defended his unintellectual wife: Cosgrave, a university friend (and the model for Lynch to whom Stephen delivers his theories in *A Portrait*), had said that Joyce 'would never make anything' of Nora, but Joyce assured Stanislaus that 'in many points in which Cosgrave and I are deficient, she does not require any making at all' (*J.J.* 210). I would submit that this realization is an important part of the 'new experience' which Stephen tells Lynch he needs. Needless to say, the spokesmen for a theory of growth and metamorphosis would be philosophers like Bergson and Bruno.

Before Stephen can accept the beauty of mortal life on earth, he must be willing to give up the belief that he can sustain the high flights of fancy which have given him the illusion of God-like self-sufficiency. We have already seen him begin to face mortality in the form of a dead dog. He takes the next step by testing himself in imagination as heroic rescuer. This theme is first broached by Mulligan, who says, 'I'm the *Uebermensch*. Toothless Kinch [Stephen] and I, the supermen' (p 22). Mulligan's plunging into the sea immediately following this comment is important because Stephen is still afraid of water. In contrast, Mulligan is a strong swimmer who has been a hero more than once. Stephen says to him, 'You saved men from drowning. I'm not a hero, however' (p 4). By the end of the Proteus episode, Stephen is very much down to earth. 'My teeth are very bad. Why I wonder? Feel. That one is going too. Shells. Ought I go to a dentist, I wonder, with that money? That one. Toothless Kinch, the superman. Why is that, I wonder, or does it mean something, perhaps?' (p 50). In fact it does mean something.

Stephen as toothless superman can most obviously be contrasted with Mulligan as physical hero. Because the superman who lives in the clouds above the earth has to be independent of the earth, he had better learn to do without food. If he does, his teeth will no longer be a necessity to him. Mulligan, on the other hand, is very much a hero of the earth. The money that Stephen has thought of putting into his teeth, Mulligan has spent on his already, as we learn at the very beginning of the novel. 'His even white teeth' glistened 'here and there with gold points' (p 3). But he cannot provide Stephen with a model for a viable relation with the world.[21]

Nor do Stephen's job and employer give him any help. While nervously waiting for Mr Deasy to pay him, Stephen lets his hand move over his employer's collection of shells, 'whelks and money, cowries.' He thinks, 'An old pilgrim's hoard, dead treasure, hollow shells' (p 29). Stephen rightly does not want to become the slave of inanimate forms. Yet without proper food and treatment, his own teeth have also turned to hollow shells. Although Stephen may feel superior to Deasy and Mulligan by sacrificing his body to purify his soul, he finally admits that he must keep his body at least alive if his soul is to be of any use to him. Similarly, Joyce had come to see that, though the forms of religion, government, and literature were empty in his day, this was only because they no longer contained the living organism they were designed to foster. Only by digging deep in the darkness of earth or into man's history or his mind could an individual find a pattern or guide for living his life, saving his soul, expressing his imagination.

In the *Odyssey* of Homer, Joyce found a shell or model elastic enough for his artistic purpose. In marriage outside the law, he found a form that satisfied his personal needs. The action of *Ulysses* takes place on 16 June, 1904, the date of its author's first tryst with Nora Barnacle (*J.J.* 162). She did for Joyce what he had not been able to do for himself, brought him down to earth, gave him a love that satisfied his longings, made it possible for his third try at living on the continent to be a success. Not having her, or a fictional character like her, Stephen Dedalus can get no farther in *Ulysses* than to be ready for her. But Joyce included at the end of the third episode of his novel a Protean cycle that alludes to her.

Stephen remembers an earlier remark, that a drowned corpse will likely be washed up a little later in the day. He imagines it floating in.

> Five fathoms out there. Full fathom five thy father lies. At one he said. Found drowned. High water at Dublin bar. Driving before it a loose drift of rubble, fanshoals of fishes, silly shells. ...
>
> Bag of corpsegas sopping in foul brine. A quiver of minnows, fat of a spongy titbit, flash through the slits of his buttoned trouser-fly. God becomes man becomes fish becomes barnacle goose becomes featherbed mountain....
>
> A seachange this. (p 50)

Shakespeare provides the clue to this sea change, but Joyce's conception is less lyric, equally concentrated but more cyclic in the manner of Bruno: 'God becomes man becomes fish becomes barnacle goose becomes featherbed mountain.' This sentence will repay investigation as a description of physical process, personal transformation, and spiritual metamorphosis.

The most accessible place to begin in the process is 'man becomes fish,' since in the sentence before, the minnow flashes through the trouser-fly of the corpse, presumably to nibble away his penis. This man becomes fish in the physical cycle of nature, what Stuart Gilbert calls 'the protean ebb and flow of living matter' (p 128). For the next phase in such a process, it would be simplest to imagine the fish swallowed by a goose. But an intermediate step seems likely. As Maurice Beebe pointed out in his interpretation of the passage, this goose gets its distinguishing name from an 'old belief' that it is 'hatched from the goose barnacle.'[22] We must first imagine the fish disintegrating until it becomes food for a barnacle and then imagine the goose as hatching from inside the shell of the barnacle. When this goose is captured and eaten by a human being, its feathers may be used to make a feather bed.

But this process must also be understood on at least two other levels. Its relevance to Stephen has been outlined by Beebe. Noting Stephen's theory of *A Portrait of the Artist* that 'the artist must be godlike, "invisible, refined out of existence"' (p 308), Beebe points out that this process has been 'ironically reversed' for Stephen: 'The godlike artist becomes human, submerges in the sea of life, enters the gullet of a bird of prey, becomes dead goose' (p 309). Beebe also sees as 'perhaps significant' the fact that Nora Joyce's maiden name was Barnacle. In the light of my earlier insistence of the importance of Nora to Joyce's 'new experience,' I would go farther.

Stephen has been and wishes to become again a 'wild goose' (p 41), that is an Irishman who lives on the continent. In Paris, however, he met a sad example of one, Kevin Egan, an old political exile who is 'loveless, landless, wifeless' (p 43). A solitary wild goose is clearly an unfortunate creature. But a barnacle goose is something else again. It has both love and a wife, because it is James Joyce plus Nora Barnacle. If we shift to the last term of the cycle, we see that Nora became Joyce's feather bed, his soft support, his place of rest. Equally important, as a Barnacle she may have been sharp and cutting at times, but she demonstrated to him that not all shells are empty, that the material filling out the form of life can be appealing, solid, sustaining. All this, however, is in the future for Stephen. He has yet to experience that love which can make him 'conscious of the beauty of mortal conditions.'

The third or spiritual level of the cycle can be most easily approached by thinking of Christ as the first step in the process of transforming god into man. We need also to remind ourselves that early in the history of Christianity, Christ was imaged as a fish. A late explanation for this symbolism is that it comes from an acrostic on the Greek words, 'Jesus Christ, God's Son, Saviour': IChThYS.[23] In the syncretism of Madame Blavatsky, 'Jesus is called the "Fish," as were Vishnu and Bacchus I H Σ , the "Saviour" of mankind being but the monogram of the god Bacchus called I X Θ Y Σ, the fish. (St Augustine says of Jesus: "He is a *fish* that lives in the midst of waters." ... "So many *fishes* bred in the *water*, and saved by *one great fish*," says Tertullian)' (*The Secret Doctrine* II, 313). Just as Christ miraculously provided loaves and fishes for his contemporary followers to eat, so his present-day followers eat secular fish and sacred bread in his memory.[24]

Although Joyce drew on the orthodox Christian tradition, he altered it in the various important ways that I earlier outlined. His god is to be found in the world, not as light, but as dark. In fact, working from Stephen's protean cycle, we can find in the third episode a dark version of Tertullian's 'great fish.' While on the beach, Stephen imagines himself back in fourteenth-century Dublin, with 'a school of turlehide whales stranded in hot noon, spouting, hobbling in the shallows. Then from the starving cagework city a horde of jerkined dwarfs, my people, with flayers' knives, running, scaling, hacking in green blubbery whalemeat' (p 45). The dwarfs feeding off the giant is an important motif in *Finnegans Wake*. In *Ulysses*, just before the vision of the stranded whale, Stephen had pictured a giant: 'Sands and stones. Heavy of the past. Sir Lout's toys. Mind you don't get one bang on the ear. I'm the bloody well gigant rolls all them bloody well boulders, bones for my steppingstones. Feefawfum. I zmellz de blodz odz an Iridzman' (pp 44-5). Alive the giant threatens to eat the dwarfs; dead his body feeds or supports them. Alive he is a demiurgic creator of the land; dead he becomes the land and its people. Early in the first episode, for instance, the reader is told that 'the blunt cape of Bray head ... lay on the water like the snout of a sleeping whale' (p 7). This description all but joins the end terms of Stephen's cycle, as mountain appears like mighty fish god.[25]

Joyce has put into Stephen's mind all the terms of a transformation cycle that he cannot yet appreciate. But by showing himself down to earth enough to enter in imagination the questing senses of a dog and the decomposed world of a drowned corpse, Stephen has taken an important step towards engagement not only in the world but also with its underlying darkness. As artist and man he needs to be both within the natural process and above it in the sense of recognizing that death is only another form of the darkness on which the universe rests. Where Stephen's earlier ideal flights into the sublime sent him crashing to earth, his present realistic empathy with death has paradoxically prepared him for the kinds of immortality granted man – fathering children, creating lasting works, suffering spiritual rebirth, and ultimately re-entering the natural cycle through dissolution.

Although Stephen is offered the same opportunity in 'Circe' that Bloom is, he does not take as much advantage of it. As I shall suggest in the chapters ahead, Stephen has glimpses of a possible way out of his dilemma, but he cannot consolidate them. In contrast Bloom finds his way home to a Molly who becomes his feather bed mountain.[26]

3 The round of nature

Following Bloom as he tries to find lunch (Lestrygonians episode), as he attends the burial of Paddy Dignam (Hades episode), and as he faces the citizen (Cyclops episode), I shall in this chapter be developing two important cycles of transformation in which Joyce involved his hero. These particular patterns can again be connected quite directly with Bruno.

Bruno's conception of transformation includes a notion of physical cycles more detailed than the conception Ovid attributed to Pythagoras. Pythagoras traces only conventional cycles, such as day and night, the waxing and waning of the moon, the succession of the four seasons, and so on. Bruno shows how one natural thing becomes another, suggesting 'that what was seed becomes stalk, and what was stalk becomes corn, and what was corn becomes bread – that out of bread comes chyle, out of chyle blood, out of blood the seed, out of the seed the embryo, and then man, corpse, earth, stone, or something else in succession – on and on, involving all natural forms' (*Cause* 102). Similarly, in *Ulysses*, Bloom thinks 'And we stuffing food in one hole and out behind: food, chyle, blood, dung, earth, food: have to feed it like stoking an engine' (p 176). Joyce's cycle, because appropriate to Bloom, lacks the philosophic drive of Bruno's process, but it does contain three of Bruno's terms (chyle, blood, and earth).[1] It also emphasizes the cyclic effect better, by being circular, beginning and ending with the same word.

Usually Bruno was quite aware of this circular effect; he could even embody a cycle in his writing. I did not comment on it in Chapter 1, but the passage from *Cause, Principle and Unity* in which Bruno tried to indicate the ubiquity of the infinite contains such a cycle. 'In infinite duration hour does not differ from day, day from year, year from century, century from moment' (p 136). The progression here swings suddenly around into a circle as 'moment' provides the link with 'hour' at the beginning. Like Joyce, though much less consistently and artistically, Bruno believed in trying to have his form reflect his content.[2]

The cycle from 'Lestrygonians' quoted above was consciously constructed by Bloom after he had eaten lunch. His own surfeit combines with his revulsion at the other eaters he has seen to provide him with a new view of the process: 'Stuffing food in one hole and out behind.' The mouth of pleasure and the anus of shame become two equivalent holes, the beginning and end of an internal process.[3] Next his mind shifts to the substances and their transformations in the larger process that includes both the inner and outer environment: 'food, chyle, blood, dung, earth, food.' As food becomes nutrient in the animal system, most of it is transformed into chyle, a milky emulsion formed in the intestines during digestion and passing through the lymph system before entering the blood stream. Waste goes out as dung which fertilizes plants which become food. Since this last part of the cycle is very much on Bloom's mind as he goes through the day, his conscious and unconscious relation to it is worth investigating in detail.

Bloom had pondered the end of the cycle as he went out to defecate after breakfast. Staring at his back yard he concluded he should 'manure the whole place over,' make a 'mulch of dung' (p 68). The subject became prominent while Bloom was in the graveyard. Looking it over, he thought, 'daresay the soil would be quite fat with corpse manure, bones, flesh' (p 108), which he then imagined decomposing. He introduced a variation of the process by substituting for dung a body sustained by blood. He even left out the body and flesh in the later cycle: 'It's the blood sinking in the earth gives new life' (p 108). A similar acceptance of the cycle caused him later to criticize money spent on burials and grave plots: 'Plant him and have done with him' (p 113). Using a common idiom, 'plant him,' Bloom implicitly shifted the view of sad death and grisly decay to glad life and physical resurrection.

Equally fatalistic was his reaction to seeing 'an obese grey rat' in the graveyard: 'One of those chaps would make short work of a fellow. ... Ordinary meat for them' (p 114). Later in the day while trying to find somewhere for lunch, Bloom encounters the opposite – men eating animals. But he is less accepting of his fellow humans' habits: 'See the animals feed' (p 169). His perceptions are in fact charged negatively with a sense of man's biological heritage. Watching the diners, he realizes that a 'hungry man is an angry man' (p 169). Seeing one man use a knife, he thinks, 'Tear it limb from limb. Second nature to him' (p 170). And as he leaves the restaurant, too revolted to eat, he concludes, 'Eat or be eaten. Kill! Kill!' (p 170). These reactions tie in with the theme of the episode, based on the parallel section of the *Odyssey* in which most of Ulysses' men are eaten by a race of cannibals. The only overt mention of cannibals in the episode occurs when Bloom thinks of Dignam, whom 'cannibals' would be willing to eat. 'White missionary too salty. Like pickled pork. Expect the chief consumes the parts of honour. Ought to be tough from exercise. His wives in a row to watch the effect. *There was a right royal old nigger. Who ate or something the somethings of the reverend Mr MacTrigger*' (p 171). Later he remembers the other three lines of the limerick: '*His five hundred wives. Had the time of their lives. ... It grew bigger and bigger and bigger*' (p 172). The 'it' of the last line is presumably *prick*; indeed the penis is associated several times with this cycle, as we have already seen it was with Stephen's.

By eating the sex organ of the missionary, the cannibal king is able to perform sexual intercourse prodigiously, gigantically. The premise here is a genuinely primitive one, as Frazer analyzed cannibalism: 'The flesh and blood of dead men are commonly eaten and drunk to inspire bravery, wisdom, or other qualities for which the men themselves were remarkable, or which are supposed to have their special seat in the particular part eaten.'[4] Bloom articulates essentially the same premise: 'I wouldn't be surprised if it was that kind of food you see produces the like waves of the brain the poetical. For example one of those policemen sweating Irish stew into their shirts; you couldn't squeeze a line of poetry out of him' (p 166). If not to Frazer, the aesthetic overtones of Bloom's formulation may owe something to Bruno. In *Cause, Principle and Unity*, the Italian philosopher had a character defend one of his own dialogues, *Ash-Wednesday Supper*. 'The setting was none other than a supper, where brains are controlled by the states of the body brought about by the effectiveness of the savours and smells of the food and drink. Such as the material and corporeal supper is, so consequently develops the verbal and spiritual one' (p 60). Joyce is, of course, using this theory throughout *Ulysses* in taking his style and form from the subjects he treats. As Budgen put it,

> Joyce in Zürich was a curious collector of facts about the human body, especially on that borderland where mind and body meet, where thought is generated and shaped by a state of the body. Bloom is led on to lunch by erotic visions. After his bread and cheese and Burgundy he lives in erotic memories. 'Sun's heat it is. Seems to a secret touch telling me memory. Touched his sense moistened remembered.' (p 106).

In the final line we find almost a natural science of thought.

The connection of sex and death, which appears again in the lunch scene, began in the graveyard. There Bloom thought, 'whores in Turkish graveyards. ... Love among the tombstones. ... In the midst of death we are in life. Both ends meet' (p 108). This is a relatively straightforward statement of Bruno's notion that extremes meet. Similarly Bloom thinks of oysters, as of other meat, with revulsion in the Lestrygonians episode. 'Unsightly like a clot of phlegm. Filthy shells. Devil to open them too. Who found them out? Garbage, sewage they feed on. Fizz and Red bank oysters. Effect on the sexual. Aphrodis. He was in the Red bank this morning. Was he oyster old fish at table. Perhaps he young flesh in bed' (pp 174-5).[5] Again transformation is important and again extremes meet, this time with an emphasis on feeding and sexual stimulation comparable to the cannibal limerick.

But Joyce gave a larger dimension to the transformations of feeding than its connection with sex. In *Dublin's Joyce*, Hugh Kenner looks at the Lestrygonians episode in a section entitled 'Who are the Cannibals?' As he points out, 'The organ of the episode is the stomach; it is into a vast stomach, seat of the appetites, the belly usurping the functions of the members, that the Body Politic has declined' (p 234). In his view, the once-spiritual kingdom in which Christ's body regularly appeared to sustain man through the Eucharist has degenerated into a materialistic city where the physical belly is fed, but where men in turn are processed for the benefit of a commercial state.

Dublin should indeed be seen as a kind of animal, as Joyce put it in the notesheets for *Ulysses*, 'State: monster fed with our blood, must be starved.'[6] In fact, however, the monster goes right on devouring in this episode. Its internal functions proceed automatically, their action being fateful and reductive. Bloom's experience of peristalsis (Joyce's technique for Lestrygonians) helps to explain his depression. Peristalsis is the contracting rhythm of the alimentary canal which causes food to pass through the stages of decomposition and assimilation until the residue reaches the hole of expulsion.[7] Bloom may be experiencing the psychological equivalent of the latter when he thinks, 'no one is anything. This is the very worst hour of the day. Vitality. Dull, gloomy: hate this hour. Feel as if I had been eaten and spewed' (p 164). Just before this, he had imagined a 'cityful passing away, other cityful coming, passing away too; other coming on, passing on.' He thus extends the image of man as food to a continuous cycle in history of people being passed through the city's system. As Avel Austin suggests, 'Dublin's streets are seen as the human "bowels," passing a stream of digestibles and indigestibles into the main drain' (p 5). Phillip Herring provides a graphic description of the picture Joyce seems to have imagined: 'A glance at a map will show that the city proper is circumscribed by canals and the North and South Circular Roads, and, with a little imagination one can picture a reclining posterior. In 1904 the river Liffey, which divides the city, would have carried away a good part of the city's sewage.'[8]

That section of Joyce's chart which lists the appropriate organs for the book could be thought of as a key to the activities of this giant body. Thus the newspaper office with its constant winds can be taken not only in its Homeric parallel with the God of the Winds, Aeolus, but in its function as Dublin's lungs breathing in the bits of information and opinion which it then passes on as lively news and rhetoric into the lifestream of the city.[9] But we can look further and see even more of Joyce's intent. As Richard Ellmann has described it, 'he conceived of his entire book as a silent, unspoken portrayal of an archetypal man who would never appear and yet whose body would slowly materialize as the book progressed, linguafied as it were into life. This creature's presence can be felt distinctly ... for the first time' in the newspaper office (*Ulysses on the Liffey* 73). Besides working backward from *Finnegans Wake* for this conception (cf. p 175 of the *Liffey*), Ellmann presumably had in mind also Joyce's comment to Budgen.

> 'Among other things,' he said, 'my book is the epic of the human body. The only man I know who has attempted the same thing is Phineas Fletcher. But then his Purple Island is purely descriptive, a kind of coloured anatomical chart of the human body. In my book the body lives in and moves through space and is the home of a full human personality. The words I wrote are adapted to express first one of its functions then another. In *Lestrygonians* the stomach dominates and the rhythm of the episode is that of the peristaltic movement.'
>
> 'But the minds, the thoughts of the characters,' I began.
>
> 'If they had no body they would have no mind,' said Joyce. 'It's all one.'[10] (p 21)

The final comment insists on unity through the resolution of seeming opposites. This insistence in Joyce's mind and art gives the novel its Brunian excellence and justifies its plenitude, its sometimes exhausting duration. How that resolution is achieved can be demonstrated by investigation of another cycle connected with Bloom. But before turning to it, we need to consider further the destructive implications of the present cycle.

We can begin to look at a destructive opposition by focusing on a creative opposition in the body: Chyle and blood in Bloom's internal cycle circulate respectively in the complimentary lymph and artery systems. Chyle is milky white, blood sanguine red. Joyce builds on this implicit contrast. At the very beginning of the episode, Bloom pictures King Edward, 'sitting on his throne, sucking red jujubes white' (p 151). The violent potential in this seemingly innocuous transformation is further hinted at when Bloom is handed a religious advertisement. The first phrase to strike his eye is 'Blood of the Lamb' (p 151), placed by Joyce as a paragraph on its own. Bloom's eye is attracted to *blood* because its first four letters are identical with those of his own name. Knowing Joyce's Homeric parallels, we realize that he is preparing us for Bloom's encounter with the Lestrygonians, as well as with the even more dangerous cannibal giant in the Cyclops episode. At the end of the latter, the narrator reports that 'the last we saw was the *bloody* car rounding the corner and old *sheep*face on it' (p 345, my emphasis). The citizen wants to make Bloom a blood victim, a bloody sheep, wash him in the blood of the lamb because he is an alien who has claimed to be related to Christ. The lamb is, of course, white until its blood is spilled.

King Edward sucking red jujubes white seems to be the opposite of the sequence I have just reconstructed. But both are connected with violence, as comes out clearly in the Circe episode. Edward the Seventh appears near the end of the episode when Stephen and Pvt Carr are about to fight. The stage directions tell us that Edward 'sucks a red jujube' (p 590). After setting up the fight, he 'levitates over heaps of slain in the garb and with the halo of Joking Jesus, a white jujube in his phospherescent face' (p 591). As Joking Jesus he is the antichrist, the whiteness of the jujube to be associated not with the lamb but with the victim drained of blood. The king who wants blood victims is one version of god, characterized earlier by Stephen as 'hangman god' (p 213). Indeed, the hangman enters the Circe episode soon after King Edward; having hanged the Croppy Boy, he says 'God save the king!' This sentiment causes Edward to sing 'with soft contentment' (p 594). Although what occurs in this scene must be connected with Stephen's distorting consciousness, part of the preparation for it comes, as we have seen, from Bloom's experience as victim.

Like Edward, the Citizen is a larger-than-life figure who wants blood victims. Characterized as a giant in one of Joyce's parody interpolations in the Cyclops episode, the citizen wants to turn the tables on the English. In return for their killing of Irishmen over the centuries, he wants to begin killing the oppressors. '– We'll put force against force, says the citizen' (p 329). When Bloom advocates peace by pointing out that violence begets more violence, the citizen scorns him and begins to build up the hostility that leads to his attack at the end of the episode.

Bloom's meditations on the physical cycle of man's body form a contrast to his thinking of the gods consuming non-physical substances: 'Nectar, imagine drinking electricity: gods' food' (p 176). The implication is that the gods are spiritual, man physical, an opposition that comes back to haunt Bloom in his encounter with the nymph during the Circe episode. As Joyce's remark to Budgen indicated, the mind-body opposition gives a faulty picture of reality. Bloom earlier came up with a hint of another possibility. Hearing of the postcard that Denis Breen has taken to his solicitor, Menton, Bloom thinks, 'Round to Menton's office. His oyster eyes staring at the postcard. Be a feast for the gods' (p 160). At first glance, the scene might be thought a *spectacle* for the gods, but in fact Menton's oyster eyes could be imagined as a *feast* for them.[11] If they were, it would merely be an extension of the motif already investigated, of kings feeding off their subjects, giants off alien inhabitants.

The suggestion is made directly by Stephen Dedalus when he and Bloom meet at the lying-in hospital (Oxen of the Sun episode). When the students discuss infant mortality, Lynch puts forward a benevolent Darwinian view: Nature 'has her own good and cogent reasons for whatever she does'; the death of young imperfect 'organisms' is thus 'in the long run beneficial to the race in general' (p 419). Stephen's bitter response implicitly counteracts Lynch's beneficent Mother Nature with a malevolent Father, 'an omnivorous being which can masticate, deglute, digest and apparently pass through the ordinary channel with pluterperfect imperturbability such multifarious aliments as cancrenous females emaciated by parturition, corpulent professional gentlemen, not to speak of jaundiced politicians and chlorotic nuns' (p 420). Stephen's multisyllabic, Latinate diction shadows forth a picture of nature as a hungry giant whose food is diseased and otherwise imperfect creatures. Presumably the physical breakdown of their terminal illness corresponds to its mastication, their burial to its deglutination (swallowing), and their decomposition in earth to its digestion.[12] Although a clearly biased view (Stephen's mother was a 'cancrenous female emaciated by parturition'), this grotesque transformation does provide another version of the life-death cycle which Joyce made an important theme in *Ulysses*.[13]

At the end of his commentary on the first six episodes of *Ulysses*, Richard Ellmann offers Three Propositions in which 'the episodes are juxtaposed in such a way as to emphasize' the 'parallelisms' between those devoted to Stephen and those to Bloom (*Ulysses on the Liffey* 57). The first of these propositions will come into my discussion of Stephen as neurotic artist in Chapter 8. The other two are relevant here.

The second proposition begins with Stephen's gloomy view that (II) *the newborn experiences corruption and dies*; then adds Bloom's sanguine corollary, that *having died, the being experiences corruption and is in some manner newborn*. 'April's green endures.'

The final proposition is more complex. (III) *God, descending, becomes flesh becomes food, is eaten, becomes faeces, then becomes food becomes flesh becomes man ascending.* (p 60)

The dependence of this last proposition on Stephen's transformation cycle at the end of 'Proteus' is clear enough. How does it include Bloom in 'Hades?' We have seen the descent of man to food, faeces, and earth in the outhouse, graveyard, and lunchroom. Ellmann does not do much to demonstrate the ascent in 'Hades' (cf. pp 51-2, 53). Yet the evidence is there in a formula as potent as Stephen's. I am thinking of the list of names that Bloom reads in the obituary column.

Since this list lacks the coherence of Stephen's self-conscious cycle, I would like to approach it by way of Joyce's attitude to words. Budgen suggests that words were more to Joyce 'than a pleasurable material out of which agreeable patterns can be made, or thought and emotion communicated. ... They have a will and life of their own.' In short, Joyce saw 'words as a mysterious means of expression as well as an instrument of communication' (Budgen 175). Part of this mystery is how all things are connected, how the universe is what the Latin word says, one turning, (all) combined into one. (Joyce enjoyed reading Skeat's etymological dictionary.) As I suggested in the last chapter, and will further demonstrate in the fifth chapter, Joyce believed that 'happenings in nature are interconnected.' The mysterious quality of words would make them able to express this side of nature. In both nature and words, the mystery is hidden, often beneath an innocuous surface. Joyce similarly filled the world of words that became *Ulysses* with a mundane surface and an underlying further reality. Those who could appreciate the surface were welcome to it (some turn to it yet for its titillating passages). Those who could decipher its mystery were encouraged, often tantalized.

We may now turn to the newspaper item which, by its 'mysterious means of expression,' presents us with another important transformation cycle.

> Mr Bloom's glance travelled down the edge of the paper, scanning the deaths. Callan, Coleman, Dignam, Fawcett, Lowry, Naumann, Peake, what Peake is that? is it the chap was in Crosbie and Alleyne's? no, Sexton, Urbright. Inked characters fast fading on the frayed breaking paper. (p 91)

These fading 'characters' are, of course, both inked words and the persons referred to, memories of whom may last no longer than the stability of the medium in which they are installed. The names of these dead people make a rather strange cast of characters. The last two, for instance, are to say the least factitious: 'Sexton, Urbright.' According to the dictionary, 'ur' occurs in English only as a prefix, either as the Hebrew verb *to shine*, of as a German prefix, *original* or *primitive*. In fact, all the names on the list demand to be deciphered. A preliminary 'reading' could be as follows: Callan – call one; Coleman – Coalman; Dignam – dig man; Fawcett – faucet; Lowry – lower; Naumann – No man; Peake – peak; Sexton – sexton; Urbright – original brightness.

A clue to the point of 'coalman' comes from Bloom's notion of a more practical way of burial than placing long boxes in the ground: 'Like down a coalshoot. Then lump them together to save time' (p 113). Man becomes a lump of coal, a source of energy underground. By association, the 'call' of the first name on the list may therefore be a call to death. In this vein Bloom thinks of omens of death: 'when you shiver in the sun. Someone walking over it [your grave]. *Call*boy's warning' (p 111, my emphasis). But the first name on the list can also lead in an entirely different direction. There is a particular character in the novel named Callan, Nurse Callan who has two connections with Bloom (cf. pp 373, 722). At the lying-in hospital, 'the amiable Miss Callan' is praised for seeing Mrs Purefoy's baby born, for her 'lustre ... at an instant the most momentous that can befall a puny child of clay' (p 406). This Callan has brought to light what was hidden; she has taken a lump of clay and, as it were, given it life. The association with the name Callan can thus be quite the opposite of that with a coalman who puts lumps back underground where the light and energy become potential.

The possible opposition between these first two names on the list is paralleled by that between the last two. The sexton is the grave-digger who helps put man into darkness, while the original brightness tries to call him back again. The connection between coal, the sun, and Ur (as primitive) is implicit in a later quasi-scientific characterization of coal by Joyce: 'masses of bituminous coal, containing in compressed mineral form the foliated fossilised decidua of *primeval* forests which had in turn derived their vegetative existence from the *sun*, primal source of heat.'[14] Similarly, on a theological level, if we remember the grave-diggers who 'flung heavy clods of clay in on the coffin' of Dignam (p 111), we can appreciate the evangelical question put during the Circe episode: 'Are you a god or a doggone clod?' (p 507). The clod is man become mere earth, gone to the dogs, ('beastly dead' as the problem appears to Stephen, p 8). Seeing a surface truth even in the evangelical, Joyce affirmed not only the natural cycle of energy reused, but also the continued transformation of a divine universe. The cycle examined in the first part of this chapter is limited to a view of the natural and has destructive overtones. The cycle we are presently investigating includes a cosmic, constructive level. But its roots are also in the soil.

The third and fifth names on the obituary list connect easily with the sexton, whom we may imagine *digging* the grave and *lowering* the corpse in it. But what purpose does the faucet serve? To get an indication, we need to look at what follows the obituary list. Bloom reads bits of prayers and commemorations of the dead:

Thanks to the Little Flower. Sadly missed. ...
On whose soul Sweet Jesus have mercy.
  It is now a month since dear Henry fled
  To his home up above in the sky
  While his family weeps and mourns his loss
  Hoping some day to meet him on high.
I tore up the envelope? Yes. ... Dear Henry fled. (p 91)

The envelope Bloom had received that morning from his pen-pal Martha. He is reminded of it because he writes her under the nomdeplume of Henry Flower. Both words appear in the memorial items he reads. The relation of the verse to Bloom is ironic. He believes in life on earth, disbelieves in heaven; yet instead of plowing his earthy wife, he has initiated a fantasy flirtation by mail with another woman. The verse applies because he has in one sense 'left' his wife and because the sentimentality of the lines applies to his temptation to rise 'on high' as Messiah. But the brute fact is that for this Flower to Bloom it is going to have to get in touch with the cycle of nature again. First the flower must be rooted in the earth; then it needs water and sun to bloom. All three elements are indirectly present in the obituary list, earth in Coleman, the sun in Urbright, and water through Fawcet. The noun *faucet* appears only once in all the pages of *Ulysses*, when Bloom turns it on late at night to get water for cocoa. This simple action sends the impersonal narrator of the Ithaca episode off on two long disquisitions about water (pp 670-2).

Of the remaining two words on the list, 'Naumann' translates as No man. One way of becoming no man is to become a corpse, to go back to earth. As we saw earlier, Bloom thinks an appropriate way to treat a corpse is to 'plant him.' Figuratively, it is also true of Bloom that he must die before he can come to life. Although Bloom is realistic about life and death in general, he has tended to escape into sexual fantasies since he pulled back from sexual relations with his wife after the death of their infant son. He is purged of his escapism and made ready for rebirth in the brothel scene. Joyce's Circe, Bella Cohen, taunts him, 'We'll manure you, Mr Flower!' (p 544). This reduction of Bloom will be the end of the process as far as the sensual whoremistress is concerned, but as shown in Chapter 11, excrement is only the step before rebirth in earth's transformation cycle.

More immediately, a means of coming to terms with earth is provided by the remaining name on the list, 'Peake.' The Gaelic word for *peak* is *ben*. But it is used by Joyce interchangeably with *hill* or *slieve*, meaning *mountain*. Thus the hill of Howth is at least twice referred to as Ben Howth. One of these times is in a humorous list where it is intended to be taken as a man's name (p 297). Later in the Nausicaa episode, Howth is described as a human figure, a kind of giant:

> Far out over the sands the coming surf crept, grey. Howth settled for slumber tired of long days, of yumyum rhododendrons (he was old) and felt gladly the night breeze lift, ruffle his fell of ferns. He lay but opened a red eye unsleeping, deep and slowly breathing, slumberous but awake. And far on Kish bank the anchored lightship twinkled, winked at Mr Bloom. (p 379)

Since Howth comes from the Old Norse word for *head* (Gilbert 69), the giant-mountain connection is traditional. It is used by Joyce as the heroic head of Dublin's impolitic body. And since it has only one red eye, it should remind us of the Cyclops, a creature Joyce embodied in the bigoted citizen to whom a long parody description had been devoted earlier.[15]

> The figure seated on a large boulder at the foot of a round tower was that of a broad-shouldered deepchested stronglimbed ... deepvoiced barekneed brawnyhanded hairy-legged ruddyfaced sinewyarmed hero. ... His rocklike mountainous knees were covered, as was likewise the rest of his body wherever visible, with a strong growth of tawny prickly hair in hue and toughness similar to the mountain gorse. (p 296)

A crude malicious person, the citizen is the kind of stupid giant who makes Ireland what it is, a land of darkness from which any non-physical person has trouble drawing light. Not having yet sunk into the landscape, like benign old Howth, the citizen is a dangerous giant, especially in his attack on Bloom.

The symbolic overtones of the mountain are thus connected with forces larger than human, creative and destructive god-like forces. Bloom himself was early but allusively associated with these forces when he identified himself with 'Slieve Bloom' (p 58), the mountain on which the mythical Irish hero Finn gained his first powers.[16] But for Bloom to become a mythic mountain he would have to admit, as Howth has, that 'he was old.' He is very much tempted to do so, to retire from the competition of life as did Rip Van Winkle, but in the end, as we shall see, he overcomes that temptation.

Another conceivable choice for Bloom is to become destructive like that other mountain, the gigantic citizen. Far from being a cannibal, like the Cyclops, or even a meat eater, Bloom orders a cheese sandwich for his lunch. Later his preaching peace and love is what finally causes the irate citizen to try to make Bloom a victim. At the end of the episode, that role is reversed when Bloom is presented, with indulgent irony, as the messiah that the citizen had earlier called him, with savage irony (p 337). One reason for the interpolating narrator's overt reference in the last paragraph to Bloom as '*Abba! Adonai!*' (p 345) can be found in the parallel scene in the *Odyssey*. As Sultan demonstrates Joyce to have known, Ulysses used a punning version of his name as he sailed away from the Cyclops: 'His name "Odusseus" is composed of close puns on the words "no one" ("Outis") and "God" (Zeus)' (Sultan 258). As victim Bloom is No one; as *Abba* ('Father,' cf. Thornton), he is God. Going back to the name cycle with which we began this section, as No one he is Naumann; as Zeus he is Urbright. The list can be understood in its imposed alphabetical order, but it can also be reconstituted from what we have discovered of Joyce's Brunian outlook. On a

Peake, the Sexton does Dig nam and Lowry him. In earth this Nau man disintegrates into lumps of Cole man, until Fawcett water shall Call an. At which point, he reappears in his Ur brightness.[17] I have picked this way of telling the archetypal story because it adds to the physical dissolution, which characterized the first Bloom cycle, a spiritual affirmation, and because the two together provide a paradigm for Bloom's experience in the Circe and Ithaca episodes.

Before considering those episodes, however, I shall have more to say about Bloom as low victim and high hero in the Cyclops episode. And before we can appreciate that opposition, we must investigate in more detail the nature of the world Joyce created in *Ulysses*; we must then consider Joyce's own transformations as artist, to discover what it is like for the heroic creator to enter that destructive-creative cycle.

4 Roads parallel and roads contrary

In this chapter I propose to bring together the experiences of Leopold Bloom and Stephen Dedalus, partly to advance our understanding of them, but mainly in order to demonstrate how Joyce tried to permeate the texture of his novel with patterns comparable to those he saw operating in the coincidences of everyday experience and in the structure of the cosmos. Since much of the focus will be on the Nighttown section, I shall begin with a consideration of Joyce's handling of the Greek god that Homer chose as Ulysses' guide in his encounters with Circe, the trickster Hermes (or as the Romans named him, Mercury).

Early in the Circe episode, Bloom notices 'a sinister figure' with 'a visage unknown, injected with dark mercury' (p 436). Later 'a dark mercurialised face appears' as a character, 'THE DARK MERCURY' (p 456). The insistent adjective 'dark' seems a strange one: it could refer to mercury as planet (not visible) or as chemical (a black sublimate) or as god (who led shades to Hades). As god, Mercury is three times associated in *Ulysses* with Mulligan, once in 'Circe' (p 580), and twice in the first episode, 'Telemachus.' He calls himself 'mercurial,' (p 17), changeable, and is described at the swimming hole as 'fluttering his winglike hands, leaping nimbly, Mercury's hat quivering in the fresh wind' (p 19). As Thornton indicates in glossing this allusion, Mulligan does have many qualities which make him an appropriate representative of that god. And the advice he gives Stephen (eg, to 'give up the moody brooding') is sound, as far as it goes.[1]

But Mulligan is as tricky as Hermes, and finally inimical to Stephen. The references to 'dark Mercury' with which we began are therefore appropriate to this aspect of mutability. Mercury, the element, is the most obviously mutable metal, and was thought by the alchemists to be the *prima materia* from which all others could be formed. In *Ulysses* its changeability (as in Quicksilver) is connected with Mulligan, but the emphasis is more towards its dark earthiness than towards the gold or silver of the alchemists.

Joyce's conscious use of Mercury the god is further reflected in a letter he wrote Frank Budgen while working on the Circe episode. He pointed out that in the *Odyssey*, the gift of *moly* to protect Ulysses from Circe's enchantment is 'the only occasion on which Ulysses is not helped by Minerva but by her male counterpart or inferior' (*Letters* I, 148). Trying to determine how to find a modern equivalent for *moly* and other aspects of Homer's episode, Joyce commented, 'Moly is the gift of Hermes, god of public ways ... [and] god of signposts: i.e. he is, specially for a traveller like Ulysses, the point at which roads parallel merge and roads contrary also' (*Letters* I, 147-8). This statement gives an important indication of Joyce's intention in constructing the Circe episode. The most obvious parallel road is that of Bloom and Stephen. Though their ways have touched from time to time, the most noticeable development, to the acute reader, is the way they have gone through parallel experiences during the day. Towards the end of 'Circe' their faces coalesce in the mirror (p 567), and they remain together during the next two episodes. In another sense, their roads are contrary; they part in 'Ithaca,' presumably to meet no more.

In 'Eumaeus' we are told, 'Though they didn't see eye to eye in everything, a certain analogy there somehow was, as if both their minds were travelling, so to speak, in the one train of thought' (p 656, cf. also p 730). From this rather muzzy point of view the parallel lines of a train track merge in the train itself, in the two minds which travel in the same direction. This metaphor can be adopted to the riddle asked in the Aeolus episode, the first in which Stephen and Bloom meet. 'What opera is like a railway line? ... *The Rose of Castille*. See the wheeze? Rows of cast steel' (p 134). Bloom, as the commercial traveller who thinks of train trips and free passes during the day, would be connected with rows of cast steel. Stephen, as the singer and would-be creator of songs, could be connected with opera. Or Bloom as Molly's husband is married to a beautiful half-Spanish singer of opera songs, while Stephen as Aristotelian logician is proceeding on rows of cast steel. In an obvious allusion to his wife, Bloom asks during 'Circe,' 'What railway opera is like a tramline in Gibraltar?' (p 491). This developed image is an illustration of Joyce's interest in the merging of 'roads parallel ... and roads contrary also.'

This statement shows traces too of Bruno's doctrine of the coincidence of contraries. From this doctrine, as we have already seen, Bruno drew the conclusion that 'there is one primal foundation both of origin and of end.' A notion very close to this is behind Joyce's comment about merging roads, and the analysis which Stephen utters 'abruptly' in the Circe episode. 'What went forth to the ends of the world to traverse not itself. God, the sun, Shakespeare, a commercial traveller, having itself traversed in reality itself, becomes that self. Wait a moment. Wait a second. Damn that fellow's noise in the street. Self which it itself was ineluctably preconditioned to become. *Ecco*!' (p 505). Where earlier he was thinking of a cycle without full understanding of it, here Stephen is trying to voice an insight using as illustration four names which will appear presently as a cycle. Man takes things outside to be alien, but as he progresses discovers that by confronting and absorbing them, they become him (he finds himself; it becomes itself), so at the end individual will, impersonal nature, and inevitable fate come together in one. This convergence is typical of Bruno: 'Necessity, fate, nature, counsel, will, in things justly and impeccably ordered, all concur' (*Heroic Frenzies* 121; cf. also McIntyre 197). But Joyce's process owes more to a passage from Croce which Richard Ellmann suggests (rightly, I believe) Stephen is echoing: 'Man creates the human world, creates it by transforming himself into the facts of society; by thinking it he re-creates his own creations, traverses over again the paths he has already traversed, reconstructs the whole ideally, and thus knows it with full and true knowledge.'[2] First one creates by immersion, then re-creates by re-traversing in the mind.

The distinction between actual and ideal creation can be connected with the four terms of Stephen's illustration. God is to sun as Shakespeare to a commercial traveller. Shakespeare as parallel to God was insisted on in the library scene. 'After God Shakespeare has created most' (p 212). As Thornton points out, this observation was made by Dumas, who also wrote, 'I recognized that, in the theatrical world, everything has come from Shakespeare, as, in the real world, all comes from the sun.' The sun sends rays of physical light for earth's nourishment, while the commercial traveller helps man in an even more mundane way. But as Stephen comes to realize in 'Eumaeus,' all are equally valid expressions of divinity. Even Bloom, the commercial traveller, has a touch of Christ in him.[3]

Stephen may still see only the demeaning side of a commercial traveller, as earlier he had criticized Shakespeare's private business dealings (pp 203, 204-5). Stephen's attitude to Shakespeare is important to an understanding of the traversing passage above. His portrait of Shakespeare's end has a certain power: 'He returns after a life of absence to that spot of earth where he was born, where he has always been, man and boy, a silent witness and there, his journey of life ended, he plants his mulberrytree in the earth. Then dies. The motion is ended' (p 213). The 'return' motif is important in *Ulysses*, especially as connected with Bloom. There as here, it takes the figure of a joined circle, considered a perfect form by both Aristotle (*Metaphysica*, Chapters 6, 7) and Bruno (*Heroic Frenzies* 156-7). It is true that, Shakespeare being dead, his motion as a man is ended. But it is untrue that *the* motion is ended. His children and his plays live on.

A similar fault creeps in towards the end of Stephen's analysis of Shakespeare's success as writer:

He found in the world without as actual what was in his world within as possible. Maeterlinck says: *If Socrates leave his house today he will find the sage seated on his doorstep. If Judas go forth tonight it is to Judas his steps will tend.* Every life is many days, day after day. We walk through ourselves, meeting robbers, ghosts, giants, old men, young men, wives, widows, brothers-in-love. But always meeting ourselves. The playwright who wrote the folio of this world and wrote it badly (He gave us light first and the sun two days later), the lord of things as they are whom the most Roman of catholics call *dio boia*, hangman god, is doubtless all in all in all of us. (p 213)

Stephen ends by making one of Bruno's key points, that the divine is everywhere; 'God is near ... each one has Him with him and within himself more than he himself can be within himself' (*Heroic Frenzies* 193). But instead of drawing Bruno's optimistic conclusion that man has divinity, Stephen is able only to emulate Antisthenes and draw the cynical conclusion that man has the killer instinct because the hangman god is within him.

Stephen had earlier defined God to Deasy as 'a shout in the street' (p 34). Later the thunder which frightens Stephen in the hospital is described in similar terms, 'a black crack of noise in the street here, alack, bawled back' (p 394). And in the passage on traversing, Stephen says 'Damn that fellow's noise in the street' (p 505). As Stanley Sultan points out (p 343), that fellow is Pvt Carr, who finally deals Stephen the blow that knocks him out and confirms his fears. As he had said of Shakespeare, 'he found in the world without as actual what was in his world within as possible' (p 213). This analysis again may be taken either optimistically or pessimistically. Believing in an executioner god, Stephen has experienced his wrath.

Stephen was led into his traversing speech by a musical observation he tried to make to his erstwhile friend Lynch. Notice how Lynch (as Cap) begins by denying Bruno's coincidence of contraries.[4]

THE CAP: (*With saturnine spleen.*) Bah! It is because it is. Woman's reason. Jewgreek is greekjew. Extremes meet. Death is the highest form of life. Bah!

STEPHEN: You remember fairly accurately all my errors, boasts, mistakes. How long shall I continue to close my eyes to disloyalty? Whetstone!

THE CAP: Bah!

STEPHEN: Here's another for you. (*He frowns.*) The reason is because the fundamental and the dominant are separated by the greatest possible interval which...

THE CAP: Which? Finish. You can't.

STEPHEN: (*With an effort.*) Interval which. Is the greatest possible ellipse. Consistent with. The ultimate return. The octave. Which.
THE CAP: Which?

The 'dominant' is the fifth note of an octave; it harmonizes with the first note and is often used as the first of a new series. But I would suggest Joyce has given us reason not to praise that harmony too highly. Stephen has been fooling at the pianola; 'with two fingers he repeats once more the series of empty fifths' (p 503). As usual Stephen, like Icarus, is getting ahead of himself. A series of fifths sounds hollow; by themselves, the fundamental and the dominant are empty: only in the curved path of the full eight notes does the octave fill itself out, the sixth note linked to the third, the seventh leading to the eighth, a return to the tonic or first note.[5]

Seeing Stephen's musical analogy in dialogue form we can appreciate Joyce's use of form to emphasize content. The pause and interruption at 'greatest possible interval' mimes the meaning of the phrase. Similarly, the second pause at 'which' echoes the first. The commercial traveller speech follows immediately. It ends with the Italian word '*Ecco!*' meaning 'here it is,' or 'I've done it.' But the English homonym is 'echo,' which is equally appropriate, since Stephen has gone through another series of statements before returning to his original end. Certainly Joyce elsewhere in 'Circe' used the idea of echo in ways such as I am indicating: 'BLOOM: Hurray for High School! THE ECHO: Fool!' (p 548); or 'MAJOR TWEEDY: Salute! THE RETRIEVER: Ute ute ute' (p 601, cf. p 602); or 'KELLEHER ... Burying the dead. Safe home! THE HORSE: Hohohohohome!' (p 607, cf. p 606). In each case the echo undercuts the unthinking optimism of the original speaker. 'Fool!' comments on Bloom's attempt to recapture the past. 'Ute, ute ute' suggests the mindlessness of Tweedy's code of the warrior. 'Hohohohohome' underlines the irony of Kelleher's parting good wish. As an undertaker, he makes it his business to get corpses safely 'home.' Of course, the retriever and the horse function at a more realistic level, too. Both respond with their animal natures to human stimulus: the retriever voices Tweedy's excitement; the horse expresses the longing of all animal bodies for safe rest. (I will say more about the implications of this point in Chapter 9).

Joyce makes significant use of the word 'echo' in other parts of the novel. Bloom later observes 'the statue of Narcissus, sound without echo, desired desire' (p 728). Narcissus fell in love with his own image in the water (as mirror) and so would not respond to the love of a woman (Echo). Since this statue is later equated by Molly with Stephen as poet (pp 775-6), we may take it as a comment on Stephen's problem. Trying to be self-sufficient, he has run into the plight of the solipsist – he is cut off from himself because he denies the part of him that must be in a warm, positive relation to the 'not itself.' Only by loving someone can he fully find himself.

Mirrors in *Ulysses* distort as much as echoes. Rather than being interchangeable with the echo, however, the mirror can be associated with the limitation of self-involvement.[6] Thus towards the end of 'Circe,' we see the merging of Stephen's and Bloom's faces into that of Shakespeare in the mirror. When I quoted from this scene earlier, I left out an important part of the context. It is no easy unity that occurs, but rather a painful and subhuman one.

LYNCH: (*Points.*) The mirror up to nature. (*He laughs.*) Hu hu hu hu hu hu.
(*Stephen and Bloom gaze in the mirror. The face of William Shakespeare, beardless, appears there, rigid in facial paralysis, crowned by the reflection of the reindeer antlered hatrack in the hall.*)
SHAKESPEARE: (*In dignified ventriloquy.*) 'Tis the loud laugh bespeaks the vacant mind. (*To Bloom.*) Thou thoughtest as how thou wastest invisible. Gaze. (*He crows with a black capon's laugh.*) Iagogo! How my Oldfellow chokit his Thursdaymomun. Iagogogo!
(p 567)

Since Bloom has just fantasied watching Boylan have intercourse with his wife, the antlers in the mirror can be taken as a cuckold's horns. Shakespeare's reference to Iago provides an appropriate analogue also for the limitation of Stephen's mind, as indicated by part of his analysis of the bard earlier in the day. 'In *Cymbeline*, in *Othello* he is bawd and cuckold. He acts and is acted on. Lover of an ideal or a perversion, like José he kills the real Carmen. His unremitting intellect is the hornmad Iago ceaselessly willing that the moor in him shall suffer' (p 212). In this sense, Stephen may also be appropriately horned, since at the end of 'Circe' he will cause himself to be punished by Pvt Carr as God.

As Schutte points out, Stephen's picture of Shakespeare as creator-artist is not only built on faulty evidence, but yields a figure who has Stephen's faults and twists. Particularly, he indicates how Stephen, who cannot believe in himself or love a woman, insists that Shakespeare cannot either, 'because Ann Hathaway has destroyed his ability to believe in himself' (*Joyce and Shakespeare* 107). Stephen uses this problem of his prototype to bolster himself in his refusal to give in to the dominant woman in his life, his mother. His battle with her image is for him (as Bloom's battle for dominance with Bella Cohen is for him) the climactic struggle in Circe's house. His settling the struggle by the destructive act of breaking the light shows, as Schutte suggests (pp 112-15), that he has (at this point) more of the *dio boia* in him than of the creator god. Naturally he finds that same god in the world without.

In short, Stephen is and remains throughout the novel far from the harmony that he professes to seek. Lynch called up Shakespeare in the mirror by quoting

Hamlet, 'The mirror up to nature' (p 567), but Stephen is unable to understand what he sees there. He can operate only in the realm of the intellect, where 'fundamental' and 'dominant' are keys to the pure form of the octave. For Joyce, it was different. Just as he did not take Aristotle's doctrine of imitation as slavish holding up of the realistic mirror, so he realized that terms such as 'fundamental' and 'dominant' were meaningless unless they were more than pure form. Bloom is also faced with the temptation of choosing a pure form, the nymph whom he has worshipped as a picture on his wall and who comes to life in this episode. Hearing him make a farting noise, she says, 'we immortals, as you saw today, have no such a place and no hair there either. We are stonecold and pure' (p 551). In his response, Bloom dwells on preparing and administering enemas, 'up the fundament' (p 551). But when Bloom's button comes off, he gets away from this neurotic fixation and down to more realistic fundamentals, thereby breaking out of the pure goddess/brute man opposition.

Bloom's other more lasting trial is with the dominant, that is with Bella Cohen, who treats him as sadistically as his masochistic tendency desires. These two figures, cold goddess and brutal madam, set the form of Bloom's ellipse, 'the greatest possible ... consistent with. The ultimate return' (p 504).[7] During his purgation, Bloom at one point demands, 'Let me go. I will return' (p 543). This was a delayed adaptation of Bello's deterministic analysis, 'No, Leopold Bloom, all is changed by woman's will since you slept horizontal in Sleepy Hollow your night of twenty years. Return and see' (p 542). After he frees himself, Bloom does return, not to see cuckoldry, as Bella suggests, but to assert himself with Molly.

Sleepy Hollow is connected with another well-known 'return' story, that of Rip Van Winkle. Irving's character first enters *Ulysses* through a charade Bloom remembers being acted out: 'Rip van Winkle we played. Rip: tear in Henry Boyle's overcoat. Van: breadvan delivering. Winkle: cockles and periwinkles. Then I did Rip van Winkle coming back. She leaned on the sideboard watching. Moorish eyes. Twenty years asleep in Sleepy Hollow. All changed. Forgotten. The young are old. His gun rusty from the dew' (p 377). I take Bloom's acting out of a word to be matched by Joyce's shadowing forth through words of a theme.[8]

The question of returning is very much in Bloom's mind when he remembers the charade. Before it, he thinks, 'The year returns. History repeats itself. ... Life, love, voyage round your own little world. ... Returning not the same. ... Nothing new under the sun' (p 377). Then immediately before the charade memory, 'Curious she an only child, I an only child. So it returns. Think you're escaping and run into yourself. Longest way round is the shortest way home. And just when he and she. Circus horse walking in a ring' (p 377). The circus ring, as an analogue of the circular return, has both positive and negative overtones. Negatively, it appears in the Circe episode when Bloom says 'all tales of circus life are highly demoralising' (p 454) and then finds himself as an animal being put through his paces.

But aside from being a demoralized animal, Bloom has another more ambiguous connection with the circus. A memory of two events in his past emerges from the question and answer technique of the Ithaca episode.

> What rendered problematic for Bloom the realisation of these mutually selfexcluding propositions?
>
> The irreparability of the past: once at a performance of Albert Hengler's circus in the Rotunda, Rutland square, Dublin, an intuitive particoloured clown in quest of paternity had penetrated from the ring to a place in the auditorium where Bloom, solitary, was seated and had publicly declared to an exhilarated audience that he (Bloom) was his (the clown's) papa. The imprevidibility of the future: once in the summer of 1898 he (Bloom) had marked a florin (2s.) with three notches on the milled edge and tendered it in payment of an account ... for circulation on the waters of civic finance, for possible, circuitous or direct, return.
>
> Was the clown Bloom's son?
>
> No.
>
> Had Bloom's coin returned?
>
> Never. (p 696)

The circle functions differently in these two incidents. The clown breaks out of his ring to offer news Bloom desires[9] (his decline in position began with the death of his son; his coming rise in position is signalled by his plan to help Stephen, a son figure). On the other hand, it was bad luck that the coin did not make a full circle back to Bloom. The impossibility of breaking out of a circle and the contradictory impossibility of linking up with the starting point of a circle are both implicit in the thoughts that accompanied Bloom's earlier memory of the Rip Van Winkle charade.

In Chapter 10 we will see Bloom discover that the circle is the cosmic form of the natural cycle and how it thus offers the possibility not just of renewal but of eternal life, in the Pythagorean sense I have already considered: 'Souls cannot die, they leave their previous dwelling and live in new homes, which they forever inhabit. All things change, but nothing perishes.' To the pessimist, the last exchange in the quotation says that all is determined, fate rules. To the optimist, it says that, because life goes on, death is not to be feared; even more important, it says that because everything is constantly made anew, man may use his will not to identify with the fixed categories of intellect, whether these are sublime ('the Archetypes are eternal') or morbid ('you can't escape dying').

That the sublime and the morbid are closely related is indicated by Stephen's admission that the cynic is a disillusioned idealist. Stephen is insulted at being connected with the animal world, but the medicals who treat animal physiology as the basis of everything are no more in tune with reality. Because they have reduced life to the mechanics of the body, their humour is reductive, limited. Without denying their vision, Joyce was able to transcend it.

The importance of this issue for Joyce is evident from a remark he made in the thirties to Jacques Mercanton: 'History repeats itself comically; this is our funanimal world' (*Kenyon Review* [1962] 96). Most obviously applicable to *Finnegans Wake*, on which Joyce was then working, this compact statement grows out of the Circe episode. The comedy of that episode I shall investigate in Chapter 8; that it is an 'animal world,' I have already indicated. Comedy makes it '*fun*animal,' but that word is also a pun on another that we have just been looking at in 'Circe,' 'fundamental.' History repeates itself like the notes in a continuing series of octaves. Aesthetically, Joyce indicated this process in incidents such as that in which a legendary figure like Moses, made into a memorable statue of 'frozen music' by Michelangelo, becomes the occasion of a memorable speech by an Irish orator, that speech being respoken and mimed by a contemporary:

> J.J. O'Molloy resumed, moulding his words:
>
> – He said of it: *that stony effigy in frozen music, horned and terrible, of the human form divine, that eternal symbol of wisdom and prophecy which if aught that the imagination or the hand of sculptor has wrought in marble of soultransfigured and of soultransfiguring deserves to live, deserves to live.*
>
> His slim hand with a wave graced echo and fall. (p 140)

O'Molloy mimes by 'moulding his words'; more particulary, when his 'hand with a wave graced echo,' he mimes the repeated verb, 'deserves to live,' which both asserts and embodies the principle of historical repetition or echo. Although the 'grace' of O'Molloy's gesture indicates a genteel miming that corresponds to his mere repetition of another's words, his rendition does have some power. Here is Stephen's response: 'His blood wooed by grace of language and gesture, blushed' (p 140).

Spiritually, we may be able to hear the music of the spheres which Pythagoras claimed was tuned to the harmonic scale. Biologically, however, we must turn our eyes down to the life around us; we must see man as fundamentally the animal he is, not with Stephen's eyes that register him as beastly dead, but with more tolerance and more insight. Joyce believed we must see man as an animal able to enjoy himself (a 'funanimal'), able to engage in life, finally able to see the divine in the low, an absurd prospect that can make us laugh and give us heart.

'The year returns. History repeats itself,' Bloom thinks as he sits on the strand watching Howth darken. 'All that old hill has seen. Names change: that's all.' He proposed to Molly on Howth. 'Take the train there tomorrow. No. Returning not the same' (p 377). In other words, history repeats itself, but man cannot recapture the past. As Bloom thought earlier, 'It's always flowing in a stream, never the same, which in the stream of life we trace' (p 153). And as he realizes later, when one action is like another, it is still 'history repeating itself with a difference' (p 655, cf. Hayman 67-8). This is the optimism of variety, as opposed to the pessimism Bloom had earlier felt; 'nothing new under the sun' (p 377). Such pessimism is connected with the biological reductionism of Virag, who tries to pull down Bloom during the Circe episode. 'To hell with the pope! Nothing new under the sun. I am the Virag who disclosed the sex secrets of monks and maidens' (p 519). Another side of this attitude is the determinism of Bella Cohen, whose fan tells Bloom, 'We have met. You are mine. It is fate' (p 528). Bloom often thinks of fate or kismet during the day, usually as a way of justifying inactivity, non-assertion of will.

The theme I have tried to trace in this chapter is a complex one, bearing as it does on the experience of Joyce's two protagonists and on both the structure of the universe and the form of Joyce's novel. Joyce causes roads contrary and parallel to come together as Stephen and Bloom meet again in the whore-house, and then to merge as their faces coalesce in Circe's mirror. But that image echoes a face from another time; Shakespeare's face returns from history to address them incomprehensibly, but with hidden meaning.[10] The paralysis of that face might indicate a bad omen: that they are fated to suffer, that all is determined. Both do suffer, but each has chosen and will choose what happens to him.

'What went forth to the ends of the world to traverse not itself ... having itself traversed in reality itself becomes that self. ... Self which it was ineluctably preconditioned to become' (p 505). From perception of subject vs object, we move to discovery of individual identity to analysis of conditioned existence. The extremes of free will and determinism meet, contraries coincide, and opposites turn out to be identical in Joyce's novel. As Bruno insisted, 'liberty itself, will, and necessity are one and the same' (McIntyre 318). Existential philosophy helps us to understand how this paradox is true for the individual. The problem of historical necessity, though related, is a slightly different question.

Granted that history moves in cycles, are not events then determined? The answer is yes and no. Certain broad patterns are repeated, but particular events may happen now or later, involving one person or another. For the future this position offers hope, but what about the past? We have already seen Bloom answering this question. Water is 'always flowing in a stream, never the same, which in the stream of life we trace.' If it is never the same, he cannot recapture the past. But he can return to recreate what was; then he will have what his will can make of what is.

Joyce's aesthetic demanded of him an attempt to recreate Dublin in the novel as a whole, music in words during the Ormond bar scene, evolutionary development during the hospital scene, and so on. Believing in echoes of the past, he used them to give form to the distortions that memory recalls or our animal nature can offer us. Believing also in the importance of activity, he tried to give the sense of an individual going 'forth to the ends of the world to traverse' what is not himself. To traverse is to pass over, across, or through, as 'to the ends of the world.' Thus traversing can be easily linked with time in Bergson's notion of duration. As commercial traveller, Bloom traverses his world of Dublin, endures through the long hours of 16 June 1904. Somewhat like him, the reader in Croce's paraphrase of Vico, 'traverses over again the paths' that Joyce 'has already traversed, reconstructs the whole ideally, and thus knows it with full and true knowledge' (cf. *Ulysses on the Liffey* 141-2). Such 'ideal' knowledge may be adequate for the reader, and intriguing to Stephen. But Bloom asks less and achieves far more. He enables us to experience vicariously the long day and varied world he traverses. And Joyce's technique is behind this experiencing of the novel, his use of words which gracefully or grossly echo other times, other minds, other natures in a world where freedom and necessity, chance, and conditioning coalesce.

Conditioning his reader, Joyce acts as Hermes, 'god of public ways' and 'god of signposts.' His word signs alert us and thus become 'the point at which roads parallel merge and roads contrary also.' Out of such magic, such verbal intensity is the structure of man's experience recreated.

5 Transformations of the creator

We can best approach Joyce's conception of the author as creator through the figure of the Demiurge. As shown in Chapter 2, this creature appears in Stephen's thoughts at the beginning of 'Proteus.' Lower than the gods, the Demiurge may hope to equal them, at least in Madam Blavatsky's system, where he plays an optimistic evolutionary role. 'At this stage of action, the Demiurge is not yet the Architect. Born in the twilight of action, he has yet to perceive the play, to realise the ideal forms which lie buried in the bosom of Eternal ideation' (*The Secret Doctrine* I, 380). In Gnostic philosophy he had a much more dubious role. The *Encyclopedia Britannica* (1911) characterizes the Demiurge as 'an imperfect, ignorant, half-evil and malicious offspring of his mother,' Sophia (Vol. 27, p 854). This conception was also known to Joyce.

Speaking to Mercanton of the aesthetic behind *Finnegans Wake*, Joyce said, 'I reconstruct the nocturnal life ... as the Demiurge goes about the business of creation, starting from a mental outline that never varies. The only difference is that I obey laws I have not chosen. While He?' Though not given directly, the answer to this question is implicit in another comment: Joyce was resigned to 'the idiotic character of the universe,' giving the adjective 'its original meaning' (Mercanton 728). 'Idiotic' comes from a Greek noun which meant a private, nonprofessional, or ignorant person. Since this characterizes the Gnostic Demiurge, the answer to Joyce's question must be that the Demiurge has not chosen his plan, that he is in Hamlet's phrase 'one of nature's journeymen.' He is thus the opposite of the artist, who while he may not have been able to choose the laws that govern him is nevertheless '*homo faber*, he who reflects and he who fashions' (Mercanton 703). As artist, then, Joyce saw himself as architect and builder, as above and within the work created.

The laws Joyce said that he obeyed but had not chosen were presumably those physical laws which determine our environment, those biological laws which limit our bodies, those psychic and spiritual laws which shape our minds and souls. Joyce reflected and created his own world (as he expressed it, cf. *J.J.* 676). His world not only imitates nature in the way he understood Aristotle – 'the artistic process is like the natural process' ('Paris Notebook,' *Workshop* 54) – it also contains some of the mystery of that world. Joyce's sense of mystery was a religious sense, his rejection of the church a reaction to its materialism (simony as in 'The Sisters'), its intolerance (for piety such as Bruno's), and its twisting of man's biological and spiritual nature (in celibacy, mariolatry, and the threat of hell-fire). To the humane teachings of the church and to some of its ritual, Joyce remained loyal. Even in the early days of his apostacy, he praised 'the mystery of the mass' to his brother Stanislaus and insisted that 'the Mass on Good Friday seems to me a very great drama.' As Stanislaus suggests, 'It was as a primitive religious drama that my brother valued it so highly' (*Brother's Keeper* 117-18).[1] As late as the thirties, Joyce told Jacques Mercanton that 'Good Friday and Holy Saturday were the two days of the year when he went to church, for the liturgies, which represented by their symbolic rituals the oldest mysteries of humanity' (Mercanton 710).

Joyce's sense of mystery and reverence for past forms (if they contained the flexibility of truth) is also apparent in his use of the *Odyssey* and his interest in philology. Besides his love of archaic, specialized, and slang terms, there was his use of puns, of cognates, and of the etymological sense of English words – all these important instances of his concern for transformation, evolution, 'the process of nature.' A statement of the transformation theme occurs to Stephen as he listens to Bloom in 'Eumaeus.' 'He could hear, of course, all kinds of words changing colour like those crabs about Ringsend in the morning, burrowing quickly into all colours of different sorts of the same sand where they had a home somewhere beneath or seemed to' (p 644). As the crabs take their colour from the wet sand in which they burrow, so words take theirs from the context in which they are put, though they also have a 'home' somewhere deep in time.

But beyond his appreciation of this natural process was Joyce's sense of 'words as a mysterious means of expression' which we saw in Chapter 3. Frank Budgen, who made this suggestion, also emphasized the influence Yeats's exposition of the doctrines of magic had on Joyce.

> Yeats held that the borders of our minds are always shifting, tending to become part of the universal mind. ... This universal mind and memory could be evoked by symbols. When telling me this Joyce added that in his own work he never used the recognized symbols, preferring instead to use trivial and quadrivial words and local geographical allusions. The intention of magical evocation, however, remained the same.[2] (p 325)

Budgen says this is 'particularly true' of *Finnegans Wake*, but it is also true of *Ulysses*. The geographical allusion might be to 'Ben Howth'; as shown in the last chapter, Joyce's trivial pun on *Ben* turns it at one point from the Irish word for 'peake' into a man's name. But the pun turns out to be serious rather than trivial when Howth (ON, *head*) breaths and opens one eye (p 379). Joyce intended a 'magical evocation.'

Joyce saw magic at work not only in the mind but outwardly in events. This kind of magic is popularly called superstition, and Joyce was a very superstitious person. As Ellmann puts it,

> He was forever trying to charm his life; his superstitions were attempts to impose sacramental importance upon naturalistic details. So too, his books were not to be taken as mere books, but as acts of prophecy. Joyce was capable of mocking his own claims of prophetic power ... but he still made the claims. For Joyce life *was* charmed; nature was both stolid and magical, its ordinary details suffused with wonder, its wonderful manifestations permeated by the ordinary. (*J.J.* 562)

The ordinary is coincidence, the wonder its meaning. Ellmann suggests the literary implications of Joyce's world view.

> The characters pass through sequences of situations and thoughts bound by coincidence with the situations and thoughts of other living and dead men and of fictional, mythical men. Do Bloom and Stephen coincidentally think the same thoughts at the same times? Do they wander and fly like Ulysses and Daedalus? They are examples of a universal process. (p 563)

A coincidence is the point in time or space where two or more things come together. It could be seen as 'the point at which roads parallel merge and roads contrary also,' as Joyce said of 'Circe.' The Brunian overtones of coincidence are underlined by Lynch's statement that 'extremes meet.'

Certainly coincidences run wild in 'Circe,' causing all kinds of trouble for critics (though not for readers I think). The ordinary coincidence is the kind cited by Ellmann in which Stephen and Bloom think the same thought at the same time. In 'Circe' this three-point connection (one thought, two minds) is telescoped to a two-point connection. For instance, as Goldman points out, J.J. O'Molloy appears in one of Bloom's fantasies in 'Circe' to paraphrase the speech on Michelangelo's Moses that Stephen (not Bloom) heard him quote earlier in the day. I would still call this a coincidence (of the two-point type, Stephen's memory in Bloom's mind), but Goldman calls it 'cross-referencing.' He uses this notion to move to his central point about what is going on in 'Circe'.

The cross-referencing which the author had injected before to remind us of similarities between characters (as, Stephen's 'Gerard's Rosery' inserted in Bloom's monologue) here takes on an appearance of autonomy, as 'characters' belonging to other contexts or even ontological levels rise up to confront the characters in the Dublin action, in the meeting ground of the author's imagination which is the true *locus* of 'Circe.' (p 99)

I would suggest a modification of this analysis. The 'author's imagination' is the obvious *source* of the novel; to move the locus of only one episode back there is probably a distortion. Instead we might say that Joyce reveals most clearly in 'Circe' that he is the creator behind his creation. (But is it really not just as clear in 'Cyclops' when the ostensible narrator keeps being interrupted by a series of inflated asides?) Rather, I would prefer to conclude that 'Circe' most clearly embodies Joyce's belief that magic and mystery underlie the universe; that the 'borders of our memory' may 'shift and form part of the universal memory' (cf. Hayman 63-4); that when our limited conscious selves relax their defensive ego-control, then roads parallel and contrary merge, then the underlying being becomes one. I believe this oneness is for Joyce the mystery of the cosmos. The creator is one in the macrocosmos; the soul is that same one in the microcosmos. But Stephen has only an intellectual awareness of this connection. Of course, full awareness that all being is one must be fleeting and difficult for man; it means evolving through the cycles of transformation that we have previously traced. In the next section, I would like to follow Joyce's own movement through one mode of transformation.

When Joyce as artist abandoned the god-like pose Stephen postulated in *A Portrait of the Artist as a Young Man*, he shifted the emphasis from the creator being above his work to the creator being within his work. This meant giving himself to the processes of the world, submitting to its multifareous transformations. He came to realize that only by submitting to the cosmic cycle could he achieve oneness, only by admitting and working through all parts of his psychological nature could he integrate them into unity, only by adopting all styles, previous and present, could he achieve an artistic wholeness. Put in more practical terms, Joyce was one of those artists who choose to use all their resources. He did this out of pride and love, and necessity. The necessity came partly from his insistent memory that 'knew by heart everything he had heard or read' (Mercanton 97). This faculty made him a more self-conscious stylist than most novelists, aware of the passages that might be influencing him in the wording of any given sentence. Combined with his tenacious will and a tendency towards emotional obsessions, this memory probably made necessary Joyce's decision to focus on styles, to work through styles by means of parody and pastiche. Through parody he could purge his mind of the shoddy, dishonest writing he had absorbed; through pastiche he could recreate the best in what he remembered. Through a combination of the two he could salvage the good in the worst, as in the vulgar evangelism of 'Are you a god or a doggone clod?' examined in Chapter 3. This sentence represents a fusion in which it is impossible to separate vulgarity from truth, colloquial rhythm from rhetorical emphasis and compression.

Such fusion was the key element in the functioning of Joyce's imagination. As already indicated, he had doubts as to the originality of that imagination, and was often apologetic about the slowness with which it worked. But his care and tenacity resulted in the artistic incorporation of feeling and polish, as he also knew. Speaking of the last half of the book, he wrote Harriet Weaver, 'it is impossible for me to write these episodes quickly. The elements needed will only fuse after a prolonged existence together' (*Letters* I, 128). Defending the radical changes of style in his next letter to her, he wrote, 'in the compass of one day to compress all these wanderings and clothe them in the form of this day is for me only possible by such variation which, I beg you to believe, is not capricious' (p 129). His mode of defence offers hints which fit in with the aims and methods I have been suggesting. To 'clothe' events in the 'form' of the day means to embody the universal in the particular, the eternal in the mundane.

In a letter to another correspondent a year later, Joyce indicated more of his intent. 'Each adventure ... should not only condition but even create its own technique' (*Letters* I, 147). Thus he might argue that the scene at the lying-in hospital, which he had finished shortly before, *had* created its technique. It was to be about creation (in the analogous scene of the *Odyssey*, Ulysses visits the island of the sun god). Joyce would therefore deal with growth and birth; the episode would therefore have to show 'the natural stages of development in the embryo and the periods of faunal evolution in general,' as Joyce wrote Frank Budgen (*Letters* I, 139); its style would therefore be based on the evolution of the English language as shown in its writers from the dark ages to the present. Obviously, it is not the adventure of each episode that creates its technique; it is Joyce.

But Joyce as Aristotelian creator understands that 'the artistic process is like the natural process'; in that sense he is interested not just in birth but in gestation as development towards birth, and needs to find a style that will be consonant with that development. But in order for the creator to be within his work, he must give himself to that process, as Joyce did even more clearly in writing 'Circe.' 'I am working like a galley-slave, an ass, a brute. I cannot even sleep. The episode of *Circe* has changed me too into an animal' (*Letters* I, 146). The humour in this, as always with Joyce, is based on recognition; in this case of what was necessary to his art. As we shall see in Chapter 7, Joyce was actually using some of his own neurotic traits in purging those of Stephen and Bloom in 'Circe.' But just as he had Bloom go through the worst that his mind wished to inflict on him, only to rise superior to his conditioned limitations, so Joyce as artist went through the process of becoming animalized (in Bloom's brute submissions, in the speeches of Virag, in Stephen's depraved Paris pimp travelogue), only to rise superior to this condition. Though he was the artist within the episode for most of its course, he was finally the artist above it as well.

Another way of understanding the different modes of creation and perceiving the divine can be inferred from a distinction made in the book by Bruno that Joyce owned, *The Heroic Frenzies*. Some people, Bruno believed,

> become habitations of the gods or divine spirits, speak and do admirable things for which neither they themselves nor anyone else understand the reason; and these commonly have been raised to this state from having first been undisciplined and ignorant and void of any spirit and sense of their own; in them, as in a room which has been scoured, is introduced a divine sense and spirit which has less chance of revealing itself in those who are endowed with their own sense and reason. (p 107, also included by McIntyre 279)

Although strictly speaking only the 'divine fool' would fittingly illustrate this type, I believe Bloom is recognized by Stephen in 'Eumaeus' as having become the 'habitation' of a god or divine spirit. Though not void of sense, Bloom is 'undisciplined and ignorant' in intellectual and spiritual ways; he has been 'scoured' by his experience in the Circe episode and thus left open for the divine spirit to move in.

Bruno's conception here comes pretty clearly from Dionysius. Speaking of God's 'incomprehensible presence' in *The Mystical Theology*, he suggested the conditions under which

> it breaks forth, even from the things that are beheld and from those that behold them, and plunges the true initiate unto the Darkness of Unknowing wherein he renounces all the apprehensions of his understanding and is enwrapped in that which is wholly intangible and invisible ... and being through the passive stillness of all his reasoning powers united by his highest faculty to Him that is wholly Unknowable, of whom thus by a rejection of all knowledge he possesses a knowledge that exceeds his understanding. (p 194)

The best example of Bloom's possessing knowledge that exceeds his understanding is his giving the name of the Gold Cup winner to Bantam Lyons. Lyons asks to look at Bloom's newspaper for a moment; Bloom suggests that he keep it since he was 'just going to throw it away' (p 85). Intent on the names of and odds on the horses, Lyons takes this as an omen that 'Throwaway' will win the race. He is correct (though he changes his mind before placing the bet). As we have seen, Joyce believed in the fact and the meaningfulness of coincidences such as this. We have also seen that he did try to show some of the divine spirit in Bloom.

The other type of character developed by Bruno allows an even more obvious application to Stephen.

> Others, because of a custom or habit of contemplation, and because they are naturally endowed with a lucid and intellectual spirit, when under the impact of an internal stimulus and spontaneous fervor ... make keen their senses and in the sulphurous cognitive faculty enkindle a rational flame which raises their vision beyond the ordinary. And these do not go about speaking and acting as mere receptacles and instruments, but as chief inventors and authors. (*Heroic Frenzies* 107-8; also McIntyre 279-80).

Clearly Stephen is 'naturally endowed with a lucid and intellectual spirit'; all he needs is 'the impact of an internal stimulus and spontaneous fervor.' I would suggest that the stimulus appears in the transformation cycle that we saw come into Stephen's mind in 'Proteus.' But the 'spontaneous fervor' he is not able to muster during *Ulysses*. He did experience something like it in *A Portrait of the Artist*, but now that his confidence in himself as superman is undercut, he has to make the transition from looking for an absolute relation with the divine to finding the divine in nature. In the library scene and elsewhere in *Ulysses*, his cynical intellect is a bar. Only when he transcends the Aristotelian positive effort to understand and accepts the negative darkness of Dionysus will he discover the love that will 'enkindle' his flame and 'raise' his vision, thus enabling him to become a 'chief inventor' (Dedalus) and author (modern Homer). Thus the word 'rational' is not to be confused with the logical reasoning of Aristotle. The phrase 'rational flame' indicates the passion in which Bruno was interested. On the other hand, we have already seen that the divine is both within and above nature. In his distinguishing of types, I believe Bruno is relying on this distinction: thus we could say that Bloom has the divine *within*, and Stephen when he finally experiences the passion he needs will, as creative artist, be *above* what he sees. Joyce, in other words, is able to take us within Bloom, but also shows him to us from above.

Another passage in the *Heroic Frenzies* would have been equally useful to Joyce. Characterizing the heroic frenzy in a Platonic manner, Bruno calls it 'a heat enkindled in the soul by the sun of intellect' so that the possessed one

> acquires the feeling of divine and internal harmony, and conforms his thoughts and acts to the common measure of the law innate in all things. He is not as one inebriated by the

vessel of Circe who goes from ditch to ditch and from rock to rock, plunging and stumbling; nor is he like a variable Proteus always changing himself from one appearance to another, without ever finding any place, or mode, or manner of settling or fixing himself, but without disturbing his balance he conquers and overcomes the terrible monsters. (*Heroic Frenzies*, 109)

In his variations of style from one episode to the next, Joyce is 'a variable Proteus always changing himself from one appearance to another' never 'fixing himself.' If he thus seems to go against Bruno's advice, it must be remembered that what is described here is the final stage; Bruno shows later that Circe and her 'glorious afflictions' do provide another way to the truth. Clearly Joyce insisted on putting his characters through both the Protean and the Circean processes, and I have argued that he also submitted himself to them before (and while) maintaining an ultimate aloofness.

In 1917, while Joyce was still working on the early chapters of *Ulysses*, he discovered he had glaucoma. It is not surprising that he investigated the word, its history and myth. In Paris he spoke of glaucoma to Sylvia Beach: 'You know, the grey eyes of Athena' (*J.J.* 426). In his notesheets for the novel, Joyce included a Greek word which Herring transliterates as 'glaucope,' and glosses as 'an adjectival form in Greek ... a standard epithet for such goddesses as Athena' (*Notesheets* 484). In Greek the word *glaukos* meant 'bluish-grey,' from which the word *glaukoma* was evolved to describe the eye condition that was evidently known to the Greeks. But Joyce would not have been content with this descriptive level. As I shall indicate presently, he was also interested in the Greek god, Glaucus.

In English we have a cognate, the word 'glaucous,' which can mean 'sea-green' or 'covered with a whitish bloom, as grapes.' Joyce uses this word once in *Ulysses*, describing one of the barmaids 'as in cool glaucous *eau de Nil*' (p 273). In the overture to this Sirens section, the motif appeared as 'pearl grey and *eau de Nil*' (p 257), thus emphasizing the undersea, white bloom overtones. Since the barmaids are sirens in the Homeric parallel, it is not surprising that 'glaucous' is associated with water. Being tied to the mast, Ulysses could not jump overboard to be drowned by the sirens, but he is plunged in the sea more than once in the *Odyssey*. As Joyce described the incident to Budgen, it is almost as though he had been drowned: In Phaecia, 'when he advanced naked, to meet the princess he hid from her maidenly eyes the parts that mattered of his brine-soaked barnacle-encrusted body' (Budgen 17). This description should remind us of Stephen on the strand, thinking of the drowned man due to be washed up, finally imagining a fish eating one of his 'parts that mattered' and thinking of God, man, fish, and *barnacle* in the cycle we investigated.

Stephen is afraid of water and afraid of death. Although he thinks of Shakespeare's famous song from *The Tempest*, he focuses on the deathly part, 'Full fathom five thy father lies' (p 50). He then pictures the corpse, its nose eaten away, and alludes to a bit more of the song. 'A seachange this, brown eyes saltblue. Seadeath, mildest of all deaths known to man' (p 50). Instead of picturing 'pearls that were his eyes,' Stephen stays on the surface. For him the process of nature ends in death rather than a beautiful transformation. Not until he learns to appreciate the full cycles of nature can he become the 'complete man' that Joyce claimed Ulysses was (Budgen 15-17).

Ulysses has been to Hades and returned. In Joyce's own evocation, he has been in water so long his body has become 'brine-soaked barnacle-encrusted,' yet he emerges as himself and more than himself. In Book VI of *The Odyssey*, much is made of Ulysses' ragged condition when he goes to face Nausicaa with a bough to conceal his parts. 'He was terrible in their eyes, being marred with the salt sea foam.'[3] He goes to the river and washes 'from his skin the salt scurf that covered his back and broad shoulders, and from his head ... the crusted brine of the barren sea' (p 99). Then, with Athena's aid, he reappears 'glowing in beauty and grace' (p 99), causing Nausicaa to comment, 'he is like the gods that keep the wide heaven' (p 100). Stephen could remember this rebirth, if he would, but he shows his unwillingness in the only mention in the novel of Homer's Ulysses: 'Shipwrecked in storms dire, tried, like another Ulysses, Pericles, prince of Tyre[.] Head, redconecapped, buffeted, brineblinded' (p 195). Neither Shakespeare's Pericles nor Homer's Ulysses is called anything like 'redconecapped' during their shipwrecks. This adjective most obviously describes the penis which Stephen had imagined the fish eating earlier in the day. It is his way of saying that Ulysses has not lost his organ of generation by immersion in the sea, but Stephen is not able to draw the positive conclusion that Ulysses' adventure offers him; instead he prefers to labour with an unmanned Shakespeare.

Similarly, there is no warrant in Homer for the epithet 'barnacle-encrusted' that Joyce used to describe Ulysses. Since we know that the word 'barnacle' had special meaning to Joyce, we could rest content with the comment his father made when he heard his son had run off with a woman named Barnacle: 'She'll never leave him' (*J.J.* 162). But Joyce was not content unless he had worked an image into all its allusions and associations. It is time therefore to take up the mythological dimensions of 'glaucous' and 'barnacle.'

Joyce would have known the story of the Greek sea god, Glaucus, from Ovid's *Metamorphoses*. Originally a fisherman, he had chanced to lay his catch on some strange grass which caused the fish to come back to life and crawl into the sea. Glaucus ate some of the grass himself, whereupon his heart 'was seized with a passionate desire for this other element, the sea' (p 310). Plunging in, he was purified by the gods of the sea after immersing himself in a hundred rivers; he then took on a form appropriate to life in the sea, 'beard of rusty green ... dark blue arms ... legs curving away at the end into a fish' (p 310).

This god is also described and discussed by Plato in *The Republic*, another book with which we know Joyce was familiar (Thornton). In a passage on the soul, Plato develops as usual his archetype of the perfect form above this world. Speaking of the soul as feminine, he says that 'we see her now marred by association with the body and other evils, but when she has regained that pure condition which the eye of reason can discern, you will find her to be a far lovelier thing.'[4] The influence of this conception on Bruno is clear enough, as it is in Plato's use of a myth to explain the point further: The soul in her present lodging is 'like the sea-god Glaucus, whose original form can hardly be discerned, because parts of his body have been broken off or crushed and altogether marred by the waves, and the clinging overgrowth of weed and rock and shell has made him more like some monster than his natural self.' Therefore the soul should follow the impulse to lift herself out of 'the sea in which she is now sunken, and disencumber her of all that wild profusion of rock and shell, whose earthy substance has encrusted her, because she seeks what men call happiness by making earth her food' (p 346). As in Bruno, we find recorded here the two impulses, first to break free of earth and fly up to the spheres, the world of archetypes, and second to submit to the appetites of earth, its cycles and processes. Plato scorns this world; Bruno is sometimes ambivalent but usually insists divinity is both in the world and more than it; Joyce follows Bruno and implicitly corrects Plato's analogy. If we see Glaucus before he became encrusted, we see only a mortal fisherman. He achieved divinity by becoming encrusted, by that process of transformation which involved giving himself to his new environment, becoming like it. In so doing, he may serve us as a paradigm for the Joyce who had to give himself to the style of each chapter, who by descending to animal state in the writing of 'Circe' became the god-like creator who could look back on that episode and say 'I think it is the best thing I have ever written' (*J.J.* 511).

Joyce's most obvious model for the god of transformation by water is Proteus. A god of the sea, he is encountered by Menelaus on an island, Pharos, off the mouth of the Nile. He advises Menelaus to sail back up 'the heaven-fed stream' of the Nile (p 66) to make sacrifice before continuing. Proteus and Glaucus may thus well come together in Joyce's description of the sirens in 'cool glaucous *eau de Nil*.' In addition to these two, Joyce referred in *Ulysses* to an Irish sea god, Mananaan MacLir, to whom he gave attributes connected with the river gods of

Ireland. Mananaan is obviously intended as a form of Proteus when he is introduced into the episode that bore the Greek god's name: 'They are coming, waves. The whitemaned seahorse, champing, brightwindbridled, the steeds of Mananaan' (p 38). In fact, as Thornton points out, Mananaan is usually considered the Irish equivalent of Proteus, a shape changer.

Besides having read of Mananaan in works such as Douglas Hyde's *Literary History of Ireland* and Lady Gregory's *Gods and Fighting Men*, Joyce would have known more literary uses of the sea god in works by two older poets who influenced him, A.E. and Yeats. A long section of Yeats's narrative poem *The Wanderings of Oisin* (1889) concerns that hero's battle with a protean sea demon. For this battle Oisin is given a sword with the word 'Manannan' written on it. As Oisin fights the demon, the latter recognizes the weapon:

> And when he knew the sword of Manannan [*sic*]
> Amid the shades of night, he changed and ran
> Through many shapes, I lunged at the smooth throat
> Of a great eel; it changed, and I but smote
> A fir-tree roaring in its leafless top;
> And thereupon I drew the livid chop
> Of a drowned dripping body to my breast;
> Horror from horror grew; but when the west
> Had surged up in a plumy fire, I drave
> Through heart and spine; and cast him in the wave.[5]

Although the demon may transform himself out of fear of Manannan's potent sword, he in a sense honours Manannan as protean shape changer.

The Mananaan of A.E. is more overtly present in *Ulysses*. In the library scene, the god pops into Stephen's mind in a paraphrase of lines from a play by A.E. (Thornton): 'Flow over them with your waves and with your waters, Mananaan, Mananaan MacLir' (p 189). The quotation occurs to Stephen because he has just heard Russell (A.E.) referring to Shakespeare's *King Lear*. Russell had been quiet during the first part of Stephen's disquisition, causing another quotation to come to Stephen's mind at his initial interruption: 'Art thou there, truepenny?' (p 189). Stephen identifies Russell as a father figure, albeit an insubstantial one. In the most impressive appearance of Mananaan, as a character in 'Circe,' his identity with A.E. is clear in his speech, with its occult terms and reference to the *Homestead* (Thornton).[6] But it is the description of Mananaan given before his speech that connects him with the sea change we have been considering.

(In the cone of the searchlight behind the coalscuttle, ollave, holyeyed, the bearded figure of Mananaan MacLir broods, chin on knees. He rises slowly. A cold seawind blows from his druid mantle. About his head writhe eels and elvers. He is encrusted with weeds and shells....) (p 510)

Encrusted with shells, Mananaan is like Ulysses in Joyce's description of him to Budgen. With weeds growing on him, he is like Glaucus with a green beard in Ovid's description. The eels in his hair may come partly from Yeats's demon, but their main source is not Joyce's reading but his observation of river-god emblems on buildings near the Liffey.[7]

As described in Chapter 9, Joyce characterizes Mananaan as comic-grotesque in 'Circe' but to one who fears water he is a threatening figure, an 'engulfer,' as Stephen had earlier characterized Russell (p 192). Another transformation of Mananaan reinforces this sense. Three pages before his appearance in 'Circe,' another sea creature is introduced: '(... Along an infinite invisible tightrope taut from zenith to nadir the end of the World, a twoheaded octopus in gillie's kilts, busby and tartan filibegs, whirls through the murk, head over heels, in the form of the Three Legs of Man)' (p 507). The 'Three Legs of Man' is the emblem of the Isle of Man, just as Mananaan draws his name from that island, whose tutelary god he was. There is also an obvious connection with A.E. here. Bloom had earlier heard Russell talking occultism with a disciple: '– Of the twoheaded octopus, one of whose heads is the head upon which the ends of the world have forgotten to come while the other speaks with a scotch accent' (p 165). Stephen's fear of death and transformation make him withdraw from A.E., whose willingness to act as druid and to consider the end of the world is a threat to Stephen's guilt and pride. Unlike him, Joyce learned to meet threats such as Proteus on his own terms, not only to wrestle with the flux of nature, but himself to become the demon or the druid Mananaan or the god Glaucus, able to change into whatever he wanted to master and learn the secret of.

Artistically, Joyce attempted to immerse himself so in his subject that he expressed it completely through his style, making the artistic process follow the natural process. Arnold Goldman has discussed the style of *Ulysses*, presenting a detailed and forceful case in the fourth chapter of his book on Joyce. His thesis is that Joyce adopts many styles in order to show the impossibility of any objective or finally authoritative view. As far as it goes, this approach is helpful in placing Joyce as a 'complete artist,' definitely above his creation. But it gives insufficient emphasis to that other side of Joyce, the artist within his work.

To demonstrate the lengths to which Joyce was willing to go in adapting the Protean principle to his form, we might look at his distortions of language to parody pretension or inanity, as in 'Cyclops,' or towards stylistic evolution in 'Oxen of the Sun.' Saving these episodes for analysis in the next chapter, I propose to focus here on the most unlovely episode in the book, 'Eumaeus,' as one in which immersion in water is both referred to and used to shape the form. For this scene in the cabman's shelter, Joyce used the most banal and disoriented style possible, trying to keep the reader's attention when neither the characters' thoughts nor their actions were interesting. As Goldman contends:

> The 'tired' clichés of 'Eumaeus' strike most readers as a let-down. Probably this was in the nature of the case, after the pyrotechnics of 'Circe,' and it must be acknowledged that Joyce has not gone out of his way to prevent the reaction – rather the opposite. The effect of the 'imitative form' (tired characters: tired prose) appears disastrous – though perhaps we ought to abandon any notion that *Ulysses* makes, read cover to cover, a beautiful experience – mainly because the style chosen contains little by way of density in itself.
>
> (pp 100-1)

Since 'imitative form' is one way of phrasing that quality in Joyce which I have been praising, this episode makes a good test case. I disagree with Goldman's contention that the style lacks 'density,' and with his later more explicit complaint that Joyce reduces 'the action to a superficial account, and the manner of it only exposes its own inability to encompass the matter' (p 104).[8]

If Stephen and Bloom are tired in the Eumaeus episode, the reader is invited to be alert. He is warned by Joyce in various ways that the low-key happenings of the episode hide a meaning. For instance, the word *rebus*, which appears in this episode, provides a clue to the general theme, which is Bruno's: *Natura est Deus in rebus* ('Nature is God in the form of a puzzle'). Bloom reads the newspaper: 'The pink edition, extra sporting, of the *Telegraph*, tell a graphic lie, lay, as luck would have it, beside his elbow and as he was puzzling again, far from satisfied, over a country belonging to him and the preceding rebus...' (p 647). The 'preceding rebus' is the *Telegraph*, tell a graphic lie'; it is technically a rebus because the latter phrase is an 'enigmatical representation' of the word '*Telegraph*' by words which have the same sound as it. The answer presumably is Ireland, which belongs to Bloom and the Dublin newspaper, but more likely 'tell a graphic lie' refers to Murphy, who is clearly a spinner of yarns, with lots of circumstantial detail: graphic lies. Since Bloom is Ulysses in Joyce's plan and Murphy is listed in Joyce's outline as Ulysses 'Pseudangelos' (false messenger), we must take it that Ireland belongs both to the exile and the ostracized, to the liar and the truth teller. And since Stephen has only two pages before announced that Ireland must be important because it belongs to him, we may take Bloom's idle thought to indicate a modification of this egocentric statement.

Joyce provided his readers with several indications of mysteries to be found beneath the surface of this episode. Bloom sized up Murphy earlier:

> Yet still, though his eyes were thick with sleep and sea air, life was full of a host of things and coincidences of a terrible nature and it was quite within the bounds of possibility that it was not an entire fabrication though at first blush there was not much inherent probability in all the spoof he got off his chest being strictly accurate gospel. (p 635)

If 'life is full of a host of things,' it may contain rebuses (actually, *rebus* is the ablative plural of Latin *res*, 'things'); life may also have in it a *hostia* (Latin word from which the 'host' as Eucharist is derived), that is a 'sacrificial victim,' a Christ such as Stephen had earlier in the episode perceived Bloom to be.

As shown in Chapter 4, despite being a graphic liar, Murphy has relevant tales to tell: his eyes 'thick with sleep,' he is transformed into Morpheus later in the episode and thus leads Bloom to sleep, dream, regression preparatory to rebirth, at the end of 'Ithaca.' We have already looked at Joyce's preoccupation with coincidences as indicators of the hidden coherence of the universe. The fact that Murphy claims to have seen a man named Simon Dedalus shooting eggs off bottles in Stockholm ten years earlier would be Joyce's rendering of such a meaningful coincidence. Like Murphy's other anecdotes of violence, this one does not augur well for the son of such a father. In this sense it might be a coincidence 'of a terrible nature,' Simon functioning as the destructive *dio boia* who demolishes eggs, that is, new life of the sort we shall later see connected with Bloom's move towards rebirth. In other words, though Murphy's stories are not 'strictly accurate gospel,' they are 'full of a host of things,' and Joyce wants the reader to be aware of this.

Another hint appears in the sentence following the one quoted above. Bloom 'had meanwhile been taking stock of the individual in front of him and Sherlockholmsing him up' (pp 635-6). The relevance of Sherlock Holmes to *Ulysses* has been discussed at some length by Hugh Kenner (*Dublin's Joyce,* Chapter 10). Kenner's case is that Holmes and Watson are an epitome of the split in Victorian conscience between romantic egoism and materialistic determinism, or between 'ratiocinative violence and sentimental virtue' (p 170). He claims that Joyce aimed to expose these contradictions, to reduce to an absurdity any individual's pretention to God-like omniscience and the whole society's avid embrace of materialism. My own view clearly differs in emphasis from this. I have tried to demonstrate how Joyce saw the artist as god-like and the material world as worthy of celebration. So where Kenner insists that 'the clue is a bogus epiphany' (p 176), I would say that Joyce tried to elevate the clue into an epiphany, and thereby redeem Holmes, or his creator. An indication that he had some such aim comes from the fact that Conan Doyle's surname appears in the name cycle considered in Chapter 2. The name 'Doyle' terminates that list, coming immediately after that of Christ. In Adam's working out of the puzzle, 'd'oyle' may be taken as 'annointed,' a modern translation of Hebrew *Messiah* or Greek *Christos*; in Holmes, Doyle created an omniscient helper of man, one who could see through the mundane world to its hidden secrets. In writing 'Eumaeus,' Joyce differs from Doyle in not being pretentious, in inviting the reader to solve the mystery himself after receiving an appropriate clue from a supercilious Stephen (when he calls Bloom *Christus*).

Murphy is even connected with Glaucus at one point in the episode. 'The sailor lugged out from a case he had a pair of greenish goggles which he very slowly hooked over his nose and both ears.' Then the narrator describes him 'staring out of sea-green portholes as you might well describe them as,' and Murphy himself reports, 'I uses goggles reading. Sand in the Red Sea done that. One time I could read a book in the dark, manner of speaking' (p 659). This thoroughgoing acceptance of the sea is in direct contrast to Stephen's fear of immersion in it. In fact, this description invites contrast with an observation by Stephen in the next episode: He is 'hydrophobe ... disliking the aqueous substances of glass and crystal, distrusting aquacities of thought and language' (p 673). In the perspective I am offering, this dislike and distrust are crippling Stephen, keeping him from growing into the mature artist Joyce had become by embracing his fate (with a February birthday, Joyce was an Aquarius).[9]

In any case, the phrase 'aquacities of thought and language' obviously characterizes the style of the Eumaeus episode very well.[10] Things are dimly seen as sentences move waveringly before our eyes. Action is reduced to slow motion by the resistence of water to rapid movement. But in this medium, another process can go on, that process of distortion and transformation by which Simon Dedalus works with a circus in Stockholm, or Murphy is turned into the ancient mariner (p 659), Sinbad (p 636), and Morpheus (pp 639, 660); even Bloom tells Stephen that his surname 'was changed too' (p 623). Stephen may distrust this process, but once involved in it he contributes to it, since he produces the list of names ending in Christ and Doyle (p 622), and even changes Bloom's name to Christ (p 643).

A stumbling block to the appreciation of 'Eumaeus' was dissolved with admirable aquacity of phrasing by Goldman: 'perhaps we ought to abandon any notion that *Ulysses* makes, read cover to cover, a beautiful experience; (pp 100-1). In fact, the new criticism has been contending for almost as long as *Ulysses* has existed that beauty, in the sense that a sunset is beautiful, has not much place in literature. As Shakespeare himself continually exemplifies, literary beauty can be achieved from harsh or revolting subjects and phrases. Joyce, as a master of language, achieved the same effects in 'Circe.' But the question here is whether he was successful with the scene, dialogue, and style of 'Eumaeus.' The answer does not lie in any logical argument based on 'the fallacy of imitative form.' Rather it lies in the reader's experience of that chapter. If he begins it expecting to be bored, he will easily find it boring. If on the other hand, he approaches it alertly, he can appreciate its comic use of tired language. If he gives himself to the element, he can by exerting his mental limbs stay afloat, at the same time keeping an eye open for hidden forms beneath its aqueous surface. I do not suggest it is Joyce's greatest triumph in the novel, but I do suggest that it is a viable episode, and a 'natural' outcome of his conception of the relation of the creator to reality. In 'Eumaeus' as in most of the later episodes, Joyce maintained a creative balance between the artist as high artificer and stage manager, and the creator as one who must join in the process of life, submit himself to the dark mundanity of the world, and win from it, show forth in it, that informing light which justifies the working cosmos.

6

The comic vision and the grotesque

I have looked in the last two chapters at the characteristic process to which Joyce committed himself in his efforts to realize and express fully the material he dealt with. In this chapter I shall offer a preliminary focus on two traditional artistic modes which Joyce found congenial. The first, the comic vision, he was consciously attracted to from his university days. He early praised it over tragedy by connecting it with the affirmation of human spirit which he saw as the justification of literature. 'Even tragic art may be said to participate in the nature of comic art so far as' it 'excites in us the feeling of joy. From this it may be seen that tragedy is the imperfect manner and comedy the perfect manner in art' ('Paris Notebook,' 1903, *Critical Writings* 144).

Of the grotesque Joyce said nothing worth recording, though many of his verbal and written remarks indicate an implicit concern with it. Since the grotesque may also be comic, the two can be seen as sharing a continuum. Formally also they have a point of connection: both tend to break up traditional forms. The comic violates accepted norms; a comedy replaces the old (rigid) order with a new (life-asserting) one. The grotesque distorts recognized forms by combining them (eg, a human shape with the animal emphasized, an animal shape evolving out of a plant). But we cannot speak of a grotesquery the way I have of a comedy. Comedy is a recognized literary genre (one of the oldest, having grown directly from ritual). A grotesquery, on the other hand, is no more than an action or a prank. In fact, far from being a formal genre in literature, the grotesque so distorts form that it is in conflict with the tendency of art towards form. Yet this tension between deforming grotesque and informing art can be a very productive one, especially in a writer like Joyce for whom the transformation process was so important.[1]

In Leopold Bloom, Joyce created quite a different kind of hero from the Stephen who stood for his portrait of the artist as a young man. Where Stephen is proud, Bloom is humble. Where Stephen is unsympathetic in many ways, Bloom has our sympathy through most of the novel. But, as David Hayman points out, though Bloom's failings may generate sympathy by being so human, his expedients and the situations he finds himself in are often ludicrous enough to generate laughter.[2] His usual role is a variant of the position that Bergson describes as essentially comic: 'Something mechanical encrusted on the living.' Another of Bergson's insights is also quite applicable to Bloom: 'We laugh every time a person gives us the impression of being a thing.'[3] I would add that the blend of pathos and humour which characterizes our response to Bloom also comes from his being treated by most Dubliners he meets as a thing, as not there (in the cab ride to the cemetery), as a creature without human feelings (in the brusqueness of the newspaper editor), as a mere beast (during some of the scenes in Nighttown), as a scapegoat (first in Barney Kiernan's pub and again in Nighttown). A scapegoat may of course be seen as a tragic figure, by those who identify with him. It is therefore partly a matter of point of view. And the question we must begin with is why Joyce took the comic view: we can then ask what the result is in the Cyclops episode.

Ernst Kris sees the roots of comedy in gesture.

> Detailed analysis reveals in all comic gesture a technique of imitation, which owes its character to the reanimation of a particular phase of reaction in the child. I refer to that stage of development in which the acquisition of motor capacities, particularly that of 'representation' by 'mimo-motor' means, receives a decisive impetus by the imitation of the motor activities of adults.[4]

In his attempts at gaining mastery, the child may imitate those he admires or those he fears. 'When a small boy who has been to the dentist plays at being a dentist for days on end, he does so not only because he is still afraid but because the pleasure he finds in dominating his fear gives real enjoyment' (Kris 210). This example has an obvious relevance to a repeated incident in Joyce's childhood. 'When James wished to punish one of his brothers or sisters for misconduct, he forced the offending child to the ground, placed a red wheelbarrow over him, donned a red stockingcap, and made grisly sounds to indicate that he was burning the malefactor in hellfire' (*J.J.* 26). Following Kris's suggestion, we can see Joyce as allaying his fear of the devil by building imitation into a dramatic scene. Where such a scene contains socially taboo material, it may become either serious (demonic) or laughable (comic).

> It is a great moment in the life of a child when for the first time it understands a joke made by an adult, or when it makes its own first joke. Illusion takes the place of reality –

> and in this world of make-believe forbidden things are suddenly permitted. ... By its play the child tries to dominate the outer world, and in fun it is looking aggressively or libidinously for a companion. In fun the child is trying to seduce the surrounding world, fun is the frame within which this instinctual drive is indulged. (Kris 211)

The comic thus offered Joyce an opportunity to fulfil two needs that were strong in him: to seduce others (to win the praise and admiration that as the first born he had once known from mother and father) and to express his concerns (to bring out his own anxieties about and aggression towards human beings, the social order, and religious practices). These two aims oppose one another, as Kris makes clear in his summary of the implications of laughter: It 'represents aggression and seduction simultaneously, is associated with birth or rebirth and procreation, is the sign of god-like strength and so of godlike privilege, but is also the sign of the rebellion of the human race' (Kris 233). When *Ulysses* was published, the praise and hostility heaped on it, the high demand and immediate banning it underwent also bear witness to Joyce's ambivalent intentions and success in writing that novel. At his most god-like, the author was celebrating creation, as he had early announced it was proper for comedy to do: 'the great human comedy in which each has share, gives limitless scope to the true artist' ('Drama and Life,' 1900, *Critical Writings* 45). At the same time, Joyce's rebellious nature and destructive impulses are also evident in the design and execution of *Ulysses*.

To investigate the negative side of comedy, we may turn to the Cyclops episode. The nameless narrator is, for instance, both hostile to Bloom and distasteful to us as readers. This could easily cause us to feel only pity and sympathy for Bloom. But in fact Joyce's parody interpolations in this episode not only appeal to our sense of the ridiculous, they also create a mood in which it is easy not to give great sympathy to anyone. The description of Bloom as Messiah at the end is overdone enough so that we cannot take it as a serious plea for pity or admiration of the persecuted man. (But I shall look at it more closely later in this section.) In addition, Bloom is not a very good supporter of his own cause of tolerance and love. Though these are virtues in which Joyce and his sympathetic reader also believe, Bloom gets tripped up on tolerance when asked to define a 'nation' (p 331), and Joyce makes fun of love.

The interpolated parody on love offers a good example of one side of Joyce's comic technique.

> Love loves to love love. Nurse loves the new chemist. Constable 14A loves Mary Kelly. Gerty MacDowell loves the boy that has the bicycle. M.B. loves a fair gentleman. Li Chi Han lovey up kissy Cha Pu Chow. Jumbo, the elephant, loves Alice, the elephant. Old

> Mr Verschoyle with the ear trumpet loves old Mrs Verschoyle with the turnedin eye. The man in the brown macintosh loves a lady who is dead. His Majesty the King loves Her Majesty the Queen. Mrs Norman W. Tupper loves officer Taylor. You love a certain person. And this person loves that other person because everybody loves somebody but God loves everybody. (p 333)

So many diverse examples ostensibly assert the ubiquity of love but in fact only make us wonder how meaningful the word is. The naïve assurance of the primer style overstates the word in the introductory generalization. (To love *love* is so idealistic as to be purile or inhumane. In fact the verb as used in this passage seems to cover everything from infatuation to adultery, from companionship to mourning.) The final generalizations are also broad clichés. The idea that 'everybody loves somebody' is superficially reassuring until we realize that if 'you love a certain person' and 'this person loves that other person,' then 'you' are a victim of unrequited love. Another look at the list suggests that half of the ten who love are in an unsatisfactory situation: Gerty MacDowell suffers neglect (as we discover in the next episode); M.B. (Marion Bloom) has just committed adultery (with Bloom's rival as Bloom knows); we know that Mrs Tupper has also (p 324); Mary Kelly is involved with another policeman; and the 'man in the brown macintosh loves a lady who is dead.' Actually none of the other couples offers much reassurance either. To investigate why this is so is to discover something about the nature of Joyce's comic technique.

In each example, Joyce finds a way of distorting the formula he has chosen so as to influence the reader not to take any statement seriously. 'Nurse loves the new chemist' depersonalizes the two involved by labelling them as occupations instead of naming them as individuals. 'Jumbo, the elephant, loves Alice, the elephant' provides both a name and a label, but the discrepancy between the delicate sentiment and the two ponderous creatures makes the reader smile. Joyce could have got the idea across by saying 'Jumbo loves Alice,' since most readers would know that Jumbo is a name usually limited to pachyderms. His insertion of the word 'elephant' twice in the short sentence is obviously intended to make the syntax as ponderous as the creatures it celebrates. Similarly with 'His Majesty the King loves Her Majesty the Queen.' Since we are dealing with humans here, the idea of love is acceptable, but the use of the titles makes the situation so formal that a verb like 'love' seems out of place to describe the relation. Once more the discrepancy causes a smile.

Looking over the list we realize that in no case has Joyce given both individuals a Christian and a given name, unless we except 'Li Chi Han lovey up kissy

Cha Pu Chow.' But here the names are foreign and the verb is demeaned in form and impact. A similar demeaning takes place with the Verschoyles. Not only are they old; they are given the physical infirmities of age. Our smile here must be based on the assumption that love is not love when there is difficulty in verbal or visual intercourse (not to mention sexual). As my use of words like 'demean' and 'depersonalize' suggests, we are faced here with examples which come under Bergson's contention that comedy arises when people are treated as things. Bergson further asserts that

> the pleasure caused by laughter, even on the stage, is not an unadulterated enjoyment; it is not a pleasure that is exclusively esthetic or altogether disinterested. It always implies a secret or unconscious intent, if not of each one of us, at all events of society as a whole. In laughter we always find an unavowed intention to humiliate.
>
> (*Laughter* in Sypher's *Comedy* 148)

The Cyclops episode is filled with incidents or comments the aim of which is to demean, depersonalize, and humiliate.

At the end of the episode, for instance, the citizen tries to humiliate Bloom. Joyce's interpolations throughout make ridiculous what the citizen stands for. And the narrator continually makes snide comments on anyone present or mentioned. One typical Irish version of this demeaning process is the cod. In *A Portrait of the Artist as a Young Man*, when Wells apologizes to Stephen for shouldering him into a cesspool, he says it was only a cod, a joke (and like most practical jokes, hardly bothering to hide its aggression). Joyce created the Cyclops episode as a series of cods, using variations on the word itself to indicate his intentions. The narrator twice asks a friend if he is codding (pp 295, 300), 'kidding' him as we would say. In fact, some of the jokes are on the narrator (whom Joyce interrupts at will); some are even on the reader (whom Joyce mystifies and tricks in various ways).[5] In this way we could say that Joyce shows himself to be what the narrator accuses Bloom of being, a master of 'codology' (p 304), that is of codding raised to the level of a science. The narrator's insinuation that in Bloom's case it is only a pseudo-science is not completely unfair, considering Bloom's bumbling attempts at explaining the working forces behind appearance.

In another of its meanings, the word 'cod' allows us to see Bloom in yet a different light. The narrator comments three times on his 'cod's eye' (pp 297, 303, 315). To consider Bloom as fish is again to reduce him to a thing. The narrator suggests, for instance, that it would 'be an act of God to take a hold of a fellow the like of that and throw him in the bloody sea' (p 338). Not long after, when Bloom is being openly attacked as a Jew, a slut shouts, 'Eh, mister! Your fly is open, mister!' (p 342). This statement of intended humiliation has the opposite effect on Bloom, who suddenly becomes assertive. '– Mendelssohn was a jew and Karl Marx and Mercadante and Spinoza. And the Saviour was a jew and his father was a jew. Your God' (p 342). Whatever causes Bloom to react with uncharacteristic intensity, the switch from low victim to high victor is prepared for in the image of Bloom as fish. If we combine the picture of him in the sea with the other of his open fly, we can connect him with Stephen's earlier vision of the drowned man whose penis was being chewed by minnows. Bloom then becomes part of Stephen's transformation cycle, 'God becomes man becomes fish...' There is even a joke involved, a pun on the key word for this episode: Bloom becomes cod fish by way of his codpiece (genitals). Although Joyce does not make the pun in this episode, he had inserted a 'buttoned codpiece' (p 211) into an earlier scene.

Once accepted, the three meanings of 'cod' provide a connecting link between the demeaning humour we have been considering and the more positive comedy that Joyce associated with his own name. Before making that connection, however, we need to investigate the elevated connection of fish with God. Stanley Sultan has demonstrated the identification of Bloom with Christ at the beginning of the Lestrygonian episode. Seeing a throwaway sheet with 'Blood of the Lamb' written on it, Bloom reacts, 'Bloo ... Me?' (p 151). Thinking of a luminous crucifix, he compares it to a phosphorescent codfish (p 151). As Sultan also points out, Bloom's boyhood nickname is 'Mackerel' (p 162), 'the name of a fish ... symbolic of Christ' (Sultan 137). All of this is relevant to the end of 'Cyclops' because Joyce works up to a joking grand finale in which Bloom is explicitly identified as the Messiah. As we saw in Chapter 3, that identification had its homeric basis in Joyce's understanding of the Greek pun on Odysseus as 'Outis' (Noman) and 'Zeus' (God). In his usual way Joyce worked this epiphany into the fabric of his work. Remembering Bloom as cod and the different meaning of the word 'cod' in the episode, we can see God as cod-fish, and No one as cod-joke or trick.[6] Like Odysseus, Bloom is spirit and matter combined, Godhood and thingness together. He can be exalted or humbled. Like Christ he can in fact be exalted through being humbled. What he represents may seem a mere cod or joke to unbelievers, but it is in fact a fish that can feed multitudes. Like any man he has a codpiece, potentially the 'father of thousands' (p 86).

The point of this excursion into Joyce's symbolism is to provide an insight into his comic structuring of the Cyclops episode. It ends with another exaggerated description of the sort Joyce had used throughout to make fun of various kinds of Irish nationalism.

When lo, there came about them all a great brightness and they beheld the chariot wherein He stood ascend to heaven. And they beheld Him in the chariot, clothed upon in the glory of the brightness, having raiment as of the sun, fair as the moon and terrible that for awe they durst not look upon Him. And there came a voice out of heaven, calling: *Elijah! Elijah!* And he answered with a main cry: *Abba! Adonai!* And they beheld Him even Him, ben Bloom Elijah, amid clouds of angels ascend to the glory of the brightness at an angle of fortyfive degrees over Donohoe's in Little Green Street like a shot off a shovel. (p 345)

Here Bloom's claim to kinship with Christ is translated into biblical language which 'blends several passages' (Thornton) from both the Old and the New testaments. The final two lines bring this heavenly ascencion down to earth. Are we to infer that Joyce wishes us to take the same attitude to Bloom as to Irish nationalism? I think not. Bloom's real elevation came when he spoke truth to the bigoted: 'Your God was a jew. Christ was a jew like me' (p 342). For Bloom, 'jew' is the common denominator; it is Joyce (as comic narrator and architect creator) and later Stephen who make 'Christ' the vehicle for a comparison. But once that point is made, we can register that Bloom has been acting like a Christian, or as the citizen says, with mistaken irony, 'a new apostle to the gentiles' (p 333). Rather than squandering his money on drink, Bloom has contributed to Dignam's family. When he goes out it is not to urinate like the narrator or to collect winnings (for a horse race on which he had not bet); it is rather to find Martin Cunningham so they can try to provide more money for the bereaved family. Bloom is secure in his humanity. In fact, he is physically untarnished by the citizen's aggression. He is also beyond the animus of the narrator.

I would see Joyce's last paragraph being shaped as an implicit answer to the one before it, a paragraph which gives us the relish of the narrator at Bloom's discomfiture. The truth about Bloom lies in neither the deflation by the narrator nor the inflation by Joyce. These two processes are connected, as I have indicated; one inevitably calls forth the other, but Bloom – though he contains both deflated thing and inflated god within him – wisely acts a creature halfway between these extremes, a human who fallibly searches for truth, who can humbly assert himself when he personally does not stand to gain. I am characterizing Bloom at his best, as he appears here and at the end of 'Circe.' When not fully himself he can slip into a less-than-human animality or inertia, or a compensatory more-than-human disembodiedness. Inert, he can let others use him as a comic butt. Flying high, he can either escape the earth or take revenge on his enemies. By treating both alternatives as comedy, Joyce allows his readers to laugh at their own similar inclinations. That laughter then frees them to feel the comic joy which is the positive human mood of mind, body and spirit in harmony.

Like the Cyclops episode, 'Oxen of the Sun' has a series of stylistic parodies. Unlike the earlier episode, 'Oxen of the Sun' consists of nothing but such imitations, presented more as pastiche than as parody. Where the parodies of 'Cyclops' inflate a point or a view from the main narrative until the pretentiousness or inanity of that view is exposed, the pastiches of 'Oxen' strive to realize the content to which they are applied. As I suggested in the last chapter, Joyce decided first that his scene in the lying-in hospital would follow the stages of the gestating embryo and second that the vehicle for imitating those stages of transformation would be the development of English prose over the centuries. Although his pastiches make for difficulties in comprehension, we should not mistakenly conclude that the episode is a failure. It is indeed one of the striking successes of the novel, not only in its virtuosity but in its expressiveness. That the result should be sometimes strained is not surprising; that it could be better expressed I would deny. Certainly it could be differently expresed, but Joyce's appropriation of the master stylists of English prose provided him not only with impressive styles but with important ways of viewing the traditional concerns of English authors.

These concerns are, most abstractly, religious, political, and social. The religious concern is appropriate to the homeric parallel that Joyce was developing: Ulysses landing at the Island of the Sun where his crew impiously slays the sacred cattle of the sun god, causing Zeus in turn to slay the crew with a thunderbolt. Religious worship, piety, and impiety are thus appropriate topics for this episode, as are the following styles and attitudes which Joyce adopted: a Roman brotherhood of priests; the Anglo-Saxon monastic translator of Homiles, Aelfric; Malory, the Middle English redactor of the tale of Arthur and the Holy Grail; various sixteenth-and seventeenth-century divines; and John Bunyan. After Bunyan the political and social enters more obviously, but the writings of Swift and Sterne also showed a clerical calling. Distorted religion enters the gothic writers, as well as Dickens, De Quincey, and Carlyle.

Perhaps the best example of Joyce's use of a style to recapture the flavour and scope of an original, while at the same time using it to give breadth to his own concerns, is the section which is a pastiche of Swift's personified history of Christian schism, *A Tale of a Tub*. Like the original, Joyce's tale is allegorical in structure but colloquial in style. It thus combines depth with surface appeal. In discussing the development of Christianity in different countries, Joyce could work in political and nationalistic concerns which were his and Ireland's. In using the bull as his image, he could also move among religious, national, and sexual implications, with a consequent gain in vitality. The distinction between subject matter and manner of presentation breaks down when we appreciate the intimate connection between word-play and the connection of ideas, between colloquialisms and theological conflict.

Out of an intoxicated competition of wits among the students in the hospital, we gain the following view of the papal bull in which Pope Nicholas gave Henry II of England permission in 1155 to invade Ireland:

> It is the same bull that was sent to our island by farmer Nicholas, the bravest cattle breeder of them all, with an emerald ring in his nose [says Dixon]. True for you, says Mr Vincent cross the table, and a bullseye into the bargain, says he, and a plumper and a portlier bull, says he, never shit on shamrock. He had horns galore, a coat of gold and a sweet smoky breath coming out of his nostrils so that the women of our island, leaving doughball and rollingpins, followed after him hanging his bulliness in daisychains. What for that, says Mr Dixon, but before he came over farmer Nicholas that was a eunuch had him properly gelded by a college of doctors, who were no better off than himself. So be off now, says he, and do all my cousin german the Lord Harry tells you and take a farmer's blessing, and with that he slapped his posteriors very soundly. But the slap and the blessing stood him friend, says Mr. Vincent, for to make up he taught him a trick worth two of the other so that maid, wife, abbess and widow to this day affirm that they would rather any time of the month whisper in his ear in the dark of a cowhouse or get a lick on the nape from his long holy tongue than lie with the finest strapping young ravisher in the four fields of all Ireland. (pp 399-400)

History is mixed here not only with sacrilege, but with envy of the priest's special position as confessor. The impiety and carnality of the students corresponds neatly with that of Ulysses' crew which used the Oxen of the Sun only to appease their appetites. Joyce is concerned, as is Stephen, with the unnaturalness of celibacy and its perverse consequences. Both also share with Bloom a willingness to celebrate life, its potency and its mystery; on the other hand, perversity and unnaturalness are more evident in this episode.

The varied historic prose styles lend themselves well to these concerns, since by the standard of our straightforward conceptions of clarity and brevity, these styles appear distorted and distorting. But the embryo itself in its organic metamorphoses is also constantly distorted, any stage appearing ugly and unrecognizable by our standard of humanness. Yet each stage is essential to the next and to the creature that we finally call human. Each of us contains within reminders of those stages both of our personal gestation and of the evolution of our species from the humanoid and anthropoid, mammalian and ultimately piscene forms of life. One of Joyce's purposes in writing 'Oxen of the Sun' clearly was to make us face the grotesque history of our evolutionary growth.

The importance of a grotesque conception to this episode can be appreciated by considering this basic definition offered by Wolfgang Kayser in *The Grotesque in Art and Literature*:

By the word *grottesco* the Renaissance, which used it to designate a specific ornamental style suggested by antiquity, understood not only something playfully gay and carelessly fantastic, but also something ominous and sinister in the face of a world totally different from the familiar one – a world in which the realm of inanimate things is no longer separated from those of plants, animals, and human beings, and where the laws of statics, symmetry, and proportion are no longer valid.[7]

Not only are lack of symmetry and proportion evident in 'Oxen,' but the reader is aware of continual gay or ominous transformations resulting from the various styles of the episode. The grotesque continually reminds us of those lower animate worlds of plant and animal with which we are connected. Through it also we can receive intimations of that fantastic and ominous mental underworld on which our orderly consciousness depends. Kayser quotes Albrecht Dürer on the grotesque distortions of dreams: 'If a person wants to create the stuff that dreams are made of, let him freely mix all sorts of creatures' (p 22). In this sense, the grotesque is to the waking mind what the dream is to the sleeping one – unrealistic pictures without sense, mingling the absurd and the menacing. Both convey feelings alienated from their normal channels or objects. In fact the sense of alienation is one of the dominant characteristics of the grotesque. In Kayser's opinion the grotesque is not simply the strange (the exotic of day-dream) but the estranged, the familiar transformed suddenly into the 'strange and ominous' (p 184).

This sense of alienation is, however, mitigated by two other important qualities of the grotesque. The first is the sense of play. As Kayser headlines another of his basic conclusions: 'THE GROTESQUE IS A PLAY WITH THE ABSURD' (p 187). When this quality is dominant, and the play is free, we have the comic grotesque. A good illustration of this effect in 'Oxen of the Sun' is Joyce's use of the Gothic novel style. Gothic effects have many similarities to the grotesque: both alienate the reader from the conventional world, the ominous and menacing being central to the Gothic. But as Joyce adopts the Gothic it becomes comic grotesque.

The secret panel beside the chimney slid back and in the recess appeared ... Haines! Which of us did not feel his flesh creep? He had a portfolio full of Celtic literature in one hand, in the other a phial marked *Poison*. Surprise, horror, loathing were depicted on all faces while he eyed them with a ghastly grin. I anticipated some such reception, he began with an eldritch laugh, for which, it seems, history is to blame. Yes, it is true. I am the murderer of Samuel Childs. And how I am punished! The inferno has no terrors for me. This is the appearance is on me. Tare and ages, what way would I be resting at all, he muttered thickly, and I tramping Dublin this while back with my share of songs and himself after me. (p 412, ellipsis Joyce's)

The false note of 'Celtic literature' allows the development of a counter style, a play on Synge's Gaelic-cadenced English. But even without treatment, there is parody in clauses like, 'Surprise, horror, loathing were depicted on all faces.' In fact, this is pastiche; *The Castle of Otranto* has many such phrases in which Walpole uses Augustan abstractions to tell the reader what to see (rather than describing it).[8] Presumably Joyce found it difficult to take the style seriously enough to parody. He did however consider it worthy of the speaker in the paragraph, the playful and superficial Mulligan.

The comic grotesque is evident in several other sections of the episode, as it is in the pastiche of Swift's papal bull, where the lifetime of one animal compresses several centuries of Irish-English relations. The jocular tale contains a number of distortions and transformations, as Henry II turns into Henry VII and then to Henry VIII. A straightforward example of the comic grotesque is Joyce's description, in the style of Mandeville, of the glasses the students are drinking from and the open sardine can from which they eat:

And there were vessels that are wrought by magic of Mahound out of seasand and the air by a warlock with his breath that he blares into them like to bubbles. And full fair cheer and rich was on the board that no wight could devise a fuller ne richer. And there was a vat of silver that was moved by craft to open in the which lay strange fishes withouten heads though misbelieving men nie that this be possible thing without they see it natheless they are so. And these fishes lie in an oily water brought there from Portugal land because of the fatness that therein is like to the juices of the olive press. (p 387)

The reader is pleased to recognize the objects described; his smile is equally at the naïveté of the style and at the way a naïve observer brings alive common objects by his wonderstruck pondering of their origin and nature.

But often the humorous tone will cover transformations basically ominous and unsettling. Often, that is, the comic grotesque is connected with the fantastic grotesque. Speaking of the latter, Kayser moves more definitely into the psychological basis of the genre:

In spite of all the helplessness and horror inspired by the dark forces which lurk in and behind our world and have power to estrange it, the truly artistic portrayal effects a secret liberation. The darkness has been sighted, the ominous powers discovered, the incomprehensible forces challenged. And thus we arrive at a final interpretation of the grotesque: AN ATTEMPT TO INVOKE AND SUBDUE THE DEMONIC ASPECTS OF THE WORLD. (p 188)

Since I have frequently insisted on the liberation of dark forces in *Ulysses*, the applicability of Kayser's thesis will obviously fit the interpretation I have been suggesting.

Two of Kayser's terms are worth remarking. The 'demonic' is more obvious in 'Circe' than in 'Oxen of the Sun'; but if we think of the demonic as based on the devil, an animalized human figure, we can connect it with the biological monstrosities discussed in one section of 'Oxen.' These monstrosities could easily be said to be 'inspired by the dark forces which lurk in and behind our world and have power to estrange it.' This last verb is the second of Kayser's terms we should consider. Joyce's styles in this episode estrange the world by making strange the ordinary events with which they deal. These styles give a strong sense of the dark forces not only that Joyce was obsessively concerned with, but that were verified by Darwin and Freud (not to mention earlier religious writers we have looked at). In providing a figurative analogue of gestation, Joyce was imitating a process that takes place in a dark world, a biological process that recapitulates, in his words, the 'faunal evolution' which Darwin had justified. Just as Darwin's version of evolution estranged many Christians, Joyce felt justified in making strange the mundane world which is also evolving continually before our eyes. If, as Bergson and Pater suggested, our failure lies in seeing what we have always seen instead of the flux that at any moment is actually in front of us, then it is exactly the obligation of art to estrange the familiar, to break up the rigidities of conscious intellect by demonstrating other ways of seeing things.

Stephen sets up one of the important grotesque themes in this episode by his continuing obsession with physical and spiritual creation. In Malory's style, Joyce has Stephen speak of 'mother Church that would cast him out of her bosom. ... He said also how at the end of the second month a human soul was infused and how in all our holy mother foldeth ever souls for God's greater glory whereas that earthly mother which was but a dam to bring forth beastly should die by canon' (p 390). The problem of his mother's death is obviously still with him. When he takes up the theme again, he is still lining up masculine and feminine, and contrasting physical and spiritual creating. 'In woman's womb word is made flesh but in the spirit of the maker all flesh that passes becomes the word that shall not pass away. This is the postcreation.' The Virgin Mary has 'an almightiness of petition because she is the second Eve and she won us, saith Augustine too, whereas that other, our grandam, which we are linked up with by successive anastomosis of navelcords sold us all, seed, breed and generation, for a penny pippin' (p 391). Faced with the immanence of physical birth in the hospital, with the knowledge of Mrs Purefoy's protracted labour, Stephen feels obliged to play down physical birth (connected inevitably with death), to give pre-eminence to the permanence of language (through which he, like God and like other literary creators, will achieve immortality).

The most obviously grotesque image in the Mary and Eve passage is the 'successive anastomosis of navelcords' which connects Eve to all of mortal humanity. 'Anastomosis' is a term from physiology referring to the union of canals within the body. This coming together of canals (as where arteries are connected to veins by capillaries) is usually thought of within one body. The umbilical cord is a variation on this concept, a canal that connects the mother with her child in the womb. We most often think of the umbilicus as something that is cut when the child is born. Stephen imagines it as the canal linking us through generations back to Eve.[9]

The concept of anastomosis is important in *Ulysses*, and became more so in *Finnegans Wake*. The word itself is derived from two Greek words, *ana*, 'again' and *stoma*, 'mouth.' But *stoma* is also the root from which we derive 'stomach.' This identity of two parts of the alimentary canal was not lost on Joyce, as we can remind ourselves by reference to the discussion in Chapter 3 of the transformation process connected with Bloom and the Lestrygonians. As discovered there, Dublin is at one level imaged as a huge creature, a devouring giant. The Liffey is an orifice which serves both to discharge the giant's wastes (sewage) and to take in food (provisions in boats). To add to this unsettling picture, we can repeat Stephen's grotesque vision of nature eating mankind: he characterizes it as

> an omnivorous being which can masticate, deglute, digest and apparently pass through the ordinary channel with pluterperfect imperturbability such multifarious aliments as cancrenous females emaciated by parturition, corpulent professional gentlemen, not to speak of jaundiced politicians and chlorotic nuns. (p 420)

Stephen's ominous estrangement of our perception presents the end of life as a huge alimentation process. In so doing he demonstrates that death orientation which later causes Lynch to accuse him of perverted Bruno-ism: 'Extremes meet. Death is the highest form of life. Bah!' (p 504). Less self-indulgent in the early part of 'Circe,' Stephen is able to give a more positive answer there, as we saw in Chapter 4.

At the end of the anastomosis paragraph, Stephen again celebrates Mary, perhaps ironically insisting that she has 'a birth without pangs, a body without blemish, a belly without bigness' (p 392). In any case, the next paragraph presents the opposite situation of a man all too filled with the deformed blemishes of an imperfect physical world. Costello starts a bawdy song and is chided by the others as 'thou chuff, thou puny, thou got in the peasestraw, thou losel, thou chitterling, thou spawn of a rebel, thou dykedropt, thou abortion thou, to shut up his drunken drool out of that like a curse of God ape' (p 392). Later, Costello is viewed by Bloom in a similar way:

> he nauseated the wretch that seemed to him a cropeared creature of a misshapen gibbosity born out of wedlock and thrust like a crookback teethed and feet first into the world, which the dint of the surgeon's pliers in his skull lent indeed a colour to, so as it put him in thought of that missing link of creation's chain desiderated by the late ingenious Mr Darwin. (p 407)

The ape and the missing link indicate Costello's part in the evolutionary dimension of the chapter. As an inferior precursor of man, he figures as a grotesque reminder (and scapegoat). Even the sober and tolerant Bloom cannot stand his crude animal expressiveness.

Grotesque transformations and unsettling shifts of view abound in 'Oxen of the Sun.' In the style of Thomas Browne, Stephen develops a view of Aristotle's (cf. Gifford):

> As the ends and ultimates of all things accord in some mean and measure with their inceptions and originals, that same multiplicit concordance which leads forth growth from birth accomplishing by a retrogressive metamorphosis the minishing and ablation towards the final which is agreeable unto nature so is it with our subsolar being. The aged sisters draw us into life: we wail, batten, sport, clip, clasp, sunder, dwindle, die: over us dead they bend. (p 394)

In this Ovidian view of metamorphosis, the process becomes a grotesque rise and fall instead of a cycle. Man grows from birth confidently towards middle age. But at that point, the 'retrospective metamorphosis' diminishes man, who as he ages shrinks back towards a grotesque parody of childhood.

A similar transformation in time occurs with Bloom, as Joyce describes it in the style of Lamb:

> No longer is Leopold, as he sits there, ruminating, chewing the cud of reminiscence, that staid agent of publicity and holder of a modest substance in the funds. He is young Leopold, as in a retrospective arrangement, a mirror within a mirror (hey, presto!), he beholdeth himself. That young figure of then is seen. ... But hey, presto, the mirror is

breathed on and the young knighterrant recedes, shrivels, to a tiny speck within the mist. Now he is himself paternal and these about him might be his sons. (p 413)

The mirror serves as the image for this transformation (as we have already seen a mirror serve in 'Circe'). But again Joyce emphasizes the receding, shriveling effect, this time achieving what we might term the pathetic grotesque. At the end of 'Ithaca,' Bloom will again shrink to a point, but by then the reader is so accustomed to his transformations that the resting point seems natural rather than grotesque.

The end of 'Oxen of the Sun' is the opposite of restful; the flood of disconnected slang and dialect carries the reader breathless and confused for a final four pages. The style and language emulate the drunken actions, speech, and perceptions of the liberated students. The effect is not only to estrange but to alienate the reader's relation to the characters and the scene. Unsettling as it is, this conclusion helps provide the episode with a shape emblematic of the grotesque retrogressive transformations just looked at. Thinking of the development of English prose, we tend, for our comfort, to focus on the growing clarity of style over the centuries. This progress could be demonstrated in Joyce's episode, as the pastiches move into the eighteenth century. Such a development seems to be confirmed in the nineteenth century, unless we ponder the fact that Carlyle is the last stylist to be imitated. I believe Joyce put Carlyle out of order so that the balanced clarity of a Newman should not precede the racy incoherence of the very end. Having Newman followed by Pater, Ruskin, and Carlyle initiates a movement back towards complexity and involution and suggests stylistic retrogression rather than progress. Carlyle is closer to Swift in rhetorical vigour and to Browne in complexity and symbolic vision than to the ultimately simple elaborations of Dickens or Huxley. If the reader cannot depend upon the progress of history to clarify his view of things, then he is perhaps more willing to follow Joyce and his characters into the unsettled visionary world of Nighttown, in the episode that immediately follows 'Oxen of the Sun.' In 'Circe' we encounter both the grotesque and the destructive comic, while in 'Ithaca' we emerge into the realm of the joyful, the great cosmic comedy.

Before we can properly appreciate the full depth of Joyce's art in 'Circe,' however, we must put ourselves in a position to appreciate how much of himself he put into that episode. Such an appreciation demands a look at Joyce's own life, his ability to perceive the complexities and nuances of his mind, and what he learned about human psychology directly and indirectly from Sigmund Freud and the psychoanalytic movement.

Part 2

Introduction

Just as the first chapter on Bruno provided the themes pursued in Part 1 of this study, so the first chapter of Part 2 will provide a Freudian view which will shape the next four chapters. This sequence poses a problem in coherence: a sixteenth-century Italian Dominican heresiarch and a nineteenth-century Austrian Jewish medical revolutionary can hardly be expected to pull in tandem. No more than a young ex-Catholic intellectual aesthete could be expected to share with a middle-aged Jewish ad-canvasser the honour of being the central characters of *Ulysses*. But we know Joyce was successful in the latter attempt, and I believe that his imagination found Bruno and Freud equally compatible and necessary.

It is not, however, that Joyce picked the most unlikely combinations; rather, his mind found connections in most sources of energy he encountered. Like Bruno he believed that contraries coincide, not because this was a grand philosophical demonstration of cosmic unity, but because he had experienced the principle in his life or had observed it in his wide reading. Freud of course also believed that contraries coincide, that dream work will often turn a feeling into its opposite.[1] But rather than enumerating interesting coincidences of doctrine between these two thinkers, I would like to say a word about Joyce's knowledge of Freud before taking a broader view of influences.

There is no doubting that Joyce was well acquainted with Freud's theories. Close friends in both Trieste and Zürich had read Freud and discussed his ideas with Joyce (cf. *J.J.* 351, 450). In addition, we can now be almost certain that Joyce had read Freud. Richard Ellmann has printed a list of the 600-odd books which made up 'Joyce's Library in 1920.'[2] The list includes in German Freud's book *Psychopathology in Everyday Life* (1917 edition) and his pamphlet, *A Childhood Memory of Leonardo da Vinci* (1910). Joyce also owned a 1911 German translation of 'the earliest version of Ernest Jones's celebrated psychoanalytic theory, *The Problem of Hamlet and the Oedipus Conflict*' (*The Consciousness of Joyce* 54). Ellmann believes the pamphlets were obtained in Trieste, probably shortly after publication. He further suggests that Joyce consciously incorporated Freudian principles into the structuring of *Ulysses* (pp 54-6). I shall be making the same point in the chapters ahead. Here I would like to look briefly at qualities in Joyce's mind that would have made Freud's views appealing.

We must always keep in mind Joyce's background of reading and belief. Schooled in medieval and classical Latin, he must have assumed the relevance of the Christian and pagan past to the twentieth century. Why else would he have imposed the framework of Homer's classical epic on his first thoroughly experimental novel? He was attracted to Vico's cyclic vision of history because he had learned from Ovid, Bruno, and the more orthodox writers to see patterns repeated through time with variations. Despite important differences, science is guided by a similar vision. The discoveries of Darwin seemed not only to secularize these patterns but to make them automatic; yet as the twentieth century began, these theories were being used, as we saw in the Prologue, to demonstrate that an evolutionary philosophy could free man from the dogma of rigid forms. Both Bergson and Joyce rejected the tendency of the intellect to set up logical categories which are called real and keep man from seeing the transformation process which is the actual reality of life and the universe.

In *Creative Evolution*, Joyce found not only a philosophic reaction to an important scientific theory but a reappearance of Bruno's key themes. Bergson's vision of life, for instance, closely approximates Bruno's views on the infinite universe and the limitation of mere intellect.

> It is a creation that goes on for ever in virtue of an initial movement. This movement constitutes the unity of the organized world – a prolific unity, of an infinite richness, superior to any that the intellect could dream of, for the intellect is only one of its aspects or products. (p 116)

Bergson's philosophy must, in fact, have gladdened the heart of any artistic innovator.

> Making a clean sweep of everything that is only an imaginative symbol, [the philosopher] will see the material world melt back into a simple flux, a continuity of flowing, a becoming. And he will thus be prepared to discover real duration there where it is still more useful to find it, in the realm of life and of consciousness ... [P]hilosophy is ... the turning of the mind homeward, the coincidence of human consciousness with the living principle whence it emanates, a contact with the creative effort. (pp 401-2)

Bergson thus offered Joyce an optimistic view of the possibilities open to someone who emulated Proteus or Glaucus and installed himself within change, within the flux of flowing and becoming. But this process of transformation has its risks, its pain, its dark underside, and it is here that Freud and psychoanalysis were both useful and important to Joyce.

Although Freud's theory about the unconscious was framed in the terminology of Victorian scientific mechanism (using terms like 'apparatus,' 'systems,' and 'determined'), it was a dynamic theory. In *Psychopathology of Everyday Life*, Freud's very first example concerned a patient's word play on *liquefy*. During the recorded interview, Freud reminded the patient, 'This *stream of thoughts* has some connection with the theme which we discussed.'[3] A term closely related to the protean implication of 'stream of thoughts' is 'plastic,' a word that appears frequently in *The Interpretation of Dreams* (1900) but also in *Psychopathology of Everyday Life* and in *Jokes and Their Relation to the Unconscious* (1905). In Chapter 6 of the latter work, 'Jokes, Dreams and the Unconscious,' Freud wrote, 'the dream-work is the name for the whole sum of *transforming processes* which have converted dream-thoughts into the manifest dream.'[4] The dream techniques which Freud established in *The Interpretation of Dreams* – distortion, condensation, displacement, substitution – are all particular examples of this transforming process.

Paralleling Bergson's contrast of intellectual categories with fluid reality, Freud wrote of dreaming: 'being freed from the hindrances of the categories of thought, it gains in pliancy, agility and versatility' (*Interpretation of Dreams* 84). But Freud was ambivalent towards unconscious thoughts. Although he considered them the basis for all conscious thought, he felt this was a dubious priority. He saw dreams as a means of regressing towards childish impulses and desires, and towards primitive thought processes (*Interpretation of Dreams* 546, 548-9). Both these views are implicit in Bloom's drifting to sleep at the end of the Ithaca episode. Equally important, Freud's view of the close connection between infantile and neurotic, between primitive and atavistic would have confirmed Joyce's perceptions of the dark impulses of his own mind, the compulsions that twisted and limited his relations with others.

Freud provided a useful corrective to Bergson in yet another area. Like Bruno, Bergson was perhaps overly optimistic about the potential of man.

> Man, then, continues the vital movement indefinitely, although he does not draw along with him all that life carries in itself. On other lines of evolution there have traveled other tendencies which life implied, and of which, since everything interpenetrates, man has, doubtless, kept something, but of which he has kept only very little. *It is as if a vague and*

formless being, whom we may call, as we will, man *or* superman, *had sought to realize himself, and had succeeded only abandoning a part of himself on the way.* The losses are represented by the rest of the animal world, and even by the vegetable world, at least in what these have that is positive and above the accidents of evolution. (p 290)

While there is a suggestion here of a connection between man and the animals, the emphasis is on man as evolving towards the as-yet-unformed superman. In contrast, Freud's emphasis, like Darwin's is on the animal substratum from which each man rises himself.

Considering the importance of slips of the tongue in *Ulysses* and the fact that Joyce owned the book in which Freud discussed such slips, I feel warranted in emphasizing an anecdote Freud quoted early in that book, *Psychopathology in Everyday Life.*[5] As recounted to Freud by his colleague Ferenczi, the anecdote focuses on two pairs of aphorisms which are relevant to *Ulysses*. '*God created man in His own image* and its changed conception, *Man created God in his own image*.' Similarly, Ferenczi reported, a 'friend said to me ... *Nothing human is alien to me.* To which I remarked, basing it on psychoanalytic experience "You should go further and acknowledge *that nothing animal is foreign to you*"' (*Psychopathology of Everyday Life* 21). The first traditional aphorism is one of the key points in Bruno's agreement with orthodox Christianity. We have seen Joyce's underlining of it in Stephen's seeming to accept Bloom as a manifestation of Christ. Joyce would also have been aware that eighteenth-century sceptics like Voltaire reversed this Christian view: 'God created man in his own image and man returned the compliment.' Stephen as cynic hovers between this view and the more bitter view of God as destructive *dio boia*.

The third aphorism, 'Nothing human is alien to me,' represents Joyce's triumph in *Ulysses*, his ability to give distinct dialogue and a personality to all his characters in their human weaknesses. And the fourth, 'Nothing animal is foreign to me,' finally brings us to the crux of Freud's contribution. We looked already at Joyce's evocation of the 'funanimal world' in which we all have our being; we should remember too his suggestion that 'Circe' is 'an animal episode' (Budgen 228). In Chapter 10 I shall be investigating this aspect of the episode in more detail. But we may note now that what happens in 'Circe' is helpfully glossed by Freud's comment on animal symbolism in *The Interpretation of Dreams*.

Wild beasts are as a rule employed by the dream-work to represent passionate impulses of which the dreamer is afraid, whether they are his own or those of other people. (It then needs only a slight displacement for the wild beasts to come to represent the people who are possessed by these passions. We have not far to go from here to cases in which a dreaded father is represented by a beast of prey or a dog or wild horse – a form of representation recalling totemism.) It might be said that the wild beasts are used to represent the libido, a force dreaded by the ego and combated by means of repression.[6]

(p 410)

Applying Ferenczi's fourth aphorism, we have the crux of Freudian therapy. If I recognize what appears to be alien and bestial in my dreams and fantasies as actually being part of me, they cease to be threatening. It is on such a principle that we shall see Bloom purging himself of masochism in 'Circe.'

But this Freudian principle would have appealed to Joyce partly because it had been anticipated by Bruno. In *The Expulsion of the Triumphant Beast*, Jove cites with approval Capricorn, who has 'given us the doctrine that ... he who does not know how to become a beast cannot maintain his superiority' (p 109). Both Bruno and Freud refused to separate high from low, a refusal that earned them initial hostility but eventual honour. The same could be said of Joyce.

A word on method. I propose not only to show Joyce's use of psychoanalytic insights but to use them myself in the next two chapters, in an attempt to understand Joyce and his work better. I shall therefore have to record the dark side of Joyce's nature. I have assumed that the cardinal Freudian principles have so permeated our culture that most readers will take these revelations in stride. (Those whose memories need refreshing on some of these principles may wish to read the first five pages of Chapter 9 before beginning Chapter 7.) Certainly Joyce as artist practised a relentless probing of the motives and emotions of his characters, and the revelations that emerged were often known to their author as self-revelations. In other words, I will be saying little about him that he was not aware of himself.

Psychological analysis does, however, open up various pitfalls. The critic must be wary not to reduce Joyce to a case history.[7] He must not fall into 'psychoanalyzing Joyce through his work.'[8] That is, the insights must flow mainly from the many biographical and autobiographical details towards the fiction, rather than vice versa. The next two chapters actually do not attempt to 'psychoanalyze Joyce,' but they do represent an application of psychoanalytic insights to documents by and about him which I shall assume reveal something of how his mind worked. The assumption that such reconstruction is possible may seem arrogant in itself, but at least with Joyce we have the excuse that he was a student of his own mind and recorded descriptions of its dreams. In addition we have the revealing letters which he wrote his wife during their separation in 1909; under considerable psychic strain he there revealed some of his sexual fantasies. Finally we have the information of various friends and of Stanislaus, plus the early biography by Gorman, and the very full biography by Ellmann.

Joyce's use of portions of his own fantasies and personal insights in creating the characters of Stephen and Bloom presents us, however, with a further pitfall:

the temptation to take them as uncritical self-portraits. As I try to demonstrate in Chapter 8, this view will not hold. Joyce saw very clearly how Stephen was trapped sexually and spiritually in the problems that his parents had inadvertently set for him. Whether Joyce saw all the way through his own similar problems is a difficult question, one that has been answered negatively by Sheldon Brivic and ambiguously by Mark Shechner. Although I am inclined to be more positive in my answer, I am well aware how dangerous it is to assume that an artist can resolve his psychological problems through the works he creates. When D.H. Lawrence said, 'Trust the tale and not the teller,' I believe he provided a valuable touchstone. The tale, if well and dynamically constructed, may include those painful and ultimately liberating patterns which provide creator and reader alike with a glimpse, a sense of fuller being. But insight is not enough; since old patterns tend to reassert their dominance, the teller may in retrospect moralize or otherwise try to limit his tale.

Critics, in their choice of emphasis, also run the risk of distorting a tale. I see destructive and constructive urges at work in *Ulysses*, but its artistic success tells me that the constructive triumphs. Accordingly, I feel warranted in emphasizing the positive, as I shall do especially in Chapters 11 and 12. Anticipating this emphasis, I would like to enter a minor caveat against the conventional psychoanalytic approach. Freudian analysis, invaluable for discovering the origin and nature of human neuroticism, too often carries over into the area of mental health and of art its determined habit of uncovering psychopathology. Seen as an example of psychic economy, a work of literature will certainly embody the writer's harmonizing of the demands of Id impulses and Super-ego imperatives, but it aims at more than establishing a stable Ego. Joyce's belief, voiced by Stephen in *Ulysses*, was that there is an 'affirmation of the spirit of man in literature' (p 666). Because this affirmation is hollow unless the spirit is tested and tempered, Joyce made *Ulysses* a novel full of difficulties, both for his main characters and for his readers. But that affirmation of spirit is what in the last analysis places a great work of art beyond the reach of ego psychology.

I shall suggest in Chapter 7 the dimension of psychology that is necessary to a fuller appreciation of art, and in Chapter 11 shall bring in Bruno and Dionysius as providing Joyce with that dimension. Briefly, while Freud is expert in following the protean and circean twists and turns of the mind, his nineteenth-century, medical-scientific training tended to cut him off from the spiritual dimension that Bruno used to balance the down-to-earth. To Bruno the stars were sublime; to Freud a poetic evocation of the stars was sublimation, preferable to repression, but still a regrettable defence against reality. To Joyce the milky way and milk in a jug were equally real, as were the sea and urine, the earth and solid excrement. He was therefore equally ready to follow Freud in connecting gold and faeces, and Bruno in connecting God with the sun. Freud is compatible with Bruno and even elucidates some transformation cycles in more detail and more compellingly than Bruno, but his world view was informed by a tragic sense of the pain of being human. As an exile and apostate, Bruno had even more reason for a tragic view than Freud, but he insisted on viewing the universe as a divine comedy in which 'all things coincide in unity and identity' (*Cause, Principle and Unity* 138). At last, as at first, therefore, Joyce would turn towards Bruno's view, combining a comic and grotesque sense of the pain of being human with a cosmic sense of the divine comedy.

7 Conditioned ego and observing self

Joyce's philosophic and aesthetic views finally rest on his psychology, of which his biographer, Richard Ellmann, is an acute if sometimes too urbane observer. If we really care about the themes and forms of a novel as complex and deep as *Ulysses*, we cannot stop short of applying to it all the knowledge – factual and theoretical, gratifying and unsavoury – that we possess. In this chapter and the next, therefore, I propose to scrutinize Joyce's family background and the liberating insights he gained into how it had conditioned him. Since Joyce took some pains with the information that went into Gorman's contemporary biography of him, that work contains some helpful indications of Joyce's insight.

He allowed Gorman to describe the young artist, for instance, being as 'sensitive as a girl' (p 39; cf. also p 27). This unexpected comparison is born out by the recollection of a contemporary of Joyce's youth. In the group that met at the Sheehy's when he was in his teens, Joyce acted different parts in 'burlesques of operas or plays'; once he 'was got up in one of Mrs Sheehy's old gowns as Carmen and, after taking off the stage manners of opera stars, sang beautifully, "*L'amour est L'enfant de Bohème*"' (*J.J.* 54). As Mercanton records from conversations in the thirties, Joyce 'was delighted that he still had the voice of a young man, even of a child, for he could not remember that it had ever changed' (p 724). Ellmann believes that Joyce's 'disclaimers of Masculinity, his assumption of "feminine" weakness, were secondary manifestations,' citing numerous 'strong' traits that Joyce had.[1] My suggestion would be that since all of us combine strength and weakness, male and female characteristics, the interesting thing about Joyce is his admitting the feminine in himself and not feeling obliged to accept his society's somewhat arbitrary definition of the traits that are and are not permitted a male.

Joyce saw clearly that an important part of the relation between him and his wife depended upon a reversal of the accepted male-female roles. He told Gorman the story of his middle name, which was supposed to be Augustine but was recorded as 'Augusta' through a mistake of the parish clerk (p 6). He also told Gorman his wife's middle name, 'Joseph' (p 117). That Joyce was aware of the partial symbolic truth in these opposite-sex names is clear from notes he wrote for his play *Exiles*. Some of these notes are about the characters in the play, but others are plainly about the events in life on which the conflicts of the play are based.

Nora had had more than one suitor in her native Galway. The one who seems to have meant the most to her (and to Joyce) was Michael Bodkin, who died perhaps partly because of her (*J.J.* 252). The note for *Exiles* reads, 'Bodkin died. Kearns died. In the convent they called her the man-killer: (woman-killer was one of her names for me).'[2] Obviously, Joyce has here moved beyond the conventional implications of 'lady-killer' to the literal meaning of 'woman-killer.' At one level, this dislike of women could be seen as cultural. Joyce's brother Stanislaus voiced what others have observed:

> Love gets a cold welcome in Ireland...
>
> For the most part, women do not interest Irishmen except as streetwalkers and housekeepers. ...
>
> My brother, I am afraid, never quite rid himself of that Iago-complex towards women, *radix malorum*, which he imbibed in youth and which is distinctive of the medieval Catholic Church.... (*Brother's Keeper* 163, 164, 248)

Whether or not we accept Stanislaus' somewhat sweeping sociological analysis, we may find more urgent psychoanalytic reasons in Joyce's youth for such a component in his nature and for linking it with his femininity.

Like most other males, Joyce experienced a number of psychic pressures which influenced him towards adopting components of an at least unconscious feminine sexual identity. The important pressures came from his father and mother, as can be observed in a generalized way from his later relation to them. But the most compelling early evidence comes in the form of two anecdotes, in which the main part is played by parent surrogates. The first incident was recorded by Joyce himself, in the form of an epiphany, one of a number of brief episodes he wrote down from life in late adolescence. This one is a memory of an incident that occurred when he was nine.

(Bray: in the parlour of the house in Martello Terrace)

Mr Vance – (*comes in with a stick*) ... O, you know, he'll have to apologize, Mrs Joyce.

Mrs Joyce – O yes ... Do you hear that, Jim?

Mr Vance – Or else – if he doesn't – the eagles'll come
and pull out his eyes.
Mrs Joyce – O, but I'm sure he will apologise.
Joyce – (*under the table, to himself*)
– Pull out his eyes,
Apologise,
Apologise,
Pull out his eyes.

Apologise,
Pull out his eyes,
Pull out his eyes,
Apologise.[3]

In strictly Freudian terms, the castrating motif is very strong here.[4] Appropriately, the father surrogate suggests violence while the mother merely pleads for submission.

The connection of eagles to destructiveness and sex is underlined in another epiphany which ends, 'What leaps, crying in answer, out of me, as eagle to eagle in mid air, crying to overcome, crying for an iniquitous abandonment?' (*Workshop* 41). If the incident under the table made a strong enough impression, Joyce's libido had two choices, either to identify with the destroying eagles, as he seems to do in the sentence above, or to accept their castration and become the passive, injured, violated one as he appears to do in some of the letters he wrote his wife. In other words, the Aristotelian logic of either/or gives way in the unconscious to a life of both/and. Identifying with Mr Vance, he becomes the aggressor with a stick (cf. Stephen with his ashplant). Identifying with his mother's admonishings he becomes a passive 'good' boy (ie, feminine). At about the time he wrote the epiphany, Joyce began to react strongly against his mother's insistence on submission, as Stanislaus reports: 'My mother had become for my brother the type of the woman who fears and, with weak insistence and disapproval, tries to hinder the adventures of the spirit'(*Brother's Keeper* 234). But this decision of creative will was taken against a deep attraction to passivity.

The other early anecdote is not so precisely located but is more obvious in its later effects. It comes to us primarily from Stanislaus.

> Until he was twelve or thirteen, my brother was always beside himself with fear during thunderstorms. He would run upstairs to our room, while my mother tried to calm him. She would close the shutters hastily, pull down the blinds and draw the curtains together.

> But even that was not enough. He would take refuge in the cupboard until the storm was over. (*Brother's Keeper* 40)

Although the mother is again prominent, in a more positive role here, it is another woman who was on the mind of Stanislaus.

> It was a direct result of the religion of terrorism that Dante had instilled into him. She used to teach us to cross ourselves at every flash of lightning and repeat the rigmarole, 'Jesus of Nazareth, King of the Jews, from a sudden and unprovided for death deliver us, O Lord.' (p 40)

Dante was Mrs Conway, a distant relative who acted as governess to the Joyce children. She took seriously the view 'that children come into the world trailing murky clouds of original sin' (pp 32-3). Stanislaus concludes, 'My brother assimilated her teaching readily and vivified it in his imagination.' In fact, 'his fear of thunderstorms never quite abandoned him' (p 41), as many observers have testified.

> In a stern ... mood, she brought us to see a picture entitled 'The Last Day' in the National Gallery. It represented a tremendous cataclysm – black thunder-clouds lowering, lurid lightning flashing, mountain-tops crashing down, and little naked figures of the wicked in all the contortions of despair ... imploring mercy, while huge rocks fell on them. (p 33)

On one level, this influence reinforced Joyce's fear of a male authority, perhaps adding more to the conscious fear of being destroyed than to the unconscious fear of being castrated (though the two are connected). Once again the child being thus indoctrinated had either to accept the role of guilty, sinful victim or find some way of escaping that role, perhaps by identifying with the authority or perhaps by refusing to admit the validity of the authority. But again it is not either/or; Joyce's life gives evidence that he tried all three solutions. On another level, this view of God could be stigmatized by connecting it with the woman who insisted on it. This response might be behind an observation reported by Stanislaus: 'Jim used to say that the church was cruel like all old whores' (p 34). Such an attitude would help explain Joyce's turning against his mother when she began trying to win him back into the church.

Joyce also had an ambivalent attitude towards males which can be observed in his relations with his father and his brother Stanislaus. That the young Stanislaus worshipped Joyce is not disputed. That he did not like him, Stanislaus recorded in his 1904 diary (p 47). He certainly had good reason, since Joyce was always belittling him (including such unfair and suggestive comments as 'I wouldn't like to be a woman and wake up to find your "goo" (face) on the pillow beside me in the morning' – *Dublin Diary* 26). But thinking over his feelings for his brother, Stanislaus reversed himself: 'I wrote once that I dislike Jim, but I see now how I was led to believe a lie' (p 101). This admitted bond connects with an aphorism of Stanislaus' which Joyce later used in 'A Painful Case': 'Love between man and man is impossible because there must not be sexual intercourse, and friendship between a man and a woman is impossible because there must be sexual intercourse' (*Brother's Keeper* 165-6). This appears to have been part of the strong and twisted connection between the two brothers (cf. Ellmann on their relations in Trieste).

In the Joyce household the main source of feeling against women was John Joyce, whose hatred of his wife frequently took the form of abuse and sometimes of violence when he was drunk (*Dublin Diary* 113). He once attempted to strangle Mrs Joyce (*Brother's Keeper* 74; cf. also pp 55-6). On her deathbed, in the presence of James and Stanislaus, he blurted out 'Die and be damned to you!' (p 230). Small wonder that with such a paternal model James as eldest son had a residue of the woman-killer in him. This ambivalence comes out clearly in the letters Joyce wrote to Nora during their separation in 1909. As persuasively analyzed by Mark Shechner, they show Joyce playing 'the voyeur, the fetishist (and true connoisseur of "drawers"), the coprophile (and lover of smells), the coprolalic (the devotee of the dirty word), the sadist, the masochist, and the homosexual.'[5] According to psychoanalytic theory, all of these characteristics are present in all males; Joyce was certainly more able and willing than most men to let them come to the surface. Our concern must be with the use made of them by the artist in him.

In the Circe episode, as we have seen, submission and dominance are tied to the problems of animality and of male-female identity. Our immediate concern is how close Joyce's understanding was to the psychoanalytic one. I would say quite close.

Budgen admits that Joyce 'made use of its practical analytical devices' in *Ulysses*, while denying that 'he adopted the theory and followed the practice of psychoanalysis' in the manner of the surrealists. As Budgen points out, the latter believed in unconscious writing, 'the passively automatic method,' while Joyce was a very conscious writer (p 320). This is an excellent distinction which yet leaves the way open for Joyce's quite consciously embodying Freudian patterns, devices, and symbols in his work, as I shall be demonstrating he did in *Ulysses*.

Joyce later expressed hostility to psychoanalysis, partly because it was a codified version of modes of self-discovery and insights that he had evolved for himself. At its best, psychoanalytic theory shows how, in the words of Frederick Crews, it is possible for the artist to achieve a 'new vision' (as Joyce undoubtedly did) by 'reconciling ... competing claims so as to *fuse perception with the expression of conflict*' (p 21, my italics). At its worst, as Joyce complained of it to a friend in 1914, psychoanalysis is 'mechanical, a home being a womb, a fire a phallus' (*J.J.* 393). The more usual phallic symbols listed by Freud in the 1909 edition of *The Interpretation of Dreams* are 'all elongated objects, such as sticks, tree-trunks and umbrellas (the opening of these last being comparable to an erection).'[6] Thus when Stephen says in the library scene that 'a brother is as easily forgotten as an umbrella' (p 211), I would see Joyce as meaning, 'Stephen thinks his brother is a mere convenience in his life, but in fact he is a necessary though hidden support.' Immediately after this statement, Stephen makes the application, asking himself, 'Where is your brother? Apothecaries hall. My whetstone' (p 211). A whetstone is for sharpening a knife; Mulligan's name for Stephen, 'Kinch,' refers to the sound of a knife being whetted. Stephen that morning had thought of his relation to Mulligan: 'he fears the lancet of my art as I fear that of his' (p 7). For the 1911 edition of *The Interpretation of Dreams*, Freud added the following to the list of phallic symbols quoted above: 'all long, sharp weapons, such as knives, daggers and pikes' (p 354). Rubbing Kinch as phallic knifeblade aganst the whetstone of a younger brother is just the kind of word-image, psychological puzzle we have seen Joyce employing in other sections of *Ulysses*.[7]

I am trying to suggest that Joyce was consciously using Freud in the Scylla and Charybdis episode; he uses such symbolism throughout the novel but particularly here because Stephen's subject is Shakespeare's sexual problem.[8] Although Stephen adapts and distorts to his own subjective ends the views of various Shakespearean critics (as Schutte lays out for the reader in Appendix A of *Joyce and Shakespeare*), he tries to keep Freud out of the picture. But Joyce includes a clue to the wary reader when he has Stephen reveal that he does know of Freud's theory. He suggests that Aquinas' view of incest differs 'from that of the Viennese school' (p 205). Since Stephen's discussion of Shakespeare is almost pathological in its focus on the bard's sexual problem and on the problem of incest, we are warranted in thinking that a Freudian view will be relevant here.

Whether Joyce got his information for such a view from the first edition (1900) of *The Interpretation of Dreams* or, as now seems most likely, from Jones's study of Oedipus and *Hamlet*, Stephen's discussion of the sexual problems of Shakespeare and Hamlet certainly reveals Joyce's knowledge of the Oedipus complex.[9] I would like to focus on Stephen's inability to face one aspect of that complex, the problem of the son's relation to the father. He certainly worries the problem like an anxious dog, but he cannot face it, though he does manage to sound as daring as any shocking psychoanalyst. Stephen is aware of something goading him but not of what it is:

– Who is the father of any son that any son should love him or he any son?
What the hell are you driving at?...
Are you condemned to do this?
– They are sundered by a bodily shame so steadfast that the criminal annals of the world, stained with all other incests and bestialities, hardly record its breach. Sons with mothers, sires with daughter, lesbic sisters, loves that dare not speak their name, nephews with grandmothers, jailbirds with key holes, queens with prize bulls. (p 207)

As Sheldon Brivic aptly comments, 'Stephen protests too much in his intense reaction against the idea of loving the father' (p 150). By indirection, Joyce indicates himself to be above this particular problem, though his attitude to women is another matter. Schechner makes a compelling case for Joyce's deep ambivalence there.

As I suggested in Chapter 2, Stephen will not be a full man or artist until he can commit himself to a woman. The investigation in this chapter enables us to see, however, that it is not simple selfishness that keeps him from loving another. Consciously Stephen has attributed to the female a bestial desire to kill or maim. Psychoanalyzing Shakespeare's problem Stephen contends, 'The tusk of the boar has wounded him,' referring both to *Venus and Adonis* and to Ann Hathaway's 'undoing' him in the cornfield (p 196). Yet, as Brivic insists, 'The threat remains a paternal one – that is indicated by its phallic nature – but it is disguised as maternal.'[10] At the same time, Stephen consciously posits a mutual dislike between fathers and sons to counteract the unconscious attraction he feels there. Even in this latter construct, he manages to cloud the castration threat of the father by emphasizing how much of a threat the son is (pp 207-8).[11] But how does this simultaneous fear of and lust for a father explain Stephen's problem? In therapeutic terms, if he could admit and feel both emotions, they would lose their hold on him.

If Stephen marries without experiencing his feelings towards his father, he can respond only neurotically to his wife, treating her as a pawn, a fetish. Of course, he may on the one hand recognize in her that soul which seems an echo of his own inner femininity, but he will, on the other hand, actually be choosing her because she possesses that masculine authority which the father was supposed to have. This was Joyce's attraction to the strong-minded, independent 'man-killer' Nora, and it was Bloom's attraction to the Molly for whom he acts the role of wife when we first see him getting breakfast in *Ulysses*.

The exposure of Bloom's neuroticism in 'Circe' has been analyzed by Stanley Sultan (pp 312-31). He shows how Joyce used Sacher-Masoch's *Venus in Furs* for important patterns and details in the delineation of a masochist and how Bloom's fantasies go through Krafft-Ebing's steps in the 'classic development of male perversion from passivity to masochism to feminization' (Sultan 317). Following Ellmann, Sultan claims, however, that Bloom does not 'crave punishment ... to any important extent for sexual gratification (the strict meaning of masochism)' but rather 'because of his sense of guilt for failure' to be a true husband to Molly (p 316). More convincingly, Sultan argues that Bloom, in his later firmness with Zoe, the nymph, and Bella, had 'rejected shabby prurience, unmanly submissiveness, masochistic pandering, and so dispelled the guilty self-reproach that they engendered' (p 328). As I have suggested, by admitting the worst of his dark hidden desires to consciousness, Bloom is purged.

A quite different view emerges from Brivic's Freudian analysis of Bloom. Seemingly aware of Sultan's case, Brivic implicitly denies it without acknowledging it; he sees the action in the latter part of the novel as an exposé of Bloom's unresolved fetishism, castration anxiety, and suicidal tendency. He believes that although Joyce 'shows a penetrating insight into Bloom's psyche' (p 160), 'Joyce's understanding is nevertheless limited' and most seriously 'in his portrayal of Bloom' (p 161). Presumably, then, Brivic would grant that Joyce's intention was more or less as Sultan demonstrates the pattern; but in Brivic's view Joyce's inability to resolve his own feelings about his father causes the main 'theme of paternity' to lose 'much of its force' (p 161). Finding unsatisfactory the atonement of Stephen and Bloom in the last few episodes, Brivic suggests a movement in the novel from 'hopeless conflict to a reconciliation based on delusion' (p 162). I think he is wrong. It is true that both Bloom and Molly are tempted by the notion of introducing Stephen as a third person in the household. Such a situation would continue Bloom's masochism and psychic castration, but in fact Stephen is not going to move in. He refuses even to stay the night, and Bloom subsequently asserts himself to Molly, asking her to prepare breakfast. Joyce was too honest to show more than this, so it would be foolish to think of Bloom as 'cured.' But it is equally blind not to see him moving towards change.

The contrast with Richard Rowan of *Exiles* is instructive. In his notes to that play, Joyce again demonstrates his psychological insight. Richard, the noble artist, desires his wife to remain with him, but only as the result of a completely free choice. Because she cannot understand this noble concept, he forces her to follow out an advance from his friend Robert to the point where she will have to make an individual rather than a conventional choice. But as Joyce saw clearly, Richard's principled manipulation hides a neurotic need.

> The bodily possession of Bertha by Robert, repeated often, would certainly bring into almost carnal contact the two men. Do they desire this? To be united, that is carnally through the person and body of Bertha as they cannot, without dissatisfaction and degradation – be united carnally man to man as man to woman? (p 123)

This vicarious contact constitutes a kind of answer to Stanislaus' complaint that 'love between man and man is impossible because there must not be sexual intercourse.' Robert is referred to in Joyce's notes as a brother to Richard (p 114). Joyce was aware of the same undercurrent of homosexuality in Bloom (cf. Budgen 315). But the contrast of the endings is the important point. Richard will not let his wife tell him whether she has been guilty. Determined to suffer, in his last speech he tells his wife, 'I have wounded my soul for you – a deep wound of doubt which can never be healed. I can never know, never in this world. I do not wish to know or to believe. I do not care. ... And now I am tired for a while Bertha. My wound tires me' (p 112). In contrast, Bloom knows that he has been cuckolded. Although he shows acceptance of this fact, he does not choose to suffer as does Richard. *Exiles* has the limitations of a clinical case study; *Ulysses* has the fullness of a vision of life that goes beyond the clinical to an affirmation of the resilience of the human spirit. Although Bloom has not completely thrown off his neurotic traits, he has used his will, which is the first step out of bondage. His demand of Molly does not mean that a woman's proper place is in the kitchen, but rather that Bloom is no longer going to play a submissive role in the marriage. That decision is affirmative.

Brivic lays another charge against *Ulysses*. 'Joyce's attempt to differentiate the two protagonists founders on the fact that they have essentially identical psychological complexes' (p 161). Pushing past the surface contrast of Stephen as a young, aloof intellectual and Bloom as a middle-aged, gregarious bourgeois, Brivic insists that their underlying psychic make-up is almost identical:

> Both men are centrally preoccupied by the idea of the father taking the mother away from them and castrating or violating her (God taking May Dedalus, Blazes taking Molly). Both consider the mother to have betrayed them; both view sex as a castrating violence; both are horrified at the thought of the woman's castrated genitals and tend to associate themselves with the mother; both feel strongly threatened and tempted by father figures; both are inclined toward fetishism and other strategies of perversion, although only Bloom has submitted to the authoritarian mother so as to placate the threat of the father. (p 161)

Trying to be sympathetic with Brivic's psychoanalytic shorthand here, I can agree in the main with his evidence; but I must disagree entirely with his conclusion. As he himself indicates through most of his essay, the value of Freudian analysis is that it reveals unconscious problems and defences which are for our purposes universal. To the extent that all men suffer from the Oedipus complex, they will be 'centrally preoccupied by the idea of the father taking the mother away from them and castrating or violating her' (the primal scene). Brivic himself refers to '*universal* patricidal desires' (p 129, my italics) and to possible variations or disguises of them. Similarly, I believe that most of the items on which the 'essentially identical psychological complexes' of Stephen and Bloom rest are the 'universal' Freudian ones that also cause the emotions of readers to respond in ways of which they are not fully conscious.

To be explicit, I claim (as I think Brivic would) that at some level of the psyche, all Western men 'consider the mother to have betrayed them ... view sex as a castrating violence' and 'feel strongly threatened and tempted by father figures.' This leaves fetishism and perversion, two ways of acting out defences against these universal male problems. But Brivic moderates his case here, claiming only that they are 'inclined toward' perversions. Bloom comes closest to acting on the tendency, but the point is that he does not. Although the action in 'Circe' may be more dynamic than Sultan allows, he is essentially correct in insisting that 'because the drama is psychic, all that really happens is that Bloom tells himself about himself' in fantasies (p 318). In other words, some of the seeming key evidence of Bloom's perversity is actually a stage in his partial release from his neurotic plight.

Brivic falls into a similar trap in his discussion of the paternity theme. 'Because Bloom is unable to think of himself as a parent and is himself bound to parental authorities, he is less a father than a son, and this is a major failure of *Ulysses*' (p 161). It is clearly illogical to call the psychological problem of a character 'a major failure' in any novel. The character's problem is rather the source of a fictional conflict.[12] In Bloom's case, it keeps him from maturing; it allows him to be homosexually attracted to Stephen; as Brivic shows, it aids the development of the plot by allowing Stephen to 'relate to him with a minimum of anxiety' (p 154). But to say these things is to get at the psychoanalytically valid basis of the temporary friendship of Stephen and Bloom. Although Joyce allows the characters to think of the friendship's continuing, it seems to me unfair of Brivic to condemn Joyce on the grounds that *if* the friendship had continued it would have shown Joyce's own neurotic need. Brivic's preoccupation with Joyce as neurotic vitiates his appreciation of Joyce as artist.

The same defect is evident to a lesser extent of Mark Shechner's psychoanalytic study *Ulysses*. Shechner presents a great many helpful insights, but he has difficulty disentangling Stephen from Joyce. In an ironic paraphrase of Stephen's theory of art, for instance, Shechner indicates its escapism and narcissism:

> The autonomous creator-God is free from the authority of the father, the treachery of the brothers, and the seductions of the mother, for he has triumphed over childhood and

sexuality. As bisexual creator of his own family, he is not only free from sexuality and guilt, but, as creator of his own parents, is free of infantile helplessness and filial dependence. He is infallible. (p 45)

Applied to Stephen, this analysis has quite a bit of validity. Shechner's next step, however, is to claim that it is also central to *Ulysses*.

Autonomy, or transcendence of family relations, then, is an ambiguous ideal that stands, in all its complexity, at the heart of *Portrait* and *Ulysses*. (p 48)

At the end of 'Scylla and Charybdis' the elaborate metaphysic of Stephen's parable is reduced to a simple joke: to copulate is human, to masturbate divine. But that joke is one of the meanings of *Ulysses*. (pp 48-9, end of chapter)

Frankly, I find Shechner unclear here. Does he suggest that 'autonomy ... is an ambiguous ideal' in the sense that the reader is invited not to share Stephen's ideal or in the sense that Joyce covertly does share that ideal? I suspect the latter. Similarly, I suspect that when he says 'that joke is one of the meanings of *Ulysses*,' Shechner means not that Joyce invites us to see the limitations of Stephen's position, but that Joyce really agrees with Stephen on the value of artistic narcissism.

Shechner has a perceptive chapter on Joyce's self-exposure in the 1909 letters to Nora, but he tries to connect the concerns of the letters and *Ulysses* in a way that overlooks Joyce's *artistic* use of his psychic problems. 'It appears that Jim found coitus a poor substitute for masturbation. And his books seem to confirm what these letters suggest' (p 93). In fact, however, what we see in *Ulysses* is Joyce viewing these problems as they appear in his alter ego Stephen with a detachment the reader is obviously invited to share. Stephen concludes one of his discourses:

In the economy of heaven, foretold by Hamlet, there are no more marriages, glorified man, an androgynous angel, being a wife unto himself.

...

– Those who are married, Mr Best, douce herald, said, all save one, shall live. The rest shall keep as they are.

He laughed, unmarried at Eglinton Johannes, of arts a bachelor.

Unwed, unfancied, ware of wiles, they fingerponder nightly each his variorum edition of *The Taming of the Shrew*. (p 213)

The last sentence belongs to Stephen, who perceives that textual criticism and masturbation are interchangeable forms of solipsistic exercise for the man who cannot otherwise stand up to a dominant woman in his background. What he does not see is that his own sexual outlet (prostitutes) is not much healthier. Neither does he register the implied criticism of his solipsist doctrine of artistic creation. Stephen will remain isolated and limited, sexually and artistically, until he is able to give himself more to life and other human beings. As Shechner suggests (pp 98-9), if Joyce shows himself in *Ulysses* as a fuller artist and human being than Stephen, it is because he had committed himself to the relation with Nora Barnacle. Despite this affirmation of Joyce's artistic integrity, Shechner's more usual judgment is that Joyce in effect shares Stephen's limitations.[13]

Any critic using the psychoanalytic approach must feel ambivalent towards a writer who engages his problems as energetically as Joyce did. But if, as such critics claim, psychoanalytic insights deserve a privileged position, the psychoanalytic critic also has a special responsibility. Shechner acknowledges this responsibility, but has difficulty living up to it. So do we all. Frederick Crews's humane advocacy of the psychoanalytic approach makes his introductory essay a helpful and subtle guide to this problem. His concluding remarks are particularly appropriate to the difficulties I have been discussing.

> Any critic can temporarily make an engaging text seem dreary – not, however, by revealing too much of it, but by revealing too little and claiming this to be the whole. The very success of psychoanalytic theory in anticipating predictable aspects of literature leaves the Freudian peculiarly vulnerable to this coasting on his assumptions.
>
> ('Anesthetic Criticism' 24)

Brivic and Shechner both err in this way when they claim that Joyce never gets beyond the neurotic traits of his characters.

Considering the importance of literature in psychoanalytic theory, one might have thought that the seventy years since the publication of *The Interpretation of Dreams* would have brought real clarification of the relation of psychoanalysis to literary criticism. But, as Crews demonstrates, we are not in any such happy position. His essay and the articles that follow it are admirable attempts towards clarification and application, but as he indicates, progress is going to continue to be slow. To keep the process going, I would like to look at a couple of points in Crews's essay.

Crews insists that psychoanalytic criticism will decline from an informing spirit to a dead hand unless it maintains 'Freud's sympathy with the way great artists court unconscious engulfment in order to recreate the conditions of a human order' (p 19). Applying this notion to Joyce, Crews suggests that Stephen as sympathetic artist 'tells us that his, and our own, creative ego must brush every hindrance from its path. In each instance we are invited, not to experience a fantasy, but to share a posture toward questionable impulses, and in the act of sharing to diffuse responsibility and stake out some unconscious territory free from the taxation of conscience' (pp 22-3). The burden of my analysis is that Joyce worked out a process for accomplishing that end: the artist descends within the flux that will become his work, lives out the process he wishes to embody there, transmutes himself stylistically into it, and yet comes out at the end above and beyond that process as well as in it.

In the passage above, Crews speaks of the 'creative ego,' a twentieth-century term for imagination, blending the notion of flexibility and change with that of stability in the here and now. Earlier in the essay, Crews spoke favourably of 'artists whose perceptiveness has not been obliterated by ego-needs' (p 21). Clearly these are two very different egos, or emphasize two different functions of that Freudian concept. In contrast to the creative ego this second version is the ego so pressed by its need to defend against repressed yet highly-charged material that it has no opportunity to relax into clear seeing or true feeling. Both phases of mind have been experienced by all artists and, one hopes, most critics. Because the difference is so great, I am not satisfied with the way ego-psychology lumps them both under the same term. This is not a complaint about Crews but about the Freudian framework. In his attempts to enlarge this framework, he points towards a possible solution by distinguishing between 'biographical data' (that record of what conditioned the ego needs) and the artist as seen through 'negative capability' (Keats's well-known view of the self that does not close off varieties of experience and possibilities of vision).[14]

Developing this distinction, I would suggest that we should see the ego on the one hand as a centre connected closely with evaluation and distantly with emotion, and the self on the other hand as an original centre gradually overlaid with social and parental injunctions and bruises, and thus hardly operable in most adults. The distinction between ego and self was a cornerstone in C.G. Jung's analytical psychology. It is also implicit in existential psychotherapy.[15] Despite differences in emphasis, such therapists urge that *analysis* of repressed feeling is not very helpful, since the rational mind will rationalize to satisfy its ego needs. Therapy must entail experiencing or living through denied and repressed feeling. The liberation then occurs at a deeper level than the analytic mind, but most important, the self that emerges is not centred in the ego, and must in fact work not to let that ego resume control, as it will tend to do when the liberated feelings lose some of their immediacy. Another aspect of the self can help at this point, its ability simply to observe the analytical mind, the ego needs which busily, repetitively, uncreatively keep up their constant round of activity. This therapeutic schema correlates with the view of Joyce as artist that I have been developing; it most clearly underlies the Circe and Ithaca episodes, as I shall demonstrate in the chapters that follow.

As an initial overview, I would suggest that the observer self (with its refined creative will) roughly corresponds to Joyce's and Bruno's conception of the creator above that which happens, while the released feelings correspond to those transformation cycles through which all things must pass. The selfish ego denies the self and represses the feelings, refuses to admit the past pain of buried hate and love or the present possibility of change and a large view. I shall investigate the problem of released feeling and change when we come to Bloom's experience during 'Circe' in Chapters 9 and 10. I shall consider his large view in Chapter 11 and Joyce's in Chapter 12. But a preliminary view of Joyce's artistic ability to distance himself from his neurotic suspicions and self-pity will be offered at the beginning of the next chapter.

8 The image of the artist: destruction, perversion, creation

In this chapter I propose to connect Joyce's superstitious belief in the meaningfulness of coincidences with a view of the traditional psychic difficulties of the Western artist. These difficulties can be observed both in Joyce and in Stephen Dedalus. At the end of this chapter and in the two that follow, I shall suggest how Joyce's view of his dirty and sacred calling made purging an important basis of his art.

We saw in Chapter 5 that Joyce's view of himself as artist involved a peculiar kind of superstition. As he wrote Harriet Weaver while writing *Ulysses*, 'the progress of the book is in fact like the progress of some sandblast. As soon as I mention or include any person in it I hear of his or her death or departure or misfortune' (*Letters* I, 129). Ellman emphasizes how Joyce's 'feeling of the book's prophetic and magical nature seized upon every corroboration' (*J.J.* 539). Another facet of this superstition is observable in what Ellmann rightly terms 'one of the strangest ideas in literary history' (*J.J.* 604).

In 1927, in response to criticism of *A Work in Progress*, Joyce decided to find someone who would agree to carry on the work if he for some reason could not. He settled on James Stephens, a Dubliner who shared his own first name and that of his *alter ego*, Stephen Dedalus. Investigating before approaching Stephens, Joyce discovered they also shared exactly the same birth date, 2 February 1882. This coincidence convinced him to approach Stephens, who finally agreed to carry on the work if something should happen to Joyce.

Another coincidence which would have appealed to Joyce was that James Stephens's nineteenth-century namesake is referred to in *Ulysses*. This Fenian organizer escaped from Ireland in 1865, purportedly by dressing as a woman. As Joyce condensed this historically dubious anecdote in *Ulysses*, it is part of Stephen's stream of consciousness. 'How the head centre got away, authentic version. Got up as a young bride, man, veil, orangeblossoms, drove out the road to Malahide. Did, faith. Of lost leaders, the betrayed, wild escapes. Disguises, clutched at, gone, not here' (p 43). Appearing in 'Proteus,' this is obviously an important thematic anecdote. It reminds Stephen of Parnell ('lost leaders, the betrayed'). Parnell, a nationalist who refused to disguise his masculine nature, became a hunted victim, as 'Mr Fox' (cf. *Ulysses* 492, and Thornton), a prey to rapacious hounds. In contrast, James Stephens, a nationalist who was willing to appear a woman, lived to carry on his work. The Joyce who had taken on the disguise of Molly Bloom through all the transformations of her amorphous consciousness in the last episode of *Ulysses* could not help being sympathetic with the James Stephens whose *Dierdre* he was reading when he made up his mind to ask that fellow Dubliner to be his *alter ego*.

Joyce's identification with the betrayed Parnell certainly contributed to his fear of living in Ireland. The idea of needing a disguise to escape recognition, betrayal, and death has an important bearing on the different voices, points of view, and puzzles which are key ingredients of *Ulysses*. We need now to connect these disguises with the superstitious view of coincidences which we have seen lying in the magical lower consciousness of Joyce. As Ernst Kris says in one of his suggestive essays, 'The Image of the Artist':

> The belief in the artist's magical power, and at the same time also the belief in the forbidden nature of his activity, is deeply rooted in the mind of man. For, it was precisely those demigods of myth who had been rebellious and punished – the imprisoned Daedalus, the lame Wieland, the crippled Hephaestus, and their great ancestor, the enchained Prometheus – whose heritage early biographers awarded to the artists.
>
> (*Psychoanalytic Explorations in Art* 78)

Kris is speaking at this point of attitudes towards the artist, but as he goes on to demonstrate, these are the same attitudes that, for various reasons, the artist himself has towards his work and his fate. The relevance to Joyce of Kris's subsequent comments becomes even more striking: 'Artistic ability is part of the power of the demiurge. He is part of a world in which magic practices comprised art; it is the time of the sacred archaic craft which contains in undivided unity mantic, magic and various specialized skills' (p 78). Joyce's skills were his memory and mastery of words; he asserted his mantic nature in insisting on the prophetic power of his works; his connection with magic is evident in his consulting the omens about Stephens and in the ritual way he enlisted the younger author as apprentice or *alter ego*.

In these beliefs, Joyce illustrates the importance of the principle Kris sees involved in magic, that the magician is competing with God in his creation of images and that he consequently runs the risk of punishment by emasculation or death (pp 81, 78, 82). This high aspirant is playing with fire as did Prometheus, Hephaestus, and Satan, and he may be cast down or chained down for meddling with the ordinances of God, as those heroic lesser gods were (Kris 78). Joyce made this sense an important part of the consciousness of Stephen Dedalus. In *A Portrait of the Artist*, Stephen mentions his fear of dogs, the sea, and thunderstorms. 'I imagine,' he confesses, 'that there is a malevolent reality behind those things I say I fear' (p 243). In *Ulysses*, Stephen turns pale at a 'black crack of noise,' the thunder outside the lying-in hospital. Costello jokingly rebukes Stephen, connecting God's voice with Stephen's preceding 'hell-prate and paganry' (p 394). Remembering Joyce's own conditioning to thunder, we can appreciate that not far below consciousness he probably expected to be blasted by the mighty hammer-hurler for daring to create such a universe as *Finnegans Wake*, with its new life, its polymorphous perversity, its blasphemy. It is as though he ensured his own life by seeing to it that the task of creation would continue if he died or were incapacitated, because such assurance meant that the projected punishment would not halt the promethean task.

We need now to return to the question of Joyce's relation to God, Satan, and the Demiurge, armed with the insights of psychoanalysis. Again we shall be turning our attention to childhood anecdotes. But first we should consider Kris's Freudian outline of the connection between childish fantasy and adult art. In 'role-play or illusory games' he contends,

> there is no indication that the child necessarily believes in the 'reality' of the play situation, but the intensity of his imaginative powers cannot be evaluated unless we realize that the 'intensity' of illusion matches that of fantasy productivity. ... Children's role-playing, the content of which emerges at a later phase in daydreams, has from the economic point of view a parallel in that behaviour of adults in which the ego has suffered a loss in its regulating and controlling functions. When the distinction between picture and depicted diminishes for the adult, he has 'regressed' to a form of behavior which we call 'magical.' He is then dominated by the belief in the omnipotence of thought. (p 77)

Taking these assumptions a step further, we may speculate that to the extent a child feels threatened or annihilated by 'reality' he will turn to a fantasy world where, thanks to the 'omnipotence of thought,' he can regain the integral wholeness and power of which his experience may have deprived him. Such 'potency' will of course hold only in that fantasy world, but the need of the adult to build it will presumably be in inverse ratio to the ability of his ego to keep off the threats of adult reality (both inner and outer). A 'weak ego' may thus be associated not only with 'nervous breakdowns' but with artistic productivity and with clear expressions of the self (that centre of consciousness which I have suggested as an alternative to the ego).

There is evidence from Joyce's youth which Kris's observations can help us to understand. Like the anecdote about the eagle that might pull out his eyes, one of these connects his righteous 'aunt,' Dante, with the neighbouring Vance family. Because Eileen Vance's parents were Protestant, Dante 'warned James that if he played with Eileen he would certainly go to hell, and he duly informed Eileen of his destination but,' as Ellmann comments, 'did not cease to merit it' (*J.J.* 25). Ellmann continues, 'Hell and its superintendent had already become useful histrionic counters for him. He loved to arrange little plays, and his brother Stanislaus's earliest memory was of playing Adam to the Eve of his sister Margaret ("Poppie"), while James crawled about them in the congenial role of serpent' (pp 25-6). This anecdote obviously ties in with the one quoted in Chapter 6: 'When James wished to punish one of his brothers or sisters for misconduct, he forced the offending child to the ground, placed a red wheelbarrow over him, donned a red stockingcap, and made grisly sounds to indicate that he was burning the malefactor in hellfire' (p 26). Psychoanalytically, we can observe that Joyce was trying out the role of the devil, as he did at times throughout his life (cf. n 11, Chapter 2). Presumably he felt compelled to do so at least partly because Dante had successfully filled him with guilt, and he chose to act as the figure of greatest power available to him within that fallen state. Fear of punishment could thus be allayed (and accepted) by taking on the role of the punisher. This is the earliest indication in Joyce of that sadomasochism which Wilhelm Stekel has argued is a unified phenomenon. No matter which role the neurotic takes, his unconscious aim is to

> experience both conditions: triumph and defeat, power and subjection, activity and passivity, male and female, resistance and the overcoming of it. The specific scene which he is always wanting to repeat is a drama, a fiction, in which he as the author feels with the actors, suffers and enjoys.[1]

A person with this urge may grow up to write fictions in which he obsessively places characters in similar situations (as in certain kinds of pornography). On the other hand, he may like Joyce become a great artist. The distinction is admirably expressed by Crews.

> Whereas symptoms are rigidly stereotyped, are usually accompanied by guilt, and subtract from an individual's rapport with his surroundings, in the highest literary enjoyment we feel that our pleasure is being sanctioned by reality itself, whose principles have been set before us. This is an illusion, but the illusion can be practiced only by artists whose perceptiveness has not been obliterated by ego-needs. A work that flouts our conscious intelligence, as symptoms do, may have an 'escape' interest but will soon be rejected for its crudeness or empty conventionality. (p 21)

Taking Crews's distinction as a guide, we may now turn to the strategy by which Joyce evaded his ego needs to attain and express the illusion of art, an illusion which the artist can create, however, only when he achieves a new vision.

The first step will be to try to consolidate the three images of divinity suggested by Kris and worked on by Joyce: Satan, the Demiurge, and God. Stephen's thoughts on Satan at the end of 'Proteus' are worth considering: 'Clouding over. No black clouds anywhere, are there? Thunderstorm. Allbright he falls, proud lightning of the intellect, *Lucifer, dico, qui nescit occasum*' (p 50). The words 'proud' and 'intellect' indicate Stephen's identification with Lucifer, as does the Latin 'who knows no fall.' But we all know that Lucifer did fall; similarly Stephen admits later that he is Icarus and has also fallen. As Thornton points out, the Latin combines the service for Holy Saturday (Joyce's favourite) and its optimistic 'morning star that knows no setting,' with derogatory New Testament references to 'Satan as lightning fall[ing] from heaven.' Since Stephen later acts out his fear of thunder and lightning, the passage as a whole seems to combine identification with Lucifer's proud intellect and power with fear of the destructiveness of that power. Later Stephen's fear becomes, as we have seen, a fear of God's vengeance, probably God as *dio boia*. Since Satan is supposed to be doing God's work in punishing malefactors, such a fusion is not difficult to effect. It brings us back to the problem Schutte and Sultan investigated. Stephen will be sure to meet such a punishing God as long as he hates Him, his hate being a sign of his belief. In psychoanalytic terms, Stephen is still attached to the sadomasochistic unity of suffering and punishing, of covertly enjoying both roles, as his thoughts in the quotation above indicate.

But Stephen (and Joyce) are not alone in this dilemma. The unconscious problem of any artist is highlighted in inferences that Kris drew from the delusions of a particular unbalanced sculptor:

> In the center of his delusion we find the thought that the gods, envious of his perfection as an artist and particularly of his knowledge of the 'divine proportion,' persecute him – a delusional thought which can easily be recognized as a projection of that other notion according to which the artist competes with God. (p 81)

If we are interested in reducing this problem to its nuclear source, we could find it in the artist's Oedipal striving with his father for the mother. In Joyce's case, since Dante was an inspirer of fear more concerned with religion than Joyce's father, we could bring her in instead or as well. Certainly the existence of such a malign deity is evident in Stephen's thoughts at various points in *Ulysses*. In addition to the ones we have seen, in 'Wandering Rocks' he demonstrates a superstitious fear of annihilation similar to that of Joyce when he chose someone to carry on his work:

> Between two roaring worlds where they swirl, I. Shatter them, one and both. But stun myself too in the blow. Shatter me you who can. Bawd and butcher, were the words. I say! Not yet awhile. A look around.
>
> Yes, quite true. Very large and wonderful and keeps famous time. You say right, sir. A Monday morning, 'twas so, indeed. (p 242)

As several critics have observed, in the second paragraph Stephen thinks 'public' thoughts designed to pacify the destructive god of things as they are who might take up his challenge. The blow that Stephen plans is the one he later delivers with ashplant in the brothel; the one that he fears is the one he receives from Pvt Carr in the street.

The second blow we have accepted as self-directed retribution for the first; Kris suggests the artist has good psychological reasons for fearing such retribution.

> The artist does not 'render' nature, nor does he 'imitate' it, but he creates it anew. He controls the world through his work. In looking at the object that he wishes to 'make,' he takes it in with his eyes until he feels himself in full possession of it. ... Every line or every stroke of the chisel is a simplification, a reduction of reality. The unconscious meaning of this process is control at the price of destruction. But destruction of the real is fused with construction of its image: When the lines merge into shape, when the new configuration arises, no 'simile' of nature is given. Independent of the level of resemblance, nature has been re-created. (pp 51-2)

Although we might carp at Kris's analysis by noting that Joyce was interested in process (and that words bear a different relation to reality than does stone), the fact remains that Joyce as artist shows a strong destructive bent, as we saw in the aggressive and demeaning comic techniques analyzed in Chapter 6. As we would expect of a great writer, Joyce was aware of the connection between creation and destruction.

In his original 'Portrait of the Artist' essay, Joyce referred to the artist as having 'annihilated and rebuilt experience' (*Workshop* 64). Speaking to Budgen of his aim in *Ulysses*, Joyce said in Zürich, 'I want ... to give a picture of Dublin so complete that if the city one day suddenly disappeared from the earth it could be reconstructed out of my book' (Budgen 67-8). Similarly, of his distortions of language in *Finnegans Wake*, he wrote a friend, 'I'll give them back their English language. I'm not destroying it for good' (*J.J.* 559). These statements over a period of thirty years clearly underline the *hubris* of the artist. Great creativity is a response to a great impulse to destroy.[2]

The act of creation may compensate for the hate that would destroy something outside; it may even provide the artist with a sense of inner self; but if his fear and guilt are strong enough, the artist will still fell obliged to propitiate the outer in order to avoid retaliation. Thus we have superstitious gestures such as Stephen's in the 'keeps famous time' passage above, or Joyce's in enlisting James Stephens. But the actual agent of punishment is internal.

Where the super-ego has been too strongly reinforced, the punishment may be submerged and transformed not merely into psychological fear (of thunder) but also into physical symptoms, such as Joyce's iritis. Then the inversion of aggression into punishment takes the form of blinding those eyes that formerly kept taking in nature until, in Kris's formulation, the individual felt himself 'in full possession of it.' Although Kris does not speak of the sexual level in this relation, he is too good a Freudian not to intend such a level in his analysis.[3] At any rate, Joyce's self-reassuring statement about possible loss of sight fits in with Kris's theory: 'What the eyes bring is nothing. I have a hundred worlds to create, I am losing only one of them' (*J.J.* 676).

In concluding this section, I would like to underline the strong stimulus that Joyce had for fear and hate by repeating Stanislaus' description of the destructiveness of God as depicted in the National Gallery and reinforced on the two brothers by Dante. *The Last Day* 'represented a tremendous cataclysm – black thunder-clouds lowering, lurid lightning flashing, mountain-tops crashing down, and little naked figures of the wicked in all the contortions of despair' (*Brother's Keeper* 33). Under such stimuli who would not identify God with destruction, Satan, and the threat of annihilation? That form of Christianity which insists on Hell and Satan makes the identification psychologically inevitable in any case, since Satan would not punish sinners unless he acceded to God's will and became his right arm, his representative in Hell, his *alter ego*. Joyce's resolution of this problem was to take a certain pleasure in emulating Satan, to rebel against the destructive God, but finally and most characteristically, I think, to defuse the destructive polarity by choosing the third divinity, the Demiurge. If the creator is an ignorant artificer, then the artist has much less need to fear retribution. At the same time, his effort at creating a new world has that much more chance of being an improvement on the old. (I will pursue this topic further in Chapters 10 and 12.)

To the compensatory theories of origin already suggested to explain Joyce's creativity, we must add another source. Fear and hate cannot in themselves account for a positive response. In *Ulysses*, I see evidence also of Joyce's use of his creative will to probe the human impulses and social forms that most people are unwilling to face or question. He probed in the belief that a full exposure would purge unreality and reveal the life-giving and life-desiring centre that is synonymous with the human spirit. Joyce also knew that some people cannot stand full exposure; in some the centre is so surrounded by unconscious fear and hate that it cannot show itself. Stephen Dedalus may be in that condition.

Having dealt with the problem of creativity somewhat theoretically, we need now to look more closely at Stephen Dedalus, Joyce's specific embodiment of the difficulties of becoming an Irish artist. Like Joyce, Stephen is also involved in an inner battle with physical and spiritual perversion. Through Stephen's wrestling with the problems of Lucifer and homosexuality, we can get another perspective on Joyce's own grappling with the problem of authority and sexual identity as they bear on the question of creativity.

I have tended to praise Bloom over Stephen, but in truth Stephen's anger is not always twisted into hate. Stephen does allow himself to feel anger in 'Circe,' while Bloom never does. Since anger is the best emotion for counteracting fear, Stephen's experience could be liberating. When his mother first appears towards the end of 'Circe,' Stephen chokes 'with fright, remorse, and horror' (p 580), three emotions which the superego uses for punishing. But when his mother herself takes on the overt role of super-ego, Stephen is able to react with a stronger, deeper feeling.

THE MOTHER

... Beware! God's hand! (*A green crab with malignant red eyes sticks deep its grinning claws in Stephen's heart.*)

STEPHEN

(*Strangled with rage.*) Shite! (*His features grow drawn and grey and old.*) ... *Ah non, par exemple*! The intellectual imagination! With me all or not at all. *Non serviam!...*

THE MOTHER

(*Wrings her hands slowly, moaning desperately.*) O Sacred Heart of Jesus, have mercy on him! Save him from hell, O divine Sacred Heart!

STEPHEN

No! No! No! Break my spirit all of you if you can! I'll bring you all to heel! (p 582)

Although his anger begins well, rather than keeping it focused on the death-dealing aspect of his mother Stephen becomes childishly defiant, retreating into pretend omnipotence. The result, as we have seen, is that 'God's hand' does strike him down at the end of the episode. He is betrayed by 'the intellectual imagination'; in fact his last words before Carr strikes him down are 'This feast of pure reason' (p 601).

Stephen's fantasies have provided him with ample evidence that he is not involved in a feast of pure reason. The climactic fantasmagoria is the Black Mass celebrated over 'Mrs Mina Purefoy, goddess of unreason' (p 599). With her 'swollen belly,' she stands for Stephen's mother, whose 'pure faith' in Catholic doctrine also brought her more children than her body could stand. Another *alter ego* for Stephen's mother is Gummy Granny (Ireland) who appears 'seated on a toadstool, the deathflower of the potato blight on her breast' (p 595). Ireland is doomed but also dooms, just as Stephen's mother, who died of cancer, sends the crab towards his heart. Both can be what Stephen calls Gummy Granny (and Joyce called Ireland), 'The old sow that eats her farrow!' (p 595). They are also *alter egos* of Biddy the Clap and Cunty Kate, who draw from Stephen a paraphrase of Blake, 'The harlot's cry from street to street / Shall weave old Ireland's windingsheet' (p 597). They in turn are one with the tart, Cissy Caffrey, whom Bloom implores as 'sacred lifegiver' (p 597) to help mediate between Stephen and Carr. All Cissy can do is call 'Police!' which brings on all the violence of armed authority; following this the stage becomes peopled for the Black Mass.

(...Laughing witches in red cutty sarks ride through the air on broomsticks. ... On an eminence, the centre of the earth, rises the field altar of Santa Barbara. Black candles rise from its gospel and epistle horns. From the high barbicans of the tower two shafts of light fall on the smokepalled altarstone. On the altarstone Mrs Mina Purefoy, goddess of unreason, lies naked, fettered, a chalice resting on her swollen belly. Father Malachi O'Flynn, in a long petticoat and reversed chasuble, his two left feet back to the front, celebrates camp mass. The Reverend Mr Hugh C. Haines Love M.A. in a plain cassock and mortar board, his head and collar back to the front, holds over the celebrant's head an open umbrella.) (pp 598-9)

In Roman Catholic tradition, Santa Barbara protects the faithful from sudden death, but she is also the patron saint of gunsmiths and gravediggers; her presence is therefore ambivalent, to say the least. To say the most, she is an appropriate saint to oversee the carnage that will soon follow when the soldiers of Ireland face those of England. She is as much connected with death as Mrs Dedalus and Gummy Granny.

The presumed sacrifice of Mrs Purefoy is also appropriate: as 'pure faith' she has sacrificed her body to doctrine and is sacrificed by apostates and unbelievers. As Adams suggests, she is the victim; pregnant, she represents 'flesh run idiotically rampant, and representative of Mother Ireland herself – fettered, teeming, and exhausted' (*Surface and Symbol* 29). But Joyce's attitude, and ours, towards this woman is not so simple as Adams's comments (and mine so far) might suggest. She is obviously present against her will, a fettered prisoner of the Black Mass communicants. The umbrella as a symbol of contraception was established in 'Oxen of the Sun' (p 405), the episode which celebrated Mrs Purefoy's giving birth. If creating life is the same as causing death, then we have to depend on Lynch's scornful Brunian logic to accept a paradox: 'Death is the highest form of life' (p 504), or more appropriately 'Giving birth is the lowest form of death.' Indeed, as Adams implies, for a mother to bring forth mouths that a father cannot feed and that neither parent will nourish properly is not forwarding the cause of life. We should certainly expect Joyce – with his many sisters, his dead brothers, his two (only) children – to suggest this view.

Since he was a lapsed Catholic, we might also expect him to be intrigued by the Black Mass. But his actual attitude to it is more complex. On the one hand its inversion does make 'Dog' into 'God' (p 599). As we saw in Chapter 2, this is an appropriate identification for Stephen. Just as he fears thunder, which speaks in the voice of a judging god, so in 'Proteus' he fears the dog, which by virtue of its mumming ability is a fit symbol of the protean divine in nature. But the mass seems really to be connected, through the witches and the horned altar, with a *Walpurgesnacht*, a liberation of demonic, destructive forces. Immediately after Adonai chants 'Gooooood!' (p 600), Orange and Green factions begin contending. Joyce clearly does not approve of this destructiveness.

In this vein, Gummy Granny tries to hand Stephen a dagger with which to kill Pvt Carr. Since another woman is the cause of their hostility, Joyce's point is obvious enough: women are really behind the violence of the world. This point appears to fit in with Brivic's accusation that Joyce tends to displace his fear of the father onto the mother, but in fact we must remember that this is Stephen's hallucination, the externalizing of Stephen's problem. Joyce is aware of male violence (Pvt Carr and the Citizen need no woman to start them); he is also aware of the homosexual implications of being anti-feminine. This awareness emerges clearly with his dramatization of the two clergymen at the Black Mass. Father O'Flynn, 'in a long petticoat and reversed chasuble' (p 599) is a transvestite, and the Reverend Love is even more perverse in his reversal. When Father O'Flynn begins to celebrate the mass, the Reverend Love 'raises high behind the celebrant's petticoats, revealing his grey bare hairy buttocks between which a carrot is stuck' (p 599). Though shocking, this grotesque act is not comic, and the symbolism of the carrot is so obvious that the reader feels less alienated from reality than revolted by naked anti-pornography. The degradation does not even have Bloom's excuse of a sadistic Bello to take some of the blame off the individual involved.

The way the Reverend Love reveals an erect (though anal) carrot under Father O'Flynn's petticoat suggests a homosexual relation. Such a liaison can be inferred also from Stephen's contribution to the food imagery of 'Circe,' the 'feast of pure reason' already mentioned. The most famous feast of pure reason is *The Symposium*, the Socratic dialogue on love in which Alcibiades bemoans Socrates' unwillingness to give in to him.[4]

During the day Stephen denies the attraction between father and son, but though he strives to maintain his daylight rationality during 'Circe,' he gets caught up in its expressive atmosphere and admits many truths, often by implication. For instance, Stephen at one point says, 'And Noah was drunk with wine. And his ark was open' (p 569). Thornton mentions that Noah's son Ham saw him thus exposed and notes that Joyce has substituted 'his ark was open' for the statement in Genesis that Noah 'was uncovered within his tent.' Thornton takes the substitution to contain a suggestion by Stephen that 'Noah fornicated with the animals of his ark' (*Allusions in Ulysses* 414), conceivable in the context. Presumably Thornton is accepting a pun on 'ark' and 'arse.' (Bloom had remembered it earlier. Thinking of a whore whom he had tried to encourage in what Shechner would call coprolalia, Bloom remembers, 'My arks she called it.' 370) If Noah's arse is open, he is inviting sodomy from one of his sons, as Stephen is aware.[5] Stephen's relation to his father and similar authorities is therefore obviously worth further investigation.

First we need to note his paranoia, which emerges several times in 'Circe.' His reaction to any group that seems to oppose him is an isolating defiance. Thus, at one point he cries out, 'My foes beneath me. And ever shall be. World without end. ... *Pater*! Free!' (p 572). Stephen's use of the Latin word for 'father' recalls the earlier explicit allusion to Ovid's Daedalus: 'Icarus. *Pater, ait*. Seabedabbled, fallen, weltering' (p 210). Simon comes as Dedalus to help, and refers to the family crest, 'an eagle gules volant in a field argent displayed' (p 572). But Joyce describes him as having 'buzzard wings'; Joyce also gives Stephen 'vulture talons' (p 572) to offset the nobility implied by the eagle. Equally ominous is the description of Simon making 'the beagle's call' especially since we are immediately presented with a fox hunt which includes 'beaglebaying' (p 572). Since the fox is the one Stephen identified with earlier (who buried his grandmother or dug up his mother), this sequence reinforces the picture drawn in Chapter 4 of Stephen as a proud, lonely, self-isolated artist, determined to fly too close to the sun or to run the mountain ridges, but doomed to be run down by the pack he scorns. This isolation can change in a short space from active superiority – 'My foes beneath me' (p 572) – to martyrdom – 'Break my spirit, will he?' (p 572). A little later he repeats, 'Break my spirit all of you if you can! I'll bring you all to heel' (p 582). To heel like dogs?

The key question is what the paranoia hides. We may begin our attempt to find out by noting that Stephen is following his father's course in presuming to be above the multitude (cf. p 572). But to say that this paranoid attitude is 'inherited' doesn't advance our understanding very much. We can, however, find a clue in one of Simon's statements about the crowd. 'Wouldn't let them within the bawl of an ass' (p 572). In the light of Stephen's intentional pun about Noah's 'ark,' I'm tempted to see this 'ass' as having a different meaning than Simon presumably intends.

I argued earlier that God as *Dio Boia* is a destructive force in Stephen projected outside; in 'Circe' He acts through His agent, Pvt Carr. But if we look more closely, we can see that there are several intermediaries between God and Pvt Carr. One is Edward the Seventh. The identification of Edward with violent slaughter that I outlined in Chapter 3 is a fantasy that comes to Stephen when Pvt Carr asks what he is saying about the King. Stephen is incapable of admitting the danger he is in or of exricating himself from the situation. His rationalization of continuing to confront Carr is that 'he provokes my intelligence' (p 592), another example of his mind's misleading him with a picture of 'pure reason' while his feelings are actually in covert control.

Stephen's real relation to these authorities can be traced through the evangelist's comment on God at the end of 'Oxen of the Sun.' 'You'll need to rise precious early, you sinner there, if you want to diddle the Almighty God' (p 428). The verb 'diddle' has two polite meanings. Overtly here it signifies 'to cheat, swindle, victimize.' Joyce also uses it early in 'Circe' in its other meaning of 'to move rapidly up and down or backward and forward.' The Bohee Brothers do a black-face act, at the end of which 'they diddle diddle cakewalk away' (p 444). But if we accept the slang meaning of 'diddle' to be synonymous with 'screw' as a verb for sexual intercourse, we can conclude as Richard Ellmann has (*Ulysses on the Liffey* 134) that Joyce is implying sodomy; a young sinner who rises early can victimize God by moving rapidly up and down on him as he lies sleeping (like Noah in a drunken stupor?). Such a notion is certainly present in more graphic terms later in 'Circe.'

PRIVATE COMPTON

(*Pulling his comrade.*) Here, bugger off, Harry. Or Bennett'll have you in the lockup.

PRIVATE CARR

(*Staggering as he is pulled away.*) God fuck old Bennett! He's a white-arsed bugger. I don't give a shit for him. (p 603)

'Bugger off' simply means 'to depart or leave,' but 'bugger' as a noun, while it can mean merely 'fellow,' is a well-established slang term for sodomite. If God fucks Bennett it will obviously be in his 'white arse.'

The foregoing connections imply a kind of hierarchy. Regularizing it, we could say that God is on top, followed by the king of England, his vicar on earth; the king in turn appoints Bennett Sergeant Major, thus giving him authority over Pvt Carr. Or as Joyce experienced it in Switzerland, the king appointed Sir Horace Rumbold Minister to Switzerland and Percy Bennett Consul-General in Zürich. Bennett thus had authority over the Henry Carr who worked in his office (cf. *J.J.* 440, 459, 461, 471-2).

Presumably Joyce's own anger at these British authorities caused him to look into himself. He would have had good reason for doing so if he remembered a story W.B. Yeats and his co-editor told of William Blake.[6] Blake included a character from his experience in one of his poems. This was the soldier who had taken Blake to court, swearing 'that Blake cursed the king' (I, 55). In fictionalizing his encounter with Carr, Joyce had moved it towards Blake's experience by making Carr a soldier and having him say loyally, 'I'll wring the neck of any fucking bastard says a word against my bleeding fucking king' (p 597). An important difference between Blake's poetic treatment of his soldier and Joyce's of Carr is that, as Blake's editors put it, 'we look in vain for any expression of rancorous feeling or personal triumph over' the soldier in Blake's poem (I, 391). In fact, the aggression of the soldier showed Blake that he should 'look kindly on Hayley' (I, 391), the friend he had begun to distrust but who came to his aid in the affair. If we substitute for Hayley the Bloom who rescues Stephen in 'Circe,' we can see the close parallel that Joyce was making between the two incidents.

This is not to say that we may expect a lack of 'rancorous feeling' towards Bennett and Carr. Joyce was not Blake. He had moved away from that Platonism which dissolves all personal feeling in art. His writing is much more personal than Blake's, and more down to earth. Carr's swearing, quoted above, is not out of harmony with the realism of *Ulysses*. Neither is it out of tune with the novel's symbolism.

'Circe,' as we shall see, is built on a dialectic of purging. Both Bloom and Stephen have projected their deepest fears and desires into hallucinations which we share with them. Carr then represents something in Stephen which he does not care to admit. Carr for instance makes no bones about fitting into the degradation of Nighttown, while Stephen acts like the intellect above his physical indulgence. Stephen showed earlier that he half grasped his dilemma when he pointed to his head and said, 'in here it is I must kill the priest and king' (p 589). If these two authorities are so potent in his head that he must kill them, they obviously represent a threat that he does not fully understand – though his statement helps us understand the violence involved in his hallucinations. Trying to be sympathetic, we might speculate that Stephen is aware of the priest as superego, as a punishing voice which makes him suffer when he tries to free himself. But by wanting to kill it, he is only turning back on it its own threats. In that game of power it must always win, as Pvt Carr's blow demonstrates.

I suggested earlier that anger would be a proper feeling by which Stephen could free himself. Blake drove the soldier from his garden in anger, and Joyce responded to Carr's petty arrogance in Zürich with anger. Both won the subsequent court cases. Stephen, in contrast, refuses to become angry. He insists on reason, which is merely a way of letting the anger inside be turned against himself as a punishment. As his *alter ego*, Carr is able to express Stephen's anger, and to verbalize in his crude way what Stephen can only hint at indirectly. As long as Stephen will not free himself of the priest and king, he is condemned to experience life as does a private in the army – that is, at the mercy of authorities in what Joyce suggests is essentially a sado-masochistic relation. Each authority passes on orders to those below, hating those above whom each must obey. The nature of the relation is startlingly clear in Carr's 'God fuck old Bennett.' Persons in the hierarchy use one another as objects. But Stephen is no better. Unable to relate to anyone, he is cut off and doomed to suffer as much outside the hierarchy as Carr does within. And he knows the reason: he is still attached to the pleasures and pains of the hierarchy's sado-masochistic order. If he could somehow admit his attraction to his father as an understandable response to his father's neurotic anti-feminism (which points to covert homosexuality), he could free himself of the unconscious hold the attraction has on him and be able to love a woman.

Joyce's connection of sado-masochism with the military and with religion is apparent in other sections of the novel (cf. *Ulysses on the Liffey* 60). During the discussion in Barney Kiernan's, for instance, the Citizen criticizes discipline in the British Navy:

> The crew of tars and officers and rearadmirals drawn up in cocked hats and the parson with his protestant bible to witness punishment and a young lad brought out, howling for his ma, and they tie him down on the buttend of a gun.
>
> – A rump and dozen, says the citizen, was what that old ruffian sir John Beresford called it but the modern God's Englishman calls it caning on the breech....
>
> – That's your glorious British navy, says the citizen, that bosses the earth. The fellows that never will be slaves. ... That's the great empire they boast about of drudges and whipped serfs. ...
>
> – But, says Bloom, isn't discipline the same everywhere? I mean wouldn't it be the same here if you put force against force? ...
>
> – We'll put force against force, says the citizen. (p 329)

Later Stephen does avoid the obvious error of Carr or the Citizen in trying to win by force, but he does not follow the analysis of Bloom to keep clear of force. Since his connection with the problem is as much religious as nationalist, we should consider a passage Joyce as super-narrator of 'Cyclops' interpolated just before Bloom's comment.

> They believe in rod, the scourger almighty, creator of hell upon earth and in Jacky Tar, the son of a gun, who was conceived of unholy boast, born of the fighting navy, suffered under rump and dozen, was scarified, flayed and curried, yelled like bloody hell, the third day he rose again from the bed, steered into haven, sitteth on his beamend till further orders when he shall come to drudge for a living and be paid. (p 329)

This parody of the Apostles' Creed makes graphic the anal overtones of a sado-masochistic arrangement.

Stephen had also parodied the Creed earlier, giving it a form appropriate to the Sabellian heresy, that 'the three persons of the Trinity are simply different modes of a single divine substance' (Thornton 25).

> He Who Himself begot, middler the Holy Ghost, and Himself sent himself, Agenbuyer, between Himself and others, Who, put upon by His fiends, stripped and whipped, was nailed like bat to barndoor, starved on crosstree, Who let Him bury, stood up, harrowed hell, fared into heaven and there these nineteen hundred years sitteth on the right hand of His Own Self but yet shall come in the latter day to doom the quick and dead when all the quick shall be dead already. (pp 197-8)

This version of the Creed would also suit Stephen, since it adds to the sadism of whipping the homosexual implication of a 'son consubstantial with his father' (p 197). The Holy Ghost is ambivalent in this ménage. He can aid the father-son pairing by himself taking up with Mary, as Stephen is aware he did in one blasphemous version of Christ's conceiving.[7] Or the Ghost can become what he is for Stephen in the library scene, Hamlet senior's ghost, a fatherly voice of duty, the potentially punishing super-ego.

The Ghost as a conscience figure takes a strange form in Stephen's mind later. When Gummy Granny materializes, Stephen knows, as Hamlet did upon the ghost's second appearance, exactly what her errand is. 'Aha! I know you grammer! Hamlet, revenge! The old sow that eats her farrow!' (p 595). Presumably the first appearance of this female ghost had been as Stephen's mother, who also begged him to do something and whom he repulsed as a 'Lemur' (Latin for 'ghost'). Gummy Granny challenges Stephen, 'You met with poor old Ireland and how does she stand?' Stephen responds immediately, displaying some of

Hamlet's antic madness but none of the anguish his mother's ghost had inspired: 'How do I stand you? The hat trick! Where's the third person of the Blessed Trinity? Soggarth Aroon? The reverend Carrion Crow' (p 595). Each of these disjointed responses contains an intellectual allusion, but together they add up to an emotional self-revelation.

The primary reference of 'the hat trick' is probably to Stephen's earlier picture of Bishop Berkeley's taking 'the veil of the temple out of his shovel hat' (p 48). As Thornton suggests, Stephen means that 'Berkeley found reality inside his head.' Applied to Stephen's reaction to Gummy Granny, this insight means Stephen is aware that she is a mental projection. In which case his question about the location of the Holy Ghost must be rhetorical. The Irish phrase '*Soggarth Aroon*' means 'Priest dear' (Thornton) and presumably ties in with his mother's repeated request to repent. The song from which this phrase comes begins 'Am I the slave they say, *Soggarth aroon*? Since you did show the way, *Soggarth aroon*' (Thornton). Stephen of course believes that he would become a slave if he gave in. He would then be treated spiritually as that British slave, Jack Tar, is treated physically in the earlier parody of the Apostles' Creed. But his allusion to Berkeley confirms that he still subscribes to the Sabellian version of the creed, according to which all punishment to himself is done by himself. He must still get to the unified stage of willing non-self-punishment rather than his present conflicted stage in which his intellect dallies with it while his emotions desire it and bring it on him.

In addition to punishment, Stephen seems attracted to death. The 'priest dear' that he names above is the Reverend Carrion Crow. In *Madame Bovary*, Homais 'compared all priests to carrion crows attracted by the smell of death' (Thornton). This allusion fits the context well, since as we saw, both Gummy Granny and May Dedalus are heavily connected with death. But if these deathly ghosts are coming to plague Stephen, and if they are projections from his head, then he himself must be death-oriented in some way. This was implied earlier in the day by Mulligan: ' – Mournful mummer, Buck Mulligan moaned. Synge has left off wearing black to be like nature. Only crows, priests and English coal are black' (p 216). Stephen is dressed in black mourning; like Hamlet he has that within which demandeth show.[8]

Towards the end of 'Oxen of the Sun,' someone comments, 'Parson Steve, apostate's creed' (p 424). Stephen is the Reverend Carrion Crow, someone who is feeding on death rather than carrying on in life, mourning for his mother instead of finding a mate. Mulligan's comparison with Synge is appropriate. By 1904 Synge had had two plays produced. His first play, *Riders to the Sea*, has references to or reports of so many deaths that the effect is almost grotesque. His second play, *The Shadow of the Glen*, has only one mock death used by the life-denying husband to test his wife. She ends up leaving her established position in society to go live abroad (in nature as Mulligan suggests) with a man she cannot marry. Significantly, her name is Nora. Also significantly, her husband is left with the man he has threatened as her supposed lover, to whom he now makes placating overtures. The choice is as clear as that represented by Mulligan himself, with his constant reference to homosexuality.

The third black item in Mulligan's list doesn't fit with the other two. Crows and priests can be parallelled as living off death; coal, being dead already, provides life-giving heat. This leads us back to the paradox investigated in Chapter 3. There we found that, symbolically, if Bloom can admit death he can find life again. The same is true for Stephen. As long as he is preoccupied with death and afraid of it (as he shows he is in the scene with his mother's ghost), it will control his life as it does the crow's and the priest's. But if he simply accepts the death and burial of the body, his life will also bloom again. Here then lies another version of the answer Stephen has sought. Fearing death is like fearing God's wrath in the thunder; it means he is attracted to the violence or dissolution that he intellectually pretends to be above. When he comes to an emotional expression of his fear of death, that fear will no longer control him, as it does now in apocalyptic fantasies of violent destruction. Although we saw him able to resist the opportunity to murder that Granny Gummy offered, we have also seen him unable to resist the equally direct threats of Pvt Carr which everyone else can see will climax in a blow. By prolonging his mourning, probably out of guilt, Stephen becomes carrion crow, no better than the priests whom he has repudiated. He must find a way to make this blackness work for rather than against him. Such a hopeful possibility is contained in the third item of Mulligan's list.

Mulligan gives the coal a nationality; it is English. As such it is to be contrasted with Irish turves, as they are pictured by Father Conmee at the beginning of the next episode. 'It was idyllic: and Father Conmee reflected on the providence of the Creator who had made turf to be in bogs where men might dig it out and bring it to town and hamlet to make fires in the houses of poor people' (p 221). We can now appreciate why forceful conflict of nationalisms is such a problem for Stephen. If he accepts Irish turf to warm himself, he must accept the sentimental and ultimately repressive sophisms of a clergy who justify things as they are. If he accepts English coal, he will be warmer, physically better off, but chained to a materialistic empire. What can he do?

Joyce faced the same problem, and solved it by becoming an exiled Irishman who wrote in English. As he said to a friend in 1918, six days after the court case with Carr: 'As an artist I am against every state. Of course I must recognize it, since indeed in all my dealings I come into contact with institutions. The state is concentric, man is eccentric. Thence arises an eternal struggle' (*J.J.* 460). More generally, he commented, 'Material victory is the death of spiritual preëminence' (*ibid.*).

But the most important dimension of the coal-vs-turf motif is that of language. This was a problem for Stephen when in *A Portrait of the Artist* he pondered the word 'tundish' (pp 188, 251). Stephen discovers that this native word is actually English, though it was not recognized by the English Dean of Studies at Stephen's college. The implication is plain: an Irishman has as much right to the fullness of the English language as does a Britisher. This is important, because Gaelic, beloved of the nationalists, Joyce would have seen as a limited language, unserviceable in the twentieth century. English, on the other hand, is rich. Having been formed over centuries under pressure, it has plenty of latent energy in it, ready like English coal to give off a blaze to him who knows how to light it. Stephen's image of the imagination and its transformations is apposite here: 'In the intense instant of imagination, when the mind, Shelley says, is a fading coal, that which I was is that which I am and that which in possibility I may come to be' (*Ulysses* 194). Joyce had learned how to use linguistic metamorphosis; in 'Oxen of the Sun' he was able to reconstruct the layers of the language back into the dark ages and bring it forward through the stages of its 'faunal evolution' (*Letters* I, 139) to the present. With the aid originally of Skeat and subsequently of other languages (including Gaelic), he was able to work with the structure and etymology of English, first to master it with coinings, original meanings, and new patterns in *Ulysses*, and then universalizing it in *Finnegans Wake*.

To do this Joyce needed to escape the temptation to be a carrion crow, gloating over the dissected body of dead language, or a sombre priest of scholarship, too concerned with laws and sinful errors to appreciate the life-giving potential of language. He needed to see language as a living growth, an evolution to which each word gives itself without qualms and to which each writer must give himself, if he is to aid the life process by making possible the transformations of the future. To return to the third term of Mulligan's trio, the writer must learn to care about the fire that is latent in words rather than worry about their dirtiness; he cannot afford being refined, being above common words, for the dirtiest ones may give off the finest blaze.

Joyce had determined to soil himself for moral-aesthetic reasons as early as 1904 when he had printed and distributed in Dublin 'The Holy Office,' a 'satirical broadside' (as it is called by Mason and Ellmann in their introduction to it – *Critical Writings* 149). This verse diatribe adopts a therapeutic principle as its premise. It begins, 'myself unto myself will give / This name, Katharsis-Purgative'; after criticising a number of writers, it continues:

But all these men of whom I speak
Make me the sewer of their clique.
That they may dream their dreamy dreams
I carry off their filthy streams
For I can do those things for them
Through which I lost my diadem,
Those things for which Grandmother Church
Left me severely in the lurch.
Thus I relieve their timid arses,
Perform my office of Katharsis.
My scarlet leaves them white as wool.
Through me they purge a bellyful. (p 151)

Joyce functions as the dark principle necessary to their 'enlightened' state, the diabolic which complements their piety, the sewer that carries off their body wastes so that they are not incommoded in their elevated spiritual state.[9] Significantly, this is a function Joyce went on to carry out more artistically and thoroughly in *Ulysses*. The novel was banned in Ireland, England, and the United States for its dirtiness, its four-letter words, its references to defecation, masturbation, and sexual intercourse. In taking such realism as his goal, Joyce saw early and clearly its moral-aesthetic basis. He also saw and embodied its psychological purging effect – as Bloom's degrading experience in 'Circe' from which he emerges a fuller human being. In taking on this psycho-social task, Joyce joined a select company. Erik Erikson focuses on significant images in classifying Freud and Luther as two of the foremost liberators of Western society from institutional repression:

Both men illustrate certain regularities in the growth of a certain kind of genius. They had, at any rate, one characteristic in common: a grim willingness to do the dirty work of their respective ages: for each kept human conscience in focus in an era of material and scientific expansion. Luther referred to his early work as '*im Schlamm arbeiten*,' 'to work in the mud,' and complained that he had worked all alone for ten years; while Freud, also a lone worker for a decade, referred to his work as labor *in der fiefe*, calling forth the plight of a miner in deep shafts and wishing the soft-hearted *eine gute Auffahrt*, 'a good ascent.'[10]
(*Young Man Luther* 9)

Early tempted to the kind of direct liberation preached by Luther and Freud in their writings, Joyce finally chose artistic expression of his need to speak the dark truths others repressed. Like Freud and Luther, Joyce was committed to being the conscience of society; he attempted to keep it human by attacking the rigidity of the super-ego and the temporal institutions which shape it. In so doing, he had less direct influence on society that either of those more systematic thinkers; on the other hand, particular works of his will probably have even longer life than some of Freud's great work. Although *Ulysses* obviously represents less of a breakthrough for Western man than *The Interpretation of Dreams*, it makes much more interesting reading today that Freud's pioneering but dull and pedantic classic.

For Joyce, the transition of the hating victim into the mature artist must have begun after 1905; in that year the expatriate included a mock prayer with paranoid overtones in a letter to Stanislaus:

> O Vague Something behind Everything!
>
> For the love of the Lord Christ change my curse-o'-God state of affairs. Give me for Christ' sake a pen and an ink-bottle and some peace of mind and then, by the crucified Jaysus, if I don't sharpen that little pen and dip it into fermented ink and write tiny little sentences about the people who betrayed me send me to hell. After all, there are many ways of betraying people. It wasn't only the Galilean suffered that. Whoever the hell you are, I inform you that this [is] a poor comedy you expect me to play and I'm damned to hell if I'll play it for you. (*Letters* II, 110, Ellmann's interpolation)

We can see here signs of the adult fantasy regression 'to a form of behaviour which we call "magical"' (Kris 77). Grabbing his 'little pen,' Joyce is able to indulge in the childhood 'omnipotence of thought.' At the same time, there is a significant focusing on the destructive aspect of creation. Like Stephen, the young Joyce will turn destruction on those who wished to cruficy him.

As we have seen, the mature Joyce dealt with destructiveness not by identifying with it nor by denying it, but by making it the prelude to creativity. We can regain a broad sense of their interconnectedness by remembering how often his later work hovers between parody (which criticizes or destroys) and pastiche (which celebrates or recreates); in either case Joyce was imitating the word constructs of the outer 'state of affairs.' By refusing to play a part in the 'poor comedy' of life, the young Joyce was attempting to deny this state of affairs. When he became more accepting of the burdens thrust on him by accident and choice (partly through recognizing that the two are interchangeable, as we saw in Chapter 4), he found that his difficulties began to turn to successes. I am not suggesting that Joyce reconciled himself to God, but I am suggesting he came to recognize that life is a poor comedy, and is best shown as such. At the same time, Joyce set out to create a better comedy. In popular understanding, to see the world as tragedy is to see oneself or others as nailed to a cross; to see it as comedy is not to push events to such an extreme, is to stay in life by finding an outlet for one's own repressed desires, at the same time presenting society with a chance to do likewise. Joyce was emphatic about this important role of the artist; in 1936, speaking of the humour of his *Work in Progress*, he commented, 'Now they're bombing Spain. Isn't it better to make a great joke instead, as I have done? (*J.J.* 706). That the joke is a creative outlet for violence is strongly implicit in this contrast, as in those quoted earlier. In Freudian terms, Joyce had found a way to trick and disarm the punishing super-ego, to liberate some impulses from the id into ego consciousness; he had also managed to dissociate the self from the defensive mind games of the ego. The comic spirit involves these and other implications about the dynamics of the psyche and the spectacle of the world, considerations to which we must turn in the next chapter.

9 Comedy in 'Circe'

When Wilhelm Fliess read the proofs of *The Interpretation of Dreams* in 1899, he complained to Freud that the dreams were too full of jokes. This was only one of many stimuli that made inevitable Freud's study, *Jokes and Their Relation to the Unconscious* (1905). The intimate connection of dreams and jokes with unconscious mental processes is augmented by Freud's demonstration that they also share important mechanisms – condensation, representation by the opposite and the use of nonsense. In *Ulysses* Joyce brings the reader to a height of comedy and a close approximation to dream narrative during the Circe episode. It is therefore to a study of that episode that I shall turn after I have investigated comedy from the psychoanalytic point of view.

In Chapter 6, I suggested that Bergson's emphasis on laughter as humiliation helped to explain much of the comedy of the Cyclops episode. Humiliation is prominent again in 'Circe,' but we are in a position now to connect it in a more detailed way with the dynamics of the psyche. A basic premise of psychotherapy is that repressed impulses (in the id) want to come to conscious awareness (the ego) but are kept from doing so, at some expense of psychic energy, by a mechanism Freud called the censor (or super-ego). Through distortion, repressed sexual and aggressive urges can become conscious in dreams, when the super-ego is lulled by sleep, or in jokes, when the social censor agrees to nod. 'The joke *will evade restrictions and open sources of pleasure that have become inaccessible*' (p 103, Freud's italics). In addition to pleasure (once available to the unsocialized child and now regained) there is a sense of relief, expressed in the usual response to a joke. 'The hearer of the joke laughs with the quota of psychical energy which has become free through the lifting of the inhibit[ion]; we might say that he laughs this quota off' (p 149).

An example of the similarity of joke and dream occurs early in 'Circe' when Bloom is commanded by one of the domineering society women to take down his pants so she can lash his buttocks with her riding crop. The masochist in Bloom will derive pleasure from this beating, but since there are others present he should obey his social conscience by keeping up his pants. What comes out of this conflict is the following reaction: 'BLOOM: (*Trembling, beginning to obey.*) The weather has been so warm' (p 469). The situation is comic not because Bloom drops his pants (that alone the super-ego would force us to find disgusting); it is the discrepancy between what he says and does that allows us to express our pleasure at the situation. We smile or laugh because we recognize the mechanism by which one part of the mind tries to rationalize to another part for an action that the remark is far from justifying. We have all seen children act in a similar manner when faced with a tempting pleasure that is socially unacceptable, and we have all done the same ourselves (usually with greater sublety than Bloom).

Freud claimed that all obscene jokes are aimed at exposing the sexual. 'A desire to see the organs peculiar to each sex exposed is one of the original components of our libido. It may itself be a substitute for something earlier and go back to a hypothetical primary desire to touch the sexual parts. As so often, looking has replaced touching' (p 98). In addition, children desire to show their sexual organs. 'It is easy to observe the inclination to self-exposure in young children. In cases in which the germ of this inclination escapes its usual fate of being buried and suppressed, it develops in men into the familiar perversion known as exhibitionism' (p 98). The connection between the exhibitionist and the child is well caught by Joyce in Bloom's action and comment.

Freud argues that the child's (and the adult's) notion of what is obscene is connected with areas or functions of the body about which the young child has been made to feel shame, that is the

> excremental in the most comprehensive sense. This is, however, the sense covered by sexuality in childhood, an age at which there is, as it were, a cloaca within which what is sexual and what is excremental are barely or not at all distinguished. Throughout the whole range of the psychology of the neuroses, what is sexual includes what is excremental, and is understood in the old, infantile, sense. (pp 97-8)

The anal, the urethral, and their products are thus included with the sexual in the obscene. Because civilized conditioning makes us denigrate lower orifices and functions, they can become a source of comedy. At the very beginning of 'Circe,' Joyce offers an undisguised example of how this type of comedy works: the low invades the high. '(*Private Carr and Private Compton, swaggersticks tight in their oxters, as they march unsteadily rightaboutface and burst together from their mouths a volleyed fart. Laughter of men from the lane....)*' (p 430). The action of the two privates is so crude that Joyce shrewdly attaches the laughter at it to some 'men from the lane'; the implication is that only loafers in a back lane at night in the red-light district would be so vulgar as to find oral flatulence humorous. As readers we presumably tolerate their response as appropriate to them, by which stratagem we make our unconscious pleasure consciously acceptable.

The beginning of this episode has a number of children in it and a lot of childishness. The shape of the children and their presence in Nighttown make for grotesque effects, as we shall see in the next chapter. But equally important, it prepares the reader for regression. One of the first things we hear is a suggestive nursery rhyme sung by Cissy Caffrey. 'I gave it to Molly / Because she was jolly, / The leg of the duck / The leg of the duck' (p 430). The innocent surface hides an obscene meaning, as Rolf Loerisch has pointed out.[1] But included with such childish smut is even more regressive material, auditory effects which sound like baby talk:'THE GONG: Bang Bang Bla Bak Blud Bugg Bloo' (p 435). This begins like cops and robbers, moves towards 'Baa, Baa, Blacksheep,' and then switches to a tongue twister (Bugs' Black Blood). Though such sounds may have thematic content, primarily they encourage us to give up our day world of sense and regress to a night world of nonsense.[2]

Freud comments on the infant's pleasure in sounds.

> He puts words together without regard to the condition that they should make sense, in order to obtain from them the pleasurable effect of rhythm or rhyme. Little by little he is forbidden this enjoyment, till all that remains permitted to him are significant combinations of words. But when he is older attempts still emerge at disregarding the restrictions. ... Words are disfigured by particular little additions being made to them, their forms are altered by certain manipulations (e.g. by reduplications...). (p 125)

Joyce employed this childish licence to the full in *Finnegans Wake*, of course, but it also emerges importantly in *Ulysses*. It is first noticeable in 'Sirens,' which contributes more than one of its distortions to 'Circe.' When Bloom is first described in the Nighttown section it is as he appears to himself in a distorting mirror, the 'lovelorn longlost lugubru Booloohoom' (p 434). His face is then referred to: the 'fatchuck cheekchops of Jollypoldy the rixdix doldy,' a description based on a child's satiric rhyming formula. In 'Circe' Joyce gives pleasurable release to his reader by having words and sounds come from a number of creatures and things which cannot in fact speak.

An important point is that we cannot enjoy such examples as those above unless we pay attention to the sound of the nonsense syllables or follow the childish rhythm of their structure. We must enter the text not just with our eyes but with our lips and ears, regress to the level of a primary school child in order to appreciate what appears on the page. In Bruno's terms we must submit to the process of nature. In Freud's we must give up the intellectual and reactivate the muscular. Freud sees the reversal as part of a natural reaction against the socializing process, which demands 'a restriction of our muscular work and an increase of our intellectual work' in 'the course of our personal development towards a higher level of civilization' (p 195). This conflict, between the individual's desire to regress to the physical and society's pressure to move him towards the mental, results in what Freud calls 'ideational mimetics' (p 192). His explanation of this concept is clearly applicable to Joyce's mimetic artistic code. When a child or other naïve person tells an anecdote 'he is not content to make his idea plain to the hearer by the choice of clear words, but ... also represents its subject-matter in his expressive movements: he combines the mimetic and the verbal forms of representation.' If he no longer gestures 'with his hands, yet for that reason he will do it with his voice ... What he is thus expressing is not his affects but actually the content of what he is having an idea of' (pp 192-3). When adapted as a conscious technique by an artist, this tendency leads to the imitative 'fallacy,' a mode of artistic miming which we have seen as the source of Joyce's most characteristic and powerful effects.

When we observe another person unconsciously indulging in ideational mimetics, we experience a simple comic reaction. In 'Circe' simple comedy becomes more complex when it includes venting of hostility towards the authority figure who originally denied that pleasure in regression to the physical. The context in which the Gong speaks its nonsense contains this complexity. Bloom is menaced by a municipal vehicle.

(... *Through rising fog a dragon sandstrewer, travelling at caution, slews heavily down upon him, its huge red headlight winking, its trolley hissing on the wire. The motorman bangs his footgong. ... The brake cracks violently. Bloom, raising a policeman's whitegloved hand, blunders stifflegged, out of the track. The motorman thrown forward, pugnosed, on the guidewheel, yells as he slides past over chains and keys.*)

THE MOTORMAN

Hey, shitbreeches, are you doing the hattrick? ... (*Bloom trickleaps to the curbstone and halts again. He brushes a mudflake from his cheek...* (p 435)

Like the earlier oral fart, the mudflake on Bloom's cheek is displaced anal, as the motorman's comment prepares us to understand. (He is crude, Joyce is decorous.) The hattrick, according to W.Y. Tindall, is an Irish practical joke: A man 'covers a turd on the curb with his hat. Telling a policeman it is a bird,' he 'goes off for help, asking the policeman to stand guard' (*A Reader's Guide to James Joyce* 209). In the child's dirty-joke version, the man asks the policeman to grab the bird when he lifts the hat. This version of the joke gives double pleasure: it satisfies the hearer's hostile feelings towards the authority that forbids playing with his faeces; it also allows the pleasure of vicariously experiencing a hand firmly grasping the turd.

This joke is, I must admit, only subliminally present in the scene. Rather we have a harassed Bloom threatened by a machine, much more of a nightmare than a joke. The 'dragon sandstrewer' is another form of the giant who appears from time to time in *Ulysses*. Its 'huge red headlight' embodies the destructive side of old Howth, whose 'red eye' (p 379) was mentioned when Bloom was on the beach. Although this Cyclopian municipal dragon almost runs Bloom down, it is Bloom who is cast in the official authority role. He raises 'a policeman's whitegloved hand' and causes the motorman to brake and squash his nose against the wheel of his vehicle. The policeman's gesture explains the motorman's reference to the hattrick, as though Bloom were an authority to be exposed. Freud claims such exposure causes degradation; 'by replacing either the exalted figures or their utterances by inferior ones,' we have the mechanism 'for *unmasking*, which only applies where someone has seized dignity and authority by a deception and these have to be taken from him in reality' (p 201). Bloom is unmasked a number of times in this episode, and Joyce manipulates our responses by a number of comic techniques.

An interesting fact about the interchange between Bloom and the motorman is that each sees the other as an authority, and each is degraded by the other. The degradation of the motorman may escape notice. He is simply 'thrown forward, pugnosed, on the guide wheel.' Later, however, 'pugnosed' is revealed as obscene when Bloom '(*docile, gurgles*) I rererepugnosed in rerererepugnant' (p 538). 'Rere,' an Irish (and British) spelling of 'rear,' serves to connect by repeated syllables (or as Freud says 'reduplications') the smelling nose with the smelly rear. We may see the motorman's earlier insult to Bloom as a reflex association caused by his squashed nose.

In this preliminary survey I have shown Joyce's almost overt use of Freudian joke situations, not only in focusing on the themes of obscenity and authority, but in my emphasis on mimetic regression in language and action. Joyce could have read *Jokes and Their Relation to the Unconscious*, and it is highly likely that he would have heard its principles from friends in Trieste and Zürich.

In fact the notesheets he drew up and used in writing the second half of the novel indicate that he knew of the book and intended to read it. For instance, one of the notes for 'Cyclops' reads, 'Wit. read Freud: (are you shitting, honey?).'[3] The first half of this note is both a reminder and an indication that during the writing of *Ulysses* Joyce was quite open to Freud's theories in *Jokes and Their Relation to the Unconscious* ('Joke' is the English version of Freud's 'Witz,' wit). The second half is tantalizing, presumably a comic tag line. Not knowing the joke it might be associated with, I can only note that it reinforces Joyce's concern with the anal as a source of comedy. Two other notes in these sheets also indicate that Joyce may have read *Jokes and Their Relation to the Unconscious*.[4] Another note indicates his knowledge of *The Interpretation of Dreams*: 'Gold turds' (p 491). This relates clearly to a comment by Freud on 'the connection between gold and faeces,' which is 'supported by copious evidence from social anthropology' (*The Interpretation of Dreams* 403). Joyce has Stephen implicitly make Freud's connection when he thinks of the coins Deasy has paid him as 'a lump in my pocket'; remembering his debts he concludes, 'The lump I have is useless' (pp 30,31). In the Freudian formulation, a miser is an anal-retentive: Money is faeces better passed on than hoarded. The connotation of 'lump' is clarified in Simon Dedalus' scurrilous reference to Crissie Goulding, whose father he hates, as 'papa's little lump of dung' (p 88). The anal takes on sexual overtones when we turn to Stephen's earlier thought about Chrissie: 'Papa's little bedpal. Lump of love' (p 39). These examples from *Ulysses* certainly indicate Joyce's awareness of the subtle connections among hate, love, excrement, and sex.

As a first step beyond the basic Freudian principles so far developed, I must shift the focus from techniques and themes to the artistic development of them. Since the episode is concerned with Bloom most of the time, I shall be investigating Joyce's pattern of elevating and degrading his principal character. I would like to suggest that this pattern is a psychological one. In the last chapter, I applied to Joyce the familiar neurotic pattern of the child's retreat into fantasy when the world proves too much for him. Intensified, this becomes ego-inflation (dreams of glory) as a compensation for actual degradation. With the activation of the super-ego, fantasies can swing from high heroism to low suffering (the pleasure of disguised self-punishment). In an adolescent's relations with women, the opposition can manifest itself as between the high ideal and the all-too-real, the virgin and the whore. These appear in Bloom's fantasies as the nymph without a cunt who pretends to admire his chastity, and the completely physical Bella, who openly promises to degrade and unman him. By following both these figures farther than in a casual daydream, Bloom will encounter the truth each hides and come to know himself better.

After the degrading encounter with the motorman, Bloom has a number of similar experiences which prefigure grander fantasies to come. He is chastised by his father, scorned by his wife, and tempted by his old friend, Josie Powell (now Mrs Breen). He plays a child's verbal game with her.

BLOOM

(*Meaningfully dropping his voice.*) I confess I'm teapot with curiosity to find out whether some person's something is a little teapot at present.

MRS BREEN

(*Gushingly.*) Tremendously teapot! London's teapot and I'm simply teapot all over me. (*She rubs sides with him.*) (p 445)

Obviously, 'teapot' means 'burning,' its sexual symbolism being as plain as the aphrodisiac effect of the game. As Freud suggests, when a man first approaches a woman, his sexual urge has to

make use of words for two reasons; firstly, to announce itself to her, and secondly, because if the idea is aroused by speech it may induce a corresponding excitement in the woman herself and may awaken an inclination in her to passive exhibitionism. A wooing speech like this is not yet smut, but it passes over into it. If the woman's readiness emerges quickly the obscene speech has a short life; it yields at once to a sexual action. (pp 98-9)

But as Bloom's fantasy continues, it becomes obvious that he actually does not want a sexual encounter. He conjures up her husband and others to break the spell; when they leave, he begins again to weave a verbal web in which she willingly entangles herself (p 449), but at the height of it, when she is 'eagerly' listening, 'she fades from his side' (p 449) and Bloom watches as 'a standing woman bent forward, her feet apart, pisses cowily' (pp 449-50). Being charitable, we could say that Bloom is brought down to earth.

In any case, the shift from the sexual to the urinal is indicative. Immediately after seeing this pissing woman, Bloom overhears an anecdote about a man who urinated into a bucket of porter. The listeners laugh, but Bloom says, 'They think it funny. Anything but that. Broad daylight. Trying to walk. Lucky no woman' (p 450). Later this incident is enlarged in the first of Bloom's mock trials, so that he is the person who did it, and it was defecation not urination. The form in which the information reaches us provides half the comedy.

(*The crossexamination proceeds* re *Bloom and the bucket. A large bucket. Bloom himself. Bowel trouble. In Beaver Street. Gripe, yes. Quite bad. A plasterer's bucket. By walking stifflegged. Suffered untold misery. Deadly agony. About noon. Love or burgundy. Yes, some spinach. Crucial moment. He did not look in the bucket. Nobody. Rather a mess. Not completely. A* Titbits *back number.*) (p 462)

The reader is forced to reconstruct the questions which elicit these responses from Bloom. In themselves innocuous, his answers gradually become quite funny, partly because their subject is obscene, but also because of the indirection. Ernst Kris's demonstration of the relation between wit and the riddle has a bearing on Joyce's effect here.

> The riddle conceals what wit reveals. In wit the matter is known and the manner is secret; in riddles, the manner is known and the matter to be discovered. The essence of the relation between wit and the riddle ... may be illustrated by reference to the behaviour of a patient; he was incapable of deriving pleasure from a joke, but was under a compulsion to read the first line only and then guess the point. He converted a joke into a riddle.
> (p 176)

Joyce forces us to do the opposite, to convert a riddle into a joke. We must work to obtain our pleasure, and yet as we read Bloom's replies, our minds are already at work without our consciously willing it. Kris gives another clue to the attraction and power of the riddle in an aside. The features common to wit and the riddle 'have their roots deep in mythical thought, as we see when we recall the special position of the riddle in all mythologies' (p 176). Freud would say that the place of the riddle in mythical or primitive thought is comparable to the child's desire for knowledge: it is a sublimation of the desire to know secrets – taboo secrets about excretion and sex which have become subject to shame and guilt. The riddle hints at such secrets while disguising them.

Bloom's guilt begins to emerge in 'Circe' when he sees two policemen; he tries to appease these super-ego figures by passing himself off as someone with more standing than he has, as 'Dr Bloom, Leopold, dental surgeon,' related to 'von Bloom Pasha. Umpteen millions' (p 455). This donning of a false mask calls down numerous denunciations on Bloom's head (pp 456-61), including one by his former maid and ending in a pseudo-legal defence of Bloom by J.J. O'Molloy (pp 463-4). But the sexual accusations become more pointed as the society ladies denounce him, and he is saved from hanging only by the appearance of the corpse of Paddy Dignam to vouch for his having been at the funeral that morning.

Approached by Zoe from Mrs Cohen's, Bloom is encouraged by her to enter the brothel, but before he does, a comment by her triggers a long fantasy in his mind. It begins with a bid for omnipotence. He becomes political, social, and religious head of Ireland, performs miracles, mixes with the populace, and answers difficult questions. But when women start killing themselves for him, the men turn on him, and again he is given a pseudo-authoritative defence, this time by the medical students. Mulligan, the first, suggests that

> Dr Bloom is bisexually abnormal. He has recently escaped from Dr Eustace's private asylum for demented gentlemen. Born out of bedlock hereditary epilepsy is present, the consequence of unbridled lust. Traces of elephantiasis have been discovered among his ascendants. There are marked symptoms of chronic exhibitionism. Ambidexterity is also latent. He is prematurely bald from self-abuse, perversely idealistic in consequence, a reformed rake, and has metal teeth. (p 493)

Joyce's sensitivity to jargon as a misuse of the language appears here to good comic effect. Sometimes this effect is achieved by a minor substitution ('bedlock' for 'wedlock') or through faulty grammar (the dangling modifier that begins the third sentence), but more often it is by illogic or nonsense. If '*hereditary* epilepsy is present' it cannot be 'the *consequence* of unbridled lust.'

Freud noted logical fallacies and sophistry as important comic techniques. Using his three-part structure of the mind, we could explain the humour of faulty reasoning by suggesting that the lawyer and the doctor are super-ego figures who establish their authority by logic and knowledge, two learned acquisitions of the ego. When used accurately, these two impress and chastise us, but when used spuriously they anger or amuse us. In 'Circe' they amuse by being ludicrously unequal to their task, appearing as a naked appropriation by the id of the trappings of logic and knowledge. In the last sentence quoted above, for instance, we know that there is no medical connection between baldness and masturbation. In one sense, Mulligan's diagnosis merely puts into medical language a post-Victorian moral attitude towards masturbation. In another sense, it may remind us of Samson, whose loss of hair meant loss of power (through Delilah, or indulgence of sex). Similarly, the phrase 'in consequence' gives the vindication of logic to a non-sequitur conclusion. The diagnosis gives itself away completely in the last two items, 'a reformed rake, and has metal teeth,' the metal teeth making a retroactive pun out of 'rake.'

Bloom's attempts to placate the super-ego are completely unsuccessful. But what is being revealed in the defence is a deeper level of Bloom's nature, an aspect of the id that had been hinted at earlier but only becomes evident at this point. Bloom's last medical defender is Dr Dixon. 'Professor Bloom is a finished example of the new womanly man. ...Many have found him a dear man, a dear person. ...I appeal for clemency in the name of the most sacred word our vocal organs have ever been called upon to speak. He is about to have a baby' (pp 493-4). Far from exposing him to further contumely, this assertion (confirmed by Bloom) has the effect of elevating him to godhood (p 497). But that elevation is also followed by his sacrifice and death. Then he finally enters the whorehouse (p 502), and the gruelling fantasies of sexual degradation begin.

We could say that Bloom has been unmasked then, but what we see is no more the real Bloom than is his everyday self. His real self emerges just after his 'back trouser's button snaps' off (p 552). At that point he is able to drop the idealizing sublimations which have gone with his self-abasement, rise to his feet, and assert himself as a realistic human being. Implicit in his reaction to the nymph and Bella (pp 553-4) is self-recognition, that he has been violating his own nature by worshipping a goddess on the one hand while having fantasies of maltreatment by an animalized woman on the other. He has allowed himself to give up his assertiveness and become a passive thing, a mental dreamer of ethereal and masochistic daydreams who becomes physically impotent, an animal victim.

I must put off until the next chapter a detailed consideration of Bloom's grotesque acceptance of animal forms under the heel of Bello. But I do need to take up here one form of the animal, the scapegoat. As animal and victim, Bloom enters another dimension of the comic by becoming what David Hayman calls a 'clownking, clownpriest and scapegoat.'[5]

To develop this new way of viewing Bloom, I must enlarge the concept of regression from the purely psychological to the social; in this way I can analyze certain primitive roles and the ritual pattern from the Bible and Greek comedy in which these roles function. Joyce provides a number of clues that these primitive roles are relevant to Bloom's experience in 'Circe,' especially during the twenty pages in which Bloom goes through a full cycle of elevation and degradation.

The cycle begins when the whore Zoe tells Bloom to 'make a stump speech' (p 478) and ends when she says, 'Till the next time' (p 499) just before they enter Bella Cohen's. The first part of his elevation is political, though it has some religious overtones. Everything is positive until some of Bloom's subjects die. Although they are happy to dedicate their lives to him, their death is a signal for an accusation (p 485). Bloom orders the accuser shot, and praise of 'Sir Leo' continues. Finally he begins making promises to his subjects:

> I stand for the reform of municipal morals and the plain ten commandments. New worlds for old. Union of all, jew, moslem and gentile. ...General amnesty, weekly carnival, with masked licence, bonuses for all ...Free money, free love and a free lay church in a free lay state.
>
> O'MADDEN BURKE
>
> Free fox in a free henroost. (pp 489-90)

This time the reversal is in earnest, and Bloom is finally sacrificed. His promise, 'weekly carnival, with masked licence ... free money, free love' reveals him as a classical type, the Lord of Misrule, the mock king of Saturnalia.[6]

The king of Saturnalia was the Roman original from which the English Lord of Misrule evolved as a Medieval and Renaissance descendant. This Lord ruled during Christmas in important households, making 'pastimes to delight the beholders' as a contemporary recorded: 'these were fine and subtle disguisings, masks and mummeries.'[7] In Rome, Saturnalia came at the same time of year, the intercalary days before a new year began. It recalled the golden reign of Saturn and turned the contemporary social order upside down. Slaves ruled as masters, and as Sir James Frazer indicates, one slave was chosen by lot to enjoy 'the title of King' and issue 'commands of a playful and ludicrous nature to his temporary subjects' (*The Scapegoat* 308). On the basis of evidence that this mock king was sometimes killed even in historical times, Frazer is convinced that it once was

> the universal practice in ancient Italy, wherever the worship of Saturn prevailed, to choose a man who played the part and enjoyed all the traditionary privileges of Saturn for a season, and then died ... in the character of the good god who gave his life for the world. (p 311)

An earlier form of this ritual is recorded of Greece.

> Whenever Marseilles, one of the busiest and most brilliant of Greek colonies, was ravaged by a plague, a man of the poorer classes used to offer himself as a scapegoat. For a whole year he was maintained at the public expense, being fed on choice and pure food. At the expiry of the year he was dressed in sacred garments, decked with holy branches, and led through the whole city, while prayers were uttered that all the evils of the people might fall on his head. He was then cast out of the city or stoned to death by the people outside of the walls. (p 253)

Drawing partly on the Old Testament, Joyce puts Bloom through a ritual similar to the one that Frazer is concerned with.

> HORNBLOWER
>
> (*In ephod and huntingcap, announces.*) And he shall carry the sins of the people to Azazel, the spirit which is in the wilderness, and to Lilith, the nighthag. And they shall stone him and defile him, yea, all from Agendath Netaim and from Mizraim, the land of Ham.
>
> (*All the people cast soft pantomime stones at Bloom. Many bonafide travellers and ownerless dogs come near him and defile him. Mastiansky and Citron approach in gaberdines, wearing long earlocks. They wag their beards at Bloom.*)

MASTIANSKY AND CITRON

Belial! Laemlein of Istria! the false Messiah! Abulafia! (p 497)

As Thornton explains, 'Azazel' is the Vulgate transliteration of a Hebrew word in Leviticus 16; the word is translated as 'the scapegoat' in the King James Bible. The description in Leviticus 16 of the ceremony and sacrifices makes clear the meaning of scapegoat (ie, 'escape goat'). It also indicates the means of atonement.

> And Aaron shall lay both his hands upon the head of the live goat, and confess over him all the iniquities of the children of Israel, and all their transgressions in all their sins, putting them upon the head of the goat, and shall send *him* away by the hand of a fit man into the wilderness. (Verse 21)

Since Bloom is by birth a Jew, this ceremony is appropriate for him, but Joyce makes it clear that he is aware the goat is a substitute for a human sacrifice such as Frazer contends was originally offered.

The connecting point of Saturnalia and scapegoat is the fate of Christ. Thornton also points out that Laemlein and Abulafia were two Mediterranean Jews who claimed to be the Messiah. With this hint, we can see that Christ was the scapegoat who triumphed, who became God by becoming a victim. Indeed, Frazer devoted a chapter of *The Golden Bough* to a discussion of Christ as a scapegoat figure.[8] And Bloom himself, despite the patriarchal insistence of Mastiansky and Citron, is able to turn the scapegoat's role into the messiah's. 'BLOOM: (*In a seamless garment marked I.H.S. stands upright amid phoenix flames.*) Weep not for me, O daughters, of Erin' (p 498). His words echo Christ's on the way to Calvary (Thornton), but after a choir sings the Alleluia chorus, 'Bloom becomes mute, shrunken, carbonised' (p 499).

The fact that the people cast stones at Bloom indicates Joyce's expansion of the scapegoat role beyond Leviticus (where there is no stoning). But the additional fact that these are 'soft pantomime stones' shows Joyce's determination not to be heavy in his use of anthropology. The reader is not allowed to feel the kind of pity for Bloom that 'real' stones might evoke. Once our mood is set by the reassurance of soft pantomime stones, we can laugh at dogs urinating on Bloom. Similarly, when Bloom is to be burnt, we have the following description. A religious brother '(*Invests Bloom in a yellow habit with embroidery of painted flames and high pointed hat. He places a bag of gunpowder round his neck and hands him over to the civil power, saying*) Forgive him his trespasses' (p 498). In this section of 'Circe' Joyce makes sure that we view Bloom the social victim as an actor in a play, a comic production.

In his book, *The Origins of Attic Comedy* (1914), Francis Cornford noted how the characters in a Greek comedy had been 'at first serious, and even awful, figures in a religious mystery: the God who every year is born and dies and rises again, his Mother and his Bride, the Antagonist who kills him, the Medicine-man who restores him to life.'[9] But looking at the surviving Greek and Roman comedies, Cornford realized that 'the general formula of progress for Comedy is a steady drift from Mystery to Mime' (p 175). Whether Joyce knew Cornford's theory or not, he seems to be acting on it in 'Circe.' Bloom as victim-god is a buffoon. The Doctors who treat him are the Medicine-man as the comic 'humbug and quack' of mime (Cornford 176). His Bride appears as the seductive woman overdone in her Eastern harem costume (*Ulysses* 439). His Mother is clothed 'in pantomime stringed mobcap, crinoline and bustle,' etc. (p 438) and speaks like a stage Irishwoman, 'Where were you at all, at all?' Although Bloom's antagonist, Boylan, is completely triumphant in 'Circe,' as he appears outside that episode, he fits Cornford's description of the development of the role: he is guilty of 'idle vaunts' earlier and suffers a 'final discomforture' (p 176) in Molly's mind at the end of the novel. But unlike Aristophanes, Joyce was concerned to include the rite of the traditional religious mystery in his drama. By combining Mime and Mystery, with the comic dominating in both, Joyce found a perfect vehicle for showing the essential absurdity of ego-fantasies. Whether paranoid or megalomaniac, such fantasies are simply reverse sides of the same desire to substitute inflated, isolating, childish thoughts for the everyday difficulties of relating to others as human beings.

For mime, Joyce substituted music hall pantomime to give his comic drama the absurdity and transformations of the Dublin locus as he had experienced it. Besides the two references to pantomime we have seen in the stage directions, extended reference is made in the Ithaca episode (p 678) to an actual pantomime put on in Dublin one Christmas season. Speaking of 'Joyce's use of the pantomime in organizing the chapter ['Circe'] and elaborating the individual hallucinations,' David Hayman gives a sketch of its ingredients:

> The Dublin Christmas Pantomime, like its British cousin, is a gaudy jumble of music hall skits and romantic tableaux, ancillary to the burlesque treatment of a child's tale or another popular form. Fundamentally discontinuous, it nevertheless has numerous conventions. For example, the principle boy is played by a girl. In 'Circe' this transvestite aspect is ... reenforced during the Bella-Bello sequence. ... The transformation scene, concluding sequence of the Pantomime, an event roughly equivalent to the *anagnorisis* in tragedy, was apparently fundamental to Joyce's view of the chapter's ending.[10]
>
> (pp 277-8)

Hayman believes that at the end of the episode, we witness 'Stephen's transformation into Bloom's long lost Rudy' (p 278). Shifting Hayman's emphasis, I would say that Bloom, by saving Stephen from harm has earned a view of his dead son. The emotion he experiences may be pathos (as Hayman suggests), but it is real and other-directed; it is thus a reward for someone who has suffered as much distress as Bloom has during the episode. This distress had, or course, been earned in its turn by Bloom's business during the day, using words and thoughts to keep off feeling.

(... *Against the dark wall a figure appears slowly, a fairy boy of eleven, a changeling, kidnapped, dressed in an Eton suit with glass shoes and a little bronze helmet*...)

BLOOM

(*Wonderstruck, calls inaudibly.*) Rudy!

RUDY

(*Gazes unseeing into Bloom's eyes and goes on reading, kissing, smiling*...) (p 609)

The important parallel with the last scene in a pantomime is that Rudy does actually *mime* his part. British pantomime, though an outgrowth of continental Harlequin (reaching back to Roman pantomime), was dominated by clowing, acting, and singing from early nineteenth century.[11] According to J.S. Atherton, 'Dublin pantomimes in the 1890s still included a harlinquinade as a final spectacle.'[12] Rudy is more a fairytale figure (thus harmonizing with the rudimentary plot of a pantomime). As a changeling, he is subject to transformation, but his silent miming is another world from Bloom's clowning.

The important transformations in 'Circe' take place within the main body of the episode. If Joyce needed a tradition for these continual metamorphoses of character and environment, he could have found it in the earlier British pantomime.

Henry Morley in *The Journal of a London Playgoer*, published in 1881, describes performances in the 1860's in which every scene was transformed: kitchens into ballrooms, streets into enchanted islands, shops into magicians' caves; and all the costumes of the actors were simultaneously altered to match their new surroundings. (Atherton 20)

This is very much the kind of change that happens constantly in 'Circe.'

In Chapter 2, I noted Joyce's comment that '*The Circe* is a costume episode. Disguises. Bloom changes clothes half a dozen times. And of course it's an animal episode, full of animal allusions, animal mannerisms' (Budgen 128). At that point we could see that the dog as mummer provided the connecting link between costume change and animal. Now we may add to that insight the connection between mumming and pantomime. As Atherton points out, in Roman times the latter word meant that one actor played all (*panto*) the parts. Stephen, we saw, is self-conscious as a mummer and is outclassed by Mulligan in crude acting. But Bloom in 'Circe' drops his pride altogether and plays all parts: father and son, hero and victim, reformer and dictator, authority and buffoon, idealist and carnalist, exhibitionist and voyeur, sadist and masochist, man and woman.[13] Unlike Ulysses, who remained a man throughout his sojourn with Circe, Bloom becomes an animal (several animals, in fact). But like all his other transformations, this one is only in passing, and he emerges from his various metamorphoses more of a whole human being than he began.

Taking Bloom as the central character in a pantomime, we remember that the one he is connected with in 'Ithaca' is *Sinbad the Sailor*. As we shall see in Chapter 11, this means that he will return with riches, primarily diamonds, which in Bloom's case will be the compressed form of his own carbonized self. (As Joyce wrote in his notes for 'Ithaca,' 'diamond cryst. carbon.' Herring 445). Only he who descends into the mind can reach stable heights, who has become dust can sparkle in heaven, who has 'rererepugnosed' can find in the 'terrestrial hemispheres ... the islands of the blest' (p 734), who has become 'Noman' (eg, an animal) can become 'Everyman' (p 727).

As I have suggested, Joyce's handling of ritual motifs suggests that his interest is much more in comic regression that in the mystery of archetypal patterns. Joyce's accurate ear, large memory, and magic word sense were put to the service of a determined regressiveness – childish rhythms and word play and imitative noises. His evocative descriptions become of characters and scenes metamorphized or created whole out of chance phrases. The episode is full of dream changes and shifts, a world where id impulses continually break through and the reality sense of the ego has only a token sway. But if Joyce has masterfully given us the sense of emerging unconscious impulses, he has not neglected the third in Freud's triad of mind functions, the super-ego, that uneasy fellow of the id in the bed of the unconscious.[14] The two make a potent couple: the id wanting pleasure, the super-ego ostensibly trying to restrain but in fact desiring to punish. Their co-operation is evident in the scene with Bella. Bloom's id gets to test out the forbidden pleasure of femininity, and his super-ego is satisfied by taking on the punishing role of the masculinized Bello. By this analysis, it is Bloom's undefensive ego (which I would call his self) that finally asserts command. The buried impulses expressed (but not acted out), the super-ego temporarily satisfied (hopefully weakened by recognition), Bloom's real self gathers enough strength to confront the existential problem in his life, the relation of

Molly to Boylan. All day he has sought not to think of their encounter, but in the last of his fantasies he finally faces his actual role in the *ménage*. His subsequent standing up to Pvt Carr and the night watch indicates not bravery but a more realistic ability to confront hostile male authority. His regression proves to have been in the service of 'ego,' the waking self in its relations to others.

10 The grotesque in 'Circe'

Joyce's use of animals and of distorted humans in 'Circe' moves many parts of that episode beyond the comic. Although they may seem monstrous, these distortions can also be seen as natural. Budgen suggests that 'the essence of the animal into man metamorphosis seems to be that man becomes an animal when he loses his many-sided human wholeness' (p 229). This many-sided wholeness is precarious, as Freud indicated, because the social is built on the natural, the man on the animal, the conscious on the unconscious. Under stress the first tends to slip back towards the second. Society therefore builds moral laws precisely against man's 'natural' inclinations. Since acting on such inclinations (incest, sodomy, bestiality) binds those involved at that level, we could conclude that society is justified. But blind taboos also restrict insight and growth.

Simultaneous attraction and repulsion is part of the mental programming that all parents unconsciously pass on to their children. Only the individual who can bring the attraction to consciousness, and see these urges without identifying with them and acting them out, can thus become free of ego defences, free to be himself. Leopold Bloom goes through such a process in 'Circe,' and James Joyce had not only the insight to see the urges but also the ability to embody them in words, if not to free himself of them.

In fact, Joyce's obsessive vision allowed him to see through the civilized veneer both of his own thoughts and of others' appearances. As he confided to a friend in Zürich, 'Human beings sometime appear to me to take the shape of animals' (*J.J.* 452). This oddity of vision suggests that Joyce possessed a deep-seated tendency towards regressive or distorted vision, a tendency to which he gave full rein in 'Circe.' The result of this ability to picture the animal in man is that 'Circe' can be characterized as an epitome of the grotesque.

In Chapter 6, I considered Wolfgang Kayser's analysis of the grotesque as based on an estranged view of conventional reality, as 'an attempt to invoke and subdue the demonic aspects of the world' (*The Grotesque in Art and Literature* 188). Enlarging 'demonic' to incorporate the insights of psychoanalysis, on pages 157-61 of this chapter I shall probe the animalizing of Bloom, and on pages 161-6 analyze Joyce's grotesque conception in an aesthetic frame. First, however, I shall turn to the means Joyce employed to create a grotesque ambiance.

In the initial stage directions for 'Circe,' Joyce carefully built up an estranged vision of Dublin.

The Mabbot street entrance of nighttown, before which stretches an uncobbled tramsiding set with skeleton tracks, red and green will-o'-the-wisps and danger signals. Rows of flimsy houses with gaping doors. Rare lamps with faint rainbow fans. Round Rabaiotti's halted ice gondola stunted men and women squabble. They grab wafers between which are wedged lumps of coal and copper snow. Sucking, they scatter slowly. Chldren. (p 429)

The mildly expressionistic background becomes grotesque when we come to a description of the creatures who inhabit it. They are stunted; they squabble; they suck lumps of coal and copper snow. We fear we have entered some ominous unearthly underground world. Then we are given temporary respite when they are identified as children, and we realize that the inhuman details were only the author's imaginative way of describing them. But in fact those details are Joyce's way of easing us into a locale where we and his main characters can expect all sorts of uncomfortable distortions.

The respite provided by the word 'children' is only temporary, for the process of estrangement is soon intensified.

(*A deafmute idiot with goggle eyes, his shapeless mouth dribbling, jerks past, shaken in Saint Vitus' dance. A chain of children's hands imprisons him.*)

THE CHILDREN

Kithogue! Salute....

THE IDIOT

(*Gobbing.*) Ghaghahest.

(*They release him. He jerks on. A pigmy woman swings on a rope slung between the railings, counting. ... On a step a gnome totting among a rubbishtip crouches to shoulder a sack of rags and bones. ... A bandy child, asquat on the doorstep with a papershuttlecock, crawls sidling after* [a crone] *in spurts, clutches her skirt, scrambles up....*) (pp 429-30)

We can now appreciate an additional effect of the non-human sounds which I analysed as regressive in the last chapter. When pleasurable, they entice us back towards the freedom of childhood, but when the circumstances are mildly threatening, they can alienate us from the safety of socialized adulthood and remind us of the dark fears of our childhood. In this scene the sense of alienation is increased by the description with its pigmy woman and gnome, its bandy child who, like a monkey, scrambles up the skirt of a crone.

Once the drama begins Joyce relates its effects mainly to his two protagonists, and I shall again be concentrating on Bloom. The most fully developed grotesque character in the play is probably Bloom's grandfather.

(... *Lipoti Virag, basilicogrammate, chutes rapidly down through the chimneyflue and struts two steps to the left on gawky pink stilts. He is sausaged into several overcoats and wears a brown macintosh under which he holds a roll of parchment. In his left eye flashes the monocle of Cashel Boyle O'Connor Fitzmaurice Tisdall Farrell. On his head is perched an Egyptian pshent. Two quills project over his ears.*) (p 511)

Virag gives a physical description of each of the three whores at whom Bloom is looking, his comments combining realism and appreciation of their shortcomings and excesses. For instance,

She is coated with quite a considerable layer of fat. Obviously mammal in weight of bosom you remark that she has in front well to the fore two protuberances of very respectable dimensions, inclined to fall in the noonday soupplate, while on her rere lower down are two additional protuberances, suggestive of potent rectum and tumescent for palpation which leave nothing to be desired save compactness. Such fleshy parts are the product of careful nurture. When coop-fattened their livers reach an elephantine size. Pellets of new bread with fennygreek and gumbenjamin swamped down by potions of green tea endow them during their brief existence with natural pin-cushions of quite colossal blubber. (p 513)

Although this begins with what Kayser calls the comic grotesque ('two protuberances ... inclined to fall in the noonday soupplate'), the later obsessive quality in Virag's description gives the reader that feeling of helplessness and horror which Kayser associates with the fantastic grotesque.

As the exchange between Bloom and Virag goes on, the latter's speech becomes less and less coherent, his characteristics less and less human.

VIRAG

(*Prompts into* [Bloom's] *ear in a pig's whisper.*) Insects of the day spend their brief existence in reiterated coition, lured by the smell of the inferiorly pulchritudinous female possessing extendified pudendal verve in dorsal region. Pretty Poll! (*His yellow parrotbeak gabbles nasally.*) (p 515)

A moth appears and Virag first eyes it and then appears to become it:

VIRAG

(*Head askew, arches his back and hunched wingshoulders, peers at the moth out of blear bulged eyes, points a horning claw and cries.*) Who's Ger Ger? Who's dear Gerald? O, I much fear he shall be most badly burned. ... (*He rushes against the mauve shade flapping noisily.*) Pretty pretty pretty pretty pretty pretty petticoats. (pp 516-17)

Though Virag as bird or moth is grotesque enough, he begins taking four-footed animal shapes as he becomes more driven, inhuman, and demonic.

(*A diabolic rictus of black luminosity contracting his visage, cranes his scraggy neck forward. He lifts a mooncalf nozzle and howls.*) *Verfluchte Goim!* He had a father, forty fathers. He never existed, Pig God! He had two left feet. He was Judas Iacchias, a Lybyan eunuch, the pope's bastard. (*He leans out on tortured forepaws, elbows bent rigid, his eye agonising in his flat skullneck and yelps over the mute world.*) A son of a whore. Apocalypse. (p 520)

This direction of his transformations reaches its height (or depth) in an outburst of physical anti-spiritualism.

LYNCH

(*Laughs.*) And to such delights has Metchnikoff innoculated anthropoid apes.

FLORRY

(*Nods.*) Locomotor ataxy.

ZOE

(*Gaily.*) O, my dictionary.

LYNCH

Three wise virgins.

VIRAG

(*Agueshaken, profuse yellow spawn foaming over his bony epileptic lips.*) She sold lovephiltres, whitewax, orange flower. Panther, the Roman centurion, polluted her with his genitories. (*He sticks out a flickering phosphorescent scorpion tongue, his hand on his fork.*) Messiah! He burst her tympanum. (*With gibbering baboon's cries he jerks his hips in the cynical spasm.*) Hik! Hek! Hak! Hok! Huk! Kok! Kuk! (p 521)

Locomotor ataxia is a disease of the spinal cord usually caused by syphilis (with which disease Metchnikoff innoculated his apes). It is characterized by an inability to co-ordinate voluntary movements. Joyce remarked to Budgen that 'the rhythm' of the Circe episode 'is the rhythm of locomotor ataxia' (p 128). Virag seems possessed by both the physical and the mental forms of this rhythm. In other words, Virag illustrates Joyce's central conception of the process of this episode, a tendency to breakdown and discontinuity, the reduction to lower forms, to mechanical unco-ordinated rhythms as first exemplified in the idiot's shamble and gabble at the beginning of the episode.[1] Remembering Joyce's later comment to Mercanton that the universe is idiotic (cf. the beginning of Chapter 5) we can keep our eyes open for at least one other incarnation of the idiot as 'ignorant person,' a demiurge figure we shall meet later in this chapter.

Bloom will follow in his own way the reductionist rhythm asserted by Virag, but he will not reach Virag's demonic depths of mechanical spasm. Although Bloom may not be attracted by 'the cynical spasm,' he is as we shall see open to other sexual abuses. Virag also represents the excess of Bloom's tendency to religious scepticism. As denigrator of Christ and Mary, he is the Jew of Catholic anti-semitism; but he is also a warning to Bloom who, in his pragmatic scientism, needs to be innoculated against this 'rationalist' exposé. Virag is a living example of the *reductio ad absurdum* of the denial of form and spirit in favour of matter, flesh, and sensation alone. His choice reduces him to a creature so alien, so openly dominated by his brute desires that he moves beyond the comic into the fantastic or horrible grotesque.

For a better discrimination of the difference between the comic and the fantastic grotesque, we need to turn now to a psychoanalytic critique of the grotesque. A concentrated attempt at such a critique has been made by Michael Steig in 'Defining the Grotesque: An Attempt at Synthesis.' Building on the work of several recent explorers in the field of grotesque theory, Steig succeeds in drawing their observations together with a neat and convincing use of Freudian principles.

The grotesque involves the arousing of anxiety by giving expression to infantile fears, fantasies and impulses ... the threatening material is distorted in the direction of harmlessness without completely attaining it. That is, the defence is still only partially successful, in that it allows some anxiety to remain, and characteristically will even contribute to the arousing of some anxiety. This is the basic paradox of the grotesque: it is double-edged, it at once allays and intensifies the effect of the uncanny; in pure comedy, at the other end of the spectrum from the uncanny, the defense is complete, and detachment is achieved.[2]

This distinction between comic detachment and grotesque anxiety will help us to understand why we react differently to Bloom's experience outside the brothel than we do to his experience inside. We looked at the comedy of the heroic-inflation, scapegoat-deflation sequences outside the brothel in the previous chapter. In this one we can come to a better appreciation of Bloom's grotesque transformations by Bella Cohen, and why we are not as detached as in the earlier sequences.

As heroic scapegoat, Bloom is acting out a childish desire for omnipotence: in Steig's analysis:

> In what is usually called the comic-grotesque, the comic in its various forms lessens the threat of identification with infantile drives by means of ridicule; at the same time, it lulls inhibitions and makes possible on a preconscious level the same identification that it appears to the conscience or superego to prevent. (pp 259-60)

Thus the infantile desire of each reader to indulge in what Kris calls omnipotence of thought is indulged to the delight of the id and made ridiculous to satisfy the super-ego.

In contrast, we have the grotesque scene in which Bloom as unmanned female under the hoof of Bello re-enacts a childhood castration fear. In Steig's distinction:

> When the infantile material is primarily threatening, comic techniques, including caricature, diminish the threat through degradation or ridicule; but at the same time, they may also enhance anxiety through their aggressive implications and through the strangeness they lend to the threatening figure. (p 259)

As Steig also indicates, in the fantastic grotesque 'comic techniques' do not always result in comic effects. Bello's putting out his cigar in Bloom's ear or squeezing his testicles are both so vicious and painful that the reader is more threatened than amused. In his final summary, Steig implicity distinguishes the fantastic from the comic grotesque: the former 'attempts a liberation from fear, while the other attempts a liberation from inhibition; but in both a state of unresolved tension is the most common result, because of the intrapsychic conflicts involved' (p 260). With the aid of Steig's schema, we are in a position to consider Bloom's animal transformations in 'Circe' and to understand better Joyce's use of the grotesque to handle the psychic threat of the bestial.

We may begin with a slip of the tongue. On the first appearance of his wife, Bloom is completely subservient. '(... *Bloom stoops his back for leapfrog.*) ... I can give you ... I mean as your business menagerer ... Mrs Marion ... if you ...' (p 440, the ellipses within Bloom's speech are Joyce's). The word *menagerer* is half French, half English a polyglot term chosen by Joyce as part of his initial conception of the episode ('business menagerer' appears in the *Notesheets*, p 328). As *ménager* in French it would mean 'an economist,' or 'a thrifty man.' But it obviously carries the English meaning of *manager*. In neither case is the extra *er* necessary. (It may indicate that he is one who is managed, as a sufferer is one who suffers.) We already know what is on Bloom's mind from an earlier Freudian slip of his – 'wife's admirers' instead of 'wife's advisers' (p 313). He was worried about Molly's committing adultery under the guise of making business arrangements with Boylan. The same worry is present in this slip. Bloom is really the one who takes care of the *ménage*, the household. He allows Boylan to enter the *ménage*, and later actively solicits a roomer (Stephen) so it will become what he fears and desires, a *ménage à trois*.

Equally important, Bloom turns his household into a *menagerie* by letting in Boylan, who ruts like a wild animal there, as Molly lets us know (p 742).[3] *Menagerie* connects Bloom's slip with the regressive tendency in this episode. Bloom himself undergoes grotesque transformations back behind childhood to animalhood; what emerges, however, is not aggressiveness, but a larger capacity for suffering. As the lion tamer says, 'Block tackle and a strangling pully will bring your lion to heel, no matter how fractious, even *Leo ferox* there, the Libyan maneater. A redhot crowbar and some liniment rubbing on the burning part produced Fritz of Amsterdam, the thinking hyena' (p 454). Bloom's first name is 'Leo,' but he has never been *ferox*. Like Fritz, he is more a 'thinking hyena,' having acted like a castrated being since the death of Rudy. To adopt Freud's analysis, his avoidance of physical sex has resulted in an increase in rationality, but his slips show a constant regressive tendency; deep down he is a wounded animal, his rationality a pathetic compensation. But like Stephen's insistence on intellect, Bloom's rationality often precipitates the suffering it is intended to hide. The narrator of 'Cyclops' is malicious, but he is also human when he expresses irritation with Bloom's know-it-all attitude to every subject that comes up.

Bloom's inner need to invite pain becomes clear inside the brothel, where his fantasy of sexual degradation unmasks him as a passive sufferer. He is not a wild beast under his civilized exterior, as a 'real man' should be. In his 'unintelligible speech,' a first self-defence early in the episode, he characterizes himself: '*He was down and out but, though branded as a black sheep, if he might say so, he meant to reform, to retrieve the memory of the past in a purely sisterly way and return to nature as a purely domestic animal*' (pp 461-2). This hope comes to pass in a very unpastoral way at the depth of his self-abasement. First Joyce transforms Bella into a man, Bello; then he has Bloom (whose middle name is 'Paula,' p 723) become a woman. Then

BELLO

Down! (*He taps her on the shoulder with his fan.*) Incline feet forward! Slide left foot one pace back. You will fall. You are falling. On the hands down!

BLOOM

(*Her eyes upturned in the sign of admiration, closing.*) Truffles!

(*With a piercing epileptic cry she sinks on all fours, grunting, snuffling, rooting at his feet, then lies, shamming dead...*) (p 531)

But Bloom does not remain a pig. When put up for auction, he is described by Bello as another animal.

Fourteen hands high. Touch and examine his points. Handle him. This downy skin, these soft muscles, this tender flesh. If I had only my gold piercer here! And quite easy to milk. Three newlaid gallons a day. A pure stockgetter, due to lay within the hour. His sire's milk record was a thousand gallons of whole milk in forty weeks. Whoa, my jewel! Beg up! Whoa! (*He brands his initial C on Bloom's croup.*) So! Warranted Cohen! (p 540)

As 'domestic animal,'Bloom here retains his nominal sex, but takes on the attributes of a cow (and hen), while being used as a thing, as Bello calls him. 'What else are you good for, an impotent thing like you? (*He stoops and peering, pokes with his fan rudely under the fat suet folds of Bloom's haunches.*) Up! Up! Manx cat! What have we here? Where's your curly teapot gone to or who docked it on you, cockyolly? (p 541).' Earlier, Bello treated Bloom even more rudely:

What offers? (*He points.*) For that lot trained by owner to fetch and carry, basket in mouth. (*He bares his arm and plunges it elbow-deep in Bloom's vulva.*) There's fine depth for you! What, boys? That give you a hardon! (*He shoves his arm in a bidder's face.*) Here, wet the deck and wipe it round! (p 539)

Bloom is treated as a thing, a sexual object, for which the animal imagery is quite appropriate, since man does treat animals as creatures of convenience. But the comedy is somewhat raw in these descriptions. For one thing Bloom is too obviously the butt of a sado-masochistic game. For another, the details are too physically realistic. Yet they are rationally impossible. We know that Bloom is not really branded, that he does not have a vulva. The surprise and ominous estrangement signal the grotesque.

But the threat involved in these descriptions places them as fantastic rather than comic grotesque. The fulfilment of Bloom's urge to degradation presumably stimulates similar unconscious desires in the reader. The change in Bloom's sex and his becoming an animal are anti-social regressions which both tempt and threaten us. The male ego can report to the super-ego, '*I*, don't act like a woman or a beast,' thus allowing conscious acceptance of these scenes in a way that would not be possible if Bloom were allowed to retain his masculinity during his degradation. At the same time (still following Steig), because Joyce makes the punishment so graphic, once the super-ego is tricked into not condemning, our feelings are much more involved than they were during Joyce's earlier treatment of Bloom as hero-victim in the sequence outside the brothel.

Having defined the grotesque as a literary device containing various psychoanalytic mechanisms, I would like now to relate it to the larger question of the destruction and transformation of nature in art. Freud has shown us the aggressive side of the comic; we need to remember Joyce's admission and Kris's insistence (cf. Chapter 7) that there is a destructive side to all art. 'The unconscious meaning of this process [of artistic selection] is control at the price of destruction. But destruction of the real is fused with construction of its image ... when the new configuration arises ... nature has been re-created' (*Psychoanalytic Explorations in Art* 52). As Kayser demonstrates, this destructive aspect of art was localized in comedy as early as the late eighteenth century: 'An ingredient of humor as Jean Paul sought to define it' is 'its "annihilating idea"' (*The Grotesque* 54). The German Romantic writer Jean Paul suggested 'that "something comparable to the audacity of the annihilating humor" exists outside of literature,' in, for instance, 'the medieval fools carnivals ... where "religious and secular matters as well as social classes and customs are turned upside down" and where all order is destroyed' (p 55). Kayser, like Joyce, would connect Saturnaliaia with the grotesque. 'The comic innocuously annihilates greatness and dignity, especially if they are wrongly assumed. It effects the annihilation by placing us on the secure level of reality. The grotesque totally destroys the order and deprives us of our foothold' (p 59). The means by which this grotesque destruction is often accomplished is through a contrast 'that ominously permits of no reconciliation. To recognize and reveal such a construct of opposites is somewhat diabolic' (p 59). To illustrate from 'Circe,' we may say the 'construct of opposites' is overtly diabolic in the Black Mass, where there is an antiphonal structure between the Christain words and chants and the demonic inversion of them. In theory then, the demonic reversal of the Black Mass 'totally destroys the order and deprives us of our foothold,' tilting us at a steep angle towards a formless subconscious. In fact, Joyce slows down the descent to terror by having the demonic chorus first, the Christian one second.

A similar irreconcilable 'construct of opposites' can be seen in Bloom's experience in 'Circe.' Before entering the brothel, he more than once moves precipitately from hero to scapegoat. Inside the brothel, his thoroughgoing animalization forms one term in a different kind of opposition – Bella as male, Bloom as female. These transformations are unexpected and ominous; they rattle a skeleton in the dark closet of each reader's unconscious nature, since in every person who calls himself male there lingers a residual biological or conditioned tendency towards being female (and vice versa). In Kayser's words, Bloom's transformation could be said to open 'an abyss ... where we thought to rest on firm ground' (p 59) after having got used to our comic distance from Bloom.

On the other hand, we must remember that Joyce's comic destructiveness includes the special aggressiveness of man towards man which Freud saw as an important part of the covert hostility of the form. Outside the brothel, Bloom is burned to a cinder, and we are not upset. Inside the brothel, we watch his less comic transformation into a woman and an animal. Kayser suggests that one of the most unsettling manifestations of twentieth-century grotesque is its focus on the loss of identity. In the Italian *teatro del grotesco*, which flourished just before and after the publication of *Ulysses*, 'the division of the Self has become the guiding principle of characterization, and the notion of the unity of personality is completely abandoned' (p 135). Reading this we realize a crucial difference between such modernism (including surrealism) and Joyce. As I have several times asserted, Joyce's splitting of Bloom's personality is in the cause of a more authentic unity. He subjects Bloom to a grotesque purging of those 'inferior' parts of his nature that, though unconscious, have been dominating Bloom's behaviour. Bloom emerges as a more integrated and authoritative person precisely after experiencing his worst transformations.

To conclude this chapter, I would like to explore a slightly different kind of 'construct of opposites.' I have suggested above that Joyce's art is not wholeheartedly grotesque. A clue to the place of the grotesque in his vision may be gained by considering the position of Victor Hugo. Hugo, Kayser points out, assigns the grotesque

> a function within a larger whole. He takes it to be one pole of a tension whose opposite pole is constituted by the sublime. He thus ceases to think of the grotesque as the only

characteristic feature of modern art and comes to look at it as a contrasting device. He defines art as a means of creating a harmonious relation between them. (p 58)

But Hugo believes that only one author ever achieved that harmony, the English playwright in whose honour he wrote a 350-page book in which he developed the concept: William Shakespeare. Only Shakespeare, Hugo suggests, 'succeeded in combining "the sublime with the grotesque, the terrible with the burlesque, and tragedy with comedy"' (p 58). I believe that Joyce was trying to achieve something similar in 'Circe.' Bloom as scapegoat could represent tragedy (Greek *tragos*, 'goat'; *oide*, 'song'). Of course, Joyce does not seriously strive for tragic effect, but as we have seen he early decided that comedy was a fuller form than tragedy. Comedy is certainly the dominant mode in *Ulysses*, not only in its humour and joy, but in its various forms as irony, parody, satire, and so on. In 'Circe,' Joyce took great pains to recreate the religious ritual from which both tragedy and comedy grew and to bend it away from its civilized artistic forms back towards its more vital impulses in homey and vulgar burlesque and pantomime.

In another similar list of qualities to be found in Shakespeare, Hugo adds one worth considering further, '*le vaste rire divin*' (Kayser 197). 'The great divine laugh' obviously corresponds to that sense of joy which Joyce early located as the essence of comedy. In distancing, it corresponds to Joyce as the writer above and beyond his work, a perspective that he invited his reader to take even in 'Circe' by, among other means, putting memories from Stephen's experience into Bloom's mind and vice versa. But we must always remember Joyce's insistence on being within his own works too, since it is the combination of involved and dispassionate attitudes that gave his art power and complexity.

In this case the other side of Hugo's divine laugh is a character from one of Hugo's novels who appears in 'Circe.' This is the Hobgoblin, who identifies himself as '*L'homme qui rit! L'homme primigéne!*' (p 506). As Thornton records, *L'Homme Qui Rit* is the title of a novel by Hugo about a child mutilated so its mouth is set in a perpetual grimace. This 'man who laughs' identifies himself here as 'primigenial man,' that is original man. He strikes us as a more active and aggressive version of the idiot who appeared at the opening of the episode, perhaps like the Gnostic Demiurge, as described by the church father Irenaeus. The Demiurge 'formed the heavens, yet was ignorant of the heavens; he fashioned man, yet knew not man ... he was ignorant of the forms of all he made' even 'imagined that he himself was all things.'[4] The Hobgoblin operates at such a level of brute ignorance.

(*His jaws chattering, capers to and fro, goggling his eyes, squeaking, kangaroohopping, with outstretched clutching arms, than all at once thrusts his lipless face through the fork of his thighs.*)

Il vient! C'est moi! L'homme qui rit! L'homme primigène! (He whirls round and round with dervish howls.) Sieurs et dames, faites vos jeux! (He crouches juggling. Tiny roulette planets fly from his hands.) Les jeux sont faits! ... (The planets, buoyant balloons, sail swollen up and away. He springs off into vacuum.) (p 506)

A grotesque creature, the Hobgoblin hovers between the comic and the fantastic. Despite being so simple and so quickly gone, he does threaten our sense of stability. Yet he appears as a kind of fate, a croupier *cum* juggler who lacks our subtle civilized sense of the cosmos. Though his gross tricks and animal nature are comic, they are also ominous because his comments are mainly commands. The implicit allegory is not hard to find: we make our play during our brief sojourn on the spinning roulette wheel of the solar system, and we take our chances. Ordinarily we know that the odds favour the house and often suspect that the wheel is fixed. But this 'authority' is so uncivilized that we cannot trust even the hidden rules to remain fixed. We are not surprised, though we are distressed, when the roulette-ball planets sail away as balloons.

The Hobgoblin scene immediately precedes another grotesque one in which 'the End of the World, a two-headed octupus ... whirls through the murk, head over heels' (p 507). Since the Hobgoblin 'bumbles in somersalts' (p 506), it is obviously connected with the octopus, the latter *being* 'the End of the World,' the former *causing* it. The third term in this related series of figures is Mananaan, whom we already connected with the octopus in Chapter 5. Joyce makes Mananaan comic in his supposedly serious and foreboding speech:

MANANAAN MACLIR

(*With a voice of waves.*) Aum! Hek! Wal! Ak! Lub! Mor! Ma! White yoghin of the Gods. Occult pimander of Hermes Trismegistos. (*With a voice of whistling seawind.*) Punarjanam Patsypunjaub! I won't have my leg pulled. It has been said by one: beware the left, the cult of Shakti. (*With a cry of stormbirds.*) Shakti, Shiva! Dark hidden Father! (*He smites with his bicycle pump the crayfish in his left hand. On its co-operative dial glow the twelve signs of the zodiac. He wails with the vehemence of the ocean.*) Aum! Baum! Pyjaum! I am the light of the homestead, I am the dreamery creamery butter. (p 510)

The impressive stage directions for his speech ('a voice of waves,' etc.) and his occult references are undercut both by the number of nonsense words he utters and by such everyday phrases as 'I won't have my leg pulled.' The effect is comic grotesque.

Joyce is here parodying A.E.'s brand of theosophism, which was an attempt to combine the Indian and the Celtic, and equally unlikely a belief in spirits with a down-to-earth commitment to better farming (cf. Thornton). Though he could not accept A.E.'s religion, Joyce could see in it elements of truth, but of an artistic rather than a spiritual sort. If the Hobgoblin is a demiurge, the ignorant creator of our world, then Mananaan is a rebirth of the same principle, the creative force as seen by theosophy. Joyce suggests that this force contains the important power of transformation (the 'eels and elvers' in his hair, the 'weeds and shells' on his body, p 510, cf. Chapter 5), but makes it clear that Mananaan is incompatible with the fixed things by which A.E. runs his life, the bicycle pump, and the watch. The accommodation of 'the twelve signs of the zodiac' to a watch dial implies a mechanization of the occult, a temporizing with eternity. As a true emblem for art, Mananaan should represent the ability to change through natural evolution, or the psychological metamorphosis of Bloom, who reverts to the animal in order to gain more of the human.

Joyce's implicit criticism of A.E. is that Shiva and Shakti are too far removed from dairy farming. Thus Western man's relation to Shiva cannot involve real belief: it is a kind of spiritual 'dreamery creamery butter' for those who would rather rest in dreams or thrill themselves with mental images of apocalypse than face the real difficulties of art and human nature. Believing that the creator of the solar system probably was a demiurgic creature, Joyce saw the pain caused man by this ignorant artificer, but he also saw the need of submitting to the processes of the natural world. That imperfect world is a challenge to the artist who has a chance to create a better world, not by reducing the natural one to a static condition of pleasant unreality, but by reproducing the vitality which social convention tries to hide, by restoring the terrible mystery that materialism tries to assuage. At its best, then, the destructiveness of art will be aimed at false idols, its constructiveness at creating not new idols but a renewed sense of the process in which all life is involved, a sense of its vitality and its potential nobility.

The destructiveness of the Hobgoblin, verbalized in his 'rien n'va plus,' incorporates the little boy who knocks down the castle he has made of wooden blocks and the writer who in Kris's view must destroy the world in order to recreate it. The subhuman destroys, the divine creates. The Hobgoblin can thus be seen as the animal underside of the high divine laugh that Joyce often invites us to share. Like Bloom and Stephen, we must face this substratum of our nature, of all nature, before we can legitimately climb to a higher view. Our pleasurable regression by means of childish songs and word-play, by dirty jokes, has been balanced from the beginning of the episode by a more fearful and threatening regression towards darkness. This regression has as its farthest aim exposing us to our fear that alimentation ends in defecation, that our origins are brutal, that the universe runs down, or worse that we will destroy it. Because each of us is born red with blood, because all of us had ancestors, because we are subject to physical laws we cannot repeal, our culture and our selves must admit these origins rather than deny them. Of course, even in denying them, cultural taboos admit the power of dark urges, as Freud has shown. But such indirect admission is not enough.

Joyce insists on as direct a confrontation as our alienated natures can stand. To achieve this confrontation, he employs all the indirections of verbal art to turn spoken sounds back towards the pleasures and fears of the id for which organized language is so early a civilized ego substitute. Once we have allowed ourselves to enter the hallucinated world of Nighttown, of the dream land where the brothel is graphically present, Joyce can not only release our inhibitions, he can also expose us to our repressions, can engage us in watching others live through both their admitted fantasies (Bloom's sado-masochism) and their unadmitted ones (Stephen's paranoid projections). Using the tricks of art he can, as Steig suggests, placate our conscience (the super-ego, the voice of our parents and society) by appearing not to condone or identify with a character or a situation, while at the same time bringing us in touch with our hidden fears, hates, and desires. Only when we have plunged far enough down into the darkness of the mind to be in touch with those root forces of our nature can we hope to gain a stable vantage from which to view our lives with detachment, to achieve the great divine laugh.

11 'Ithaca': reduction and sublimation

After the high drama of 'Circe,' with its low comedy, painful grotesqueries, intricate integration of motifs, and active human encounters, the reader feels as purged as Bloom, as groggy as Stephen. Never one to stop short with a climax that falsely pretends to be a conclusion, Joyce persevered through three more episodes, a section of the novel that corresponds in Homer's work to the adventures of Odysseus after his return (Nostos) home to Ithaca. The first of these episodes, 'Eumaeus,' is a deliberate anticlimax, the second, 'Ithaca,' an exercise in distancing, and the last, 'Penelope,' a tour de force whose immediacy attempts to counterbalance the shifting of attention away from character and plot in the previous two. To appreciate Joyce's aim and evaluate his success in these three episodes, we shall need to incorporate the psychoanalytic and aesthetic findings particularly of Chapters 5, 6, 7, and 8 as we take up again the relation of form to matter.

In 'Circe,' Joyce tested his ability to handle a disintegrating plot with sensational actions and lurid thoughts while bringing into focus the important themes of the novel; in 'Eumaeus,' he tested his artistic ability in the opposite way, as shown in Chapter 5: action and thought are slow and dull; although the interest of both characters and readers is at a low ebb, Joyce included in the slow current of his aqueous prose intimations of submerged activity, a potential light.

In contrast to 'Eumaeus,' the last episode of *Ulysses* has never been called dull; Molly's soliloquy in 'Penelope' is what male voyeurs read for cheap thrills. Conversely, some conventional women are upset by Molly's soiled vulgarity, while more liberated women condemn her as a male chauvinist's picture of a woman. Actually, Molly's realism makes her in many ways much less bound by sexual stereotypes than are many of her readers even today. Most critics agree that

Molly brings the book down to earth; her sensuous and sensual evocations of man and nature serve as a refreshing contrast to the the rarefied abstractions of the 'Ithaca' episode, on which we will be concentrating for most of this chapter.

In a provocative article on 'Penelope,' Joseph Voelker has suggested that Bruno's conception of Nature was Joyce's main source for working out the nature of Molly Bloom. Voelker notes that Bruno saw Nature as the 'mother of all things,' the creative force in the universe.[1] Although he does not address the form of 'Penelope,' Voelker does offer as a possible key to Joyce's conception of the episode the following quotation from McIntyre's 1903 book on Bruno.

> All things are in flow; the parts of the earth, seas, and rivers vary their positions, by a certain ebbing and flowing order of Nature. As matter wanders, flowing in and out, now here, now there, so the forms travel through matter. For there is not any form which, once occupying a portion of matter, retains it always, nor any matter which, once obtaining form, maintains it forever. (McIntyre, 205-6)[2]

This evocation of the ubiquity of transformation sounds like the substratum of Anna Livia, the flowing one of *Finnegans Wake*. Even though Molly is imaged as the earth (rather than a river), Bruno's words certainly fit her monologue, which flows on and on, and her mind, in which one male form is replaced by another before the reader is aware.

Voelker also finds in Bruno a way of justifying Molly's ignorance and self-contradiction, qualities which have bothered some readers of the last episode. As seen in Chapter 1, the doctrines of learned ignorance and the coincidence of contraries are two paradoxes which Bruno used to point up the limits of conventional philosophy. Voelker suggests that Joyce embodied these paradoxes in Molly's monologue to create a salutary contrast to the rationalism of Stephen and Bloom and the pedantry of question and answer in 'Ithaca.' He parallels Stephen's affirmation of Bloom ('a rational animal proceeding syllogistically from the known to the unknown,' *Ulysses* 697) with a McIntyre paraphrase of Bruno:

> Being itself eternal, unchangeable, the divine truth reveals itself to the few to whom it is revealed – not as in the physical sciences, which are acquired by the natural light of sense and reason, proceeding from the known to the unknown, in successive stages, but – suddenly, and at one stroke. (McIntyre 292-3)[3]

Voelker uses this parallel to place Bloom as rational scientist, but we must remember that the characterization of Bloom is by Stephen and is probably a projection. Bloom's sense of himself is quite opposite to Stephen's: 'A competent keyless citizen he had proceeded energetically from the unknown to the known through the incertitude of the void' (p 697). This characterization distinguishes Bloom from both Stephen and Molly.

In a study of *Ulysses* that puts great emphasis on the importance of 'The Void, Incertitude' (*The Book as World* 34), Marilyn French sees Molly as an important exception: 'She fills the void or presents its opposite aspect because she requires no "reason" for existence, no *raison d'être* beyond her own vital animal drive to stay alive and to be alive' (p 245). French contrasts her with the two protaganists of the novel: 'It is contradictions that are destroying Stephen, while Bloom is spending all his time trying to resolve them. ... Joyce's point in Penelope as well as elsewhere in *Ulysses* is that the unremitting intellect is the cause of much human torment' (pp 249-50). This point of view is congruent with Bergson's that the void is a product of the limited and insecure intellect, that nature and consciousness are both in fact full when man is in tune with process, as Molly is. The full stream of consciousness that Joyce rendered only in her section embodies this process.

I have argued that Stephen's attachment to the logic of Aristotle is a bar to his development as an artist. Applying the ideas that Bruno developed in *The Heroic Frenzies*, I would suggest Stephen has yet to learn that 'the divine truth ... does not submit its arrival to measurements' or to 'the discursive mode one calls argumentation.'[4] And yet Stephen does have the potential, as I insisted in Chapter 1, for an intuitive vision of nature. As we saw in Chapter 5, his mode would be to fuse the two contraries, contemplation and fervor, to kindle what Bruno called 'a rational flame' (p 108). Instead, in 'Circe,' he has tried to pretend he is involved in a feast of reason and has ended by putting out a flame (the gas light). His subsequent experience with Bloom may help him get back in touch with his true nature.

Also in Chapter 5, I argued that Bloom could be seen as, among other things, a type of the divine fool, one of those who 'show a divine sense' and 'speak and do admirable things for which neither they themselves nor anyone else understands the reason' (p 107). An example would be Bloom's unexpectedly standing up to the bigoted citizen in 'Cyclops' and asserting that Christ was a Jew. French points out that when Stephen in 'Ithaca' 'sees Bloom as the "traditional figure of hypostasis",' (*Ulysses* 689), he is seeing a 'figure depicting the two natures of Christ as god and man' (*The Book as World* 228). Like Stephen, Bloom actually has a double nature; consciously he is interested in the physical world and has a fund of information about it. Since, as many readers have noted, what he possesses is often *mis*information, I would de-emphasize this side of Bloom. As Voelker suggests, it is Bloom's 'acceptance, not his knowledge, of Molly as Nature, which brings him to the state of equanimity ... in "Ithaca"' (p 44).

Voelker's contrast of the merely verbal learning of 'Ithaca' to the 'symphonic ... immanence' (p 41) of the Penelope monologue finds a backing in Bruno; however, where Voelker criticizes 'Ithaca' and praises 'Penelope,' Joyce would have followed Bruno in appreciating both modes of understanding, discoursing or being:

> Let the [flesh] feed according to the law of ... the flesh ... the reason according to the law of the reason; let them not be confused or troubled with one another. It suffices that one does not at all alter or prejudice the law of the other. For if it is unjust that the sense outrage the law of reason, it is equally blameable that the reason tyrannize over the law of the senses, inasmuch as the intellect is the greater wanderer and the sense more domestic and as though in its own abode (*The Heroic Frenzies* 135).

Although Molly is not a good housewife, her flesh and senses are domestic, well-ensconced in her abode. Similarly, although I have tried to demonstrate that pure intellect is an inadequate term for both Stephen and Bloom, they are both imaged as great wanderers in the narrator's highly rational dialogue of 'Ithaca.'

Unlike Molly's down-to-earth attitude, the point of view Joyce adopted in 'Ithaca' is cosmic, sometimes confusingly so, sometimes appealingly so, as when Bloom is characterized as a cosmic body: 'Ever he would wander, selfcompelled, to the extreme limit of his cometary orbit ... to the extreme boundary of space, passing from land to land, among peoples, amid events. Somewhere imperceptibly he would hear and somehow reluctantly, suncompelled, obey the summons of recall' (p 728). We could see Bloom as 'suncompelled' in the sense that he returns either to be a sun or to beget a son. When he returns, the paragraph continues, it will be as 'an estranged avenger, a wreaker of justice on malefactors, a dark crusader, a sleeper awakened, with financial resources (by supposition) surpassing those of Rothschild or of the silver king.' The first two of these epithets refer most obviously to Ulysses' slaughter of the suitors. The sleeper awakened is Rip Van Winkle, whom I shall investigate presently. The 'financial resources' with which Bloom will return must be figurative. I shall also follow out this motif, but must first consider Bloom as a 'dark crusader.'

On the page following the foregoing characterization, Bloom blows out his candle. 'What selfevident enigma pondered with desultory constancy during 30 years did Bloom now, having effected natural obscurity by the extinction of artificial light, silently suddenly comprehend? Where was Moses when the candle went out?' (p 729). The light dawns in Bloom's mind when he enters the dark. To put it another way, he learns by doing (not as Stephen by thinking). Bloom's admiration of Moses (a 'seeker ... of the pure truth') was mentioned earlier in the episode (p 687), and even earlier Bloom was compared to Moses in a passage where the conjunction of light and dark was again emphasized. His coincidental naming of the winner of the Gold Cup race is resumed as follows: 'a dark man had placed in his hand a throwaway (subsequently thrown away), advertising Elijah, restorer of the church in Zion'; Bloom had mentioned it to Bantam Lyons and had then 'proceeded towards the oriental edifice of the Turkish and Warm Baths, 11 Leinster street, with the light of inspiration shining in his countenance and bearing in his arms the secret of the race, graven in the language of prediction' (p 676). This description of Bloom is a variation on the earlier oratorical conclusion to Taylor's speech quoted by J.J. O'Molloy: Moses came down from Sinai 'with the light of inspiration shining in his countenance and bearing in his arms the tables of the law, graven in the language of the outlaw' (p 143). Exodus 34: 29 reads: 'When Moses came down from mount Sinai with the two tables of testimony in Moses' hand ... the skin of his face shone.' Taylor's 'tables of the law' (cf. *J.J.* 95) is in the tradition of the 'Mosaic law,' while the 'secret of the race' describing Bloom allows Joyce to refer to the Jews as a race while at the same time by a pun to refer to the Gold Cup.

Joyce is partly making fun of Bloom, but he is also continuing that Brunian notion of the common man who unconsciously embodies truth. Moses similarly was unaware that his face shone with God's reflected light (though he was aware of the less spiritual fact that he bore God's word on social conduct). Exodus emphasized that God is hidden from all but Moses not only by clouds but by 'the thick darkness where God *was*' (pp 20, 21). Bloom is similarly given the truth by 'a dark man.' Bloom himself is a dark man, of course; Molly refers to him as 'a dark man in some perplexity' (p 778). In the Catholic view Bloom as Jew would be connected with the forces of darkness, as comes out in an exchange about him at the end of 'Oxen of the Sun.' 'Whisper, who the sooty hell's the johnny in the black duds? Hush! Sinned against the light and even now that day is at hand when he shall come to judge the world by fire' (p 428). Bloom is of the race that not only sinned against Christ but also will bring forth the Messiah. In fact the ambiguous pronoun reference in this passage allows the possibility of Bloom's being the Messiah. He may thus contain divinity whether he is dark or has a shining countenance.[5]

But such a conclusion is too easy; it is balanced by an opposite quality Bloom is given in 'Ithaca,' one linked more obviously with the style or process by which we receive our information about Bloom. The technique in the episode was listed by Joyce as 'catechism (impersonal),' Joyce's questions and answers are indeed very impersonal. Occasionally instead of a question Joyce simply gives directions, as in this variation on a mathematical problem.

> Reduce Bloom by cross multiplication of reverses of fortune, from which these supports protected him, and by elimination of all positive values to a negligible negative irrational unreal quantity.
>
> Successively, in descending helotic order: Poverty: that of the outdoor hawker of imitation jewellery, the dun for the recovery of bad and doubtful debts, the poor rate and deputy cess collector. Mendicancy: that of the fraudulent bankrupt with negligible assets paying 1s. 4d. in the £, sandwichman, distributor of throwaways, nocturnal vagrant.... (p 725)

The last two terms refer again to the dark man/throwaway incident, but as part of a general pattern of degradation. The key word is the first one in the problem, the verb 'reduce.' The method of the episode is reductive, and by its end Bloom is merely a 'negligible ... unreal quantity,' a black dot on the page. The question which follows the problem quoted above is answered by further reduction until Bloom is 'worth little or nothing or less than nothing' (p 726). It is in this episode that Bloom becomes that 'nonentity ... Noman' (p 727, cf. Chapter 3). The process builds on his own thoughts of decline: 'from existence to nonexistence gone he would be by all as none perceived' (p 668). Just prior to this he has viewed life implicitly as a preparation for death (p 667). The same view reappears later in a broader scientific perspective which can view with equanimity 'the annihilation of the world and consequent extermination of the human species, inevitable but impredictable' (p 680). The feel of this description is somewhat different from Bloom's nostalgic contemplation of dying. Both are removed, but the phrase 'inevitable but impredictable' suggests an impersonality so great as to be superhuman rather than inhumane. Indeed, Joyce's insistence on a cosmic level, a univeral view point in this episode, though it often reduces man, begins finally to have the effect of reconciling him to his physical demise.

Reduction thus turns into sublimation, a word Joyce himself used to characterize the effect he was striving for in the episode (*Letters* I, 164). As he wrote Budgen in 1921,

> I am writing *Ithaca* in the form of a mathematical catechism. All events are resolved into their cosmic, physical, psychical etc. equivalents ... so that the reader will know everything and know it in the baldest and coldest way, but Bloom and Stephen thereby become heavenly bodies, wanderers like the stars at which they gaze. (*Letters* I, 159-60)

Bloom in fact shows 'the various constellations to his companion' Stephen (p 698), including the possibility of the

> influence of celestial on human bodies: the appearance of a star (1st magnitude) of exceeding brilliancy dominating by night and day (a new luminous sun generated by the collision and amalgamation in incandescence of two nonluminous exsuns) about the period of the birth of William Shakespeare over delta in the recumbent neversetting constellation of Cassiopeia. (p 700)

He then adds the appearance of other stars at his own birth, Stephen's, and Rudy's. One way in which Joyce intended to implement his notion that Bloom and Stephen 'became heavenly bodies,' was recorded in his notes on the episode: 'S D & L B a double sun.'[6] We need therefore to look a little more carefully at the 'two nonluminous exsuns' which became 'a new luminous sun' at the birth of Shakespeare. More important, this loss of individual identity also fits in with the relation of father to son. I take the 'amalgamation' of the two 'exsuns' to be a pun, remembering it took place in Shakespeare's time and that Stephen's and Bloom's face merged into Shakespeare's in the mirror in 'Circe.' Similarly, Stephen and Bloom achieve, in their 'nocturnal perambulation to and from the cabman's shelter ... atonement' (p 729). They also reach it for a second as they gaze at each other (p 702). They reach it most sublimely in the heavens, where all is harmonized.

Joyce's concern with the cosmos comes out most directly in a poetic evocation of the night sky as 'the heaventree of stars' (p 698). This image is less mystical than Swedenborg's spiritual vision of heaven, which Joyce had evoked sympathetically in his essay on Blake: 'Eternity ... appeared to the Swedish mystic in the likeness of a heavenly man, animated in all his limbs by a fluid angelic life that forever leaves and re-enters, systole and diastole of love and wisdom' ('William Blake,' *Critical Writings* 221-2). Both Swedenborg's heavenly man and Joyce's heaventree are implicitly rejected by the prosaic Bloom, whose 'logical conclusion' is

> That it was not a heaven tree, not a heavengrot, not a heavenbeast, not a heavenman. That it was a Utopia, there being no known method from the known to the unknown: an infinity renderable equally finite by the suppositious probable apposition of one or more bodies equally of the same and of different magnitudes: a mobility of illusory forms immobilised in space, remobilised in air: a past which possibly had ceased to exist as a present before its future spectators had entered actual present existence. (p 701)

Bloom sees the stars as the astronomer does, light impulses sent out millions of years ago by stars that we can 'see,' even though they may no longer in fact exist. But Bloom's infinity is not quite so different from Swedenborg's as might at first appear.

Mathematics, man's means of grasping the cosmos, allows conclusions more mystic than scientific. For instance, when Bloom remembers a face, the questioner seems to connect 'recurrent impressions' of the face with a mathematical 'hypothesis': 'parallel lines meeting at infinity' (p 730). Similarly, we are shown Bloom as a comet which disappears and then reappears 'reborn above delta in the constellation of Cassiopeia' (p 728). The next question is 'What would render such return irrational?' (p 728). Although neatly answered, the question opens up another area: mathematically speaking, a solution with an irrational number in it is, if not elegant, acceptable. The atonement of Stephen and Bloom is irrational, yet it happens; I believe that part of Joyce's purpose in the episode is to suggest a projection of their mutual attraction until their parallel lines meet at infinity, their two suns fuse into one over delta in Cassiopeia.

I suggested in Chapter 4 that Bloom and Stephen are both involved in Lenehan's riddle. It becomes apparent in this episode (p 695) that Bloom would like Stephen to get close to Molly. Perhaps Molly as the Rose of Castille would be that finite point where the parallel tracks of the two men could come together. Perhaps Bloom is motivated, as Joyce speculates Richard Rowan might be, by the unconscious realization that 'bodily possession' of the female by the other male 'would certainly bring into almost carnal contact the two men,' husband and lover. From this point of view, a parallel action by Stephen and Bloom in the garden is significant.[7] 'At Stephen's suggestion, at Bloom's instigation both, first Stephen, then Bloom, in penumbra urinated, their sides contiguous, their organs of micturition reciprocally rendered invisible by manual circumposition' (p 702). In the next answer we are told that 'the trajectories of their, first sequent, then simultaneous urinations were dissimilar' (p 703), but they are parallel, and if extended to infinity would meet.[8]

Must we conclude then, that Bloom like Richard Rowan is covertly homosexual? Yes and no, I would say. Yes, Bloom is attracted to Stephen, but no, not consciously. Joyce is of course quite conscious of the implications, as we saw in his handling of Stephen's similar problem (in Chapters 7 and 8). He had earlier described Bloom's 'firm full masculine feminine passive active hand' (p 674). This description gives us another side of Bloom as Ulysses – that is, as 'complete man,' a 'full human personality' (Budgen 17,21) and therefore possessing attributes of both sexes. His middle name, 'Paula,' is given in this episode (p 723).

Bloom as masculine actively asserts himself finally with Molly, but she who has valued him mainly for his feminine passive qualities (p 782) must learn to accept this other side of his nature.

As discussed in Chapter 6, Joyce intended *Ulysses* to be 'the epic of the human body' (Budgen 21). But that body can be spiritual as well as physical. As Joyce said to Budgen, 'It's all one' (p 21). In the Ithaca episode this meant that Joyce was humanizing the mystic, by planting Swedenborg's symbolic 'heavenly man' with his 'fluid angelic life' squarely in Dublin in the body of a thirty-eight-year-old ad canvasser. In so doing, he also improved on Blake who, Joyce claimed in 1912, used Swedenborg to kill 'the dragon of experience and natural wisdom, and, by minimizing space and time and by denying the existence of memory and the senses ... tried to paint his work on the void of the divine bosom' (*Critical Writings* 222).

I have discussed Joyce's attraction to and reservations about the void (in the Prologue). His reservation can be inferred in this passage from the other terms present. *Ulysses*, begun the same year this was written, is dedicated to a celebration, not a minimizing or denying of space and time, memory and the senses. Yet if mind and body are one, as Joyce insisted, then it is a matter of perspective and balance which gets emphasis or how they are harmonized.[9] After the eighteenth-century deists had denied the soul, it was necessary for Blake and Swedenborg to affirm it. After Victorian society had denied the body, it was necessary for Freud and Joyce to affirm the senses. But Joyce was trying to harmonize body, mind, and spirit. He could not rest content with either Freud's reductionism or Swedenborg's sublimation. We therefore need to examine Bloom's further reactions to the stars. When he first looks at the constellations above, Bloom also thinks

> of the universe of human serum constellated with red and white bodies, themselves universes of void space constellated with other bodies, each, in continuity, its universe of divisible component bodies of which each was again divisible in divisions of redivisible component bodies, dividends and divisors ever diminishing without actual division till, if the progress were carried far enough, nought nowhere was never reached. (p 699)

Perhaps Joyce is implicitly contrasting Blake's mystic sublimation with Bloom's scientific reductionism, but if we look more closely I think we will find that the two views are quite close. The meeting place is Bruno's material-spiritual philosophy. 'Each of the infinity of great and vast worlds, each of the infinity of lesser worlds, is equally sustained and nourished afresh' (*Infinite Universe* 378).

Looking at Bloom's consciousness, we realize that if nought (zero or nothing) is never reached, we always have something, just as Bergson insisted. The universe is infinite; though man's life is finite, this meditation stresses that he belongs to the infinite life of the universe. It also suggests that no matter how far intellectual 'progress' is carried, certitude is unattainable. Once the artist admits this fact, he will stop taking his intellect and pride as seriously as Stephen tends to do. By insisting on being 'a conscious rational animal preceding syllogistically' in his laudatory journey 'from the known to the unknown' (p 697), Stephen emulates Gulliver in his madness after being brainwashed by the Houyhnhnms. Bloom is much less pretentious in his paralleled affirmation: 'he had proceeded energetically from the unknown to the known through the incertitude of the void' (p 697). He shares Stephen's picture of the universe, but he differs in his approach to it. Since creation encompasses rational knowledge, man in his efforts to understand the universe will always be confronted with mystery. Stephen chooses to puzzle or boast about the void; Bloom treats it as Bergson advocates, like a pseudo-problem. Bloom is energetic, like Ulysses in his attempt to reach home (the known). Partly because he lacks so concrete a goal, Stephen is not energetic. If he were less syllogistic and more active, he would fare better in his journey.

But Stephen still seems to hold by the views he expressed in *A Portrait of the Artist* that 'dramatic emotion' should be static.

> The feelings excited by improper art are kinetic, desire or loathing. Desire urges us to possess, to go to something; loathing urges us to abandon, to go from something. These are kinetic emotions. The arts which excite them, pornographical or didactic, are therefore improper arts. (p 205)

This piece of beautifully rational, conscious knowledge is what separates Stephen from actual people, the real world, and significant creation. As Gilbert pointedly emphasized in his book on *Ulysses*, 'the conflict of deliberate indifference (*stasis*) with the loathing of disgust (*kinesis*) is apparent throughout *Ulysses*. Of this conflict in the mind of Stephen Dedalus the author of *Ulysses* is fully aware' (p 23). In other words, Joyce intends it to be the character's conflict, not his own. Gilbert implied that the Greek terms that Stephen uses are from Aristotle. Arnold Goldman points out that at the beginning of *Ulysses* there is a specific sign of the conflict Gilbert referred to. In the classroom scene, Stephen registers that 'movement' is important because it is, in 'Aristotle's phrase,' 'an actuality of the possible as possible' (p 25). Goldman locates Aristotle's phrase in the *Physics*, and identifies Stephen's word 'movement' as a translation of Aristotle's *kinesis* (Goldman 141). Following Gilbert, Goldman asks, 'Given Stephen's redefined situation, in which both static and kinetic response are brought up short against an existential paradox, is any further development of the subject, in respect of art or of life, either possible or brought to bear in *Ulysses*?' (p 151). His answer, contained in the last fifteen pages of his book, is both stimulating and too involved to trace out here. Instead, I will follow along the path I have been trying to clear.

Briefly, I would suggest that the way out of the paradox of existence is in action, not thought. The creator must choose a possible and by acting on it, make it actual, create a particular work of art. *Kinesis* then is of the *essence* of a work of art as of any other action in life, but *kinesis* should not, as Stephen rightly claims, be the *aim* of a work of art.

Bloom, for instance, is labelled a 'kinetic poet' in 'Ithaca.'[10] His first poem is clearly kinetic in the pejorative sense:

An ambition to squint
At my verses in print
Makes me hope that for these you'll find room.
If you so condescend
Then please place at the end
The name of yours truly, L. Bloom (p 678)

Because his proclaimed aim is selfish desire, his action does not arrest the reader. His second poem is another matter.

Poets oft have sung in rhyme
Of music sweet their praise divine.
Let them hymn it nine times nine.
Dearer far than song or wine,
You are mine. The world is mine. (p 678)

With its acrostic and its last line, this poem is as self-centred as the other. Although technically better (mainly by virtue of its poeticisms), its real success lies in another kinetic quality. Its aim is not to move the reader to a particular action; at the same time, its essence is a celebration of commitment, an actualizing of the possible. As Joyce confirms, by committing himself to Molly, Bloom does gain 'the world,' symbolically (Molly as *Gea*, earth, 737) and concretely (the hemispheres of her rump, p 734).

Joyce includes in 'Ithaca' a further indication that he sees the aesthetic relevance of the kinetic. In his handling of the problem of squaring the circle, Bloom demonstrates an existential solution to that paradox. Joyce mentions that problem twice in the episode (pp 699, 718) and embodies it at least twice more (pp 696, 737). The first reference that we will be concerned with occurs just after Bloom's meditation on 'the universe of human serum.'

In 1886 when occupied with the problem of the quadrature of the circle he had learned of the existence of a number computed to a relative degree of accuracy ... that ... 33 closely printed volumes of 1000 pages each ... would have to be requisitioned in order to contain the complete tale of its printed integers of units, tens, hundreds, thousands, tens of thousands, hundreds of thousands, millions, tens of millions, hundreds of millions, billions, the nucleus of the nebula of every digit of every series containing succinctly the potentiality of being raised to the utmost kinetic elaboration of any power of any of its powers.

(p 699)

This paragraph brings up again the problem we have encountered before in looking at this episode: the daunting effect of knowledge, in this case the difficulty of coping with the mathematical multitudes necessary to 'solving' the problem. But in truth, the problem is insoluble, or as I suggested above, logic and knowledge cannot solve it. Rather than feeling reduced by the prospect of endless numbers, we can take the paragraph in another way. After all, the end of the sentence does say explicitly that 'the nucleus of the nebula of every digit of every series' contains 'succinctly the potentiality of being raised to the utmost kinetic elaboration of any power of any of its powers.' Taking our clue from the word 'tale' earlier in the paragraph, we realize that Joyce has made it possible for us both to admit that we will never know 'the complete tale' of the universe – whether external (stars) or internal (bloodstream) – and to affirm that each of us (a digit in an unending series) contains 'the nucleus [centre of atom] of a nebula [largest astronomical body]' with the potential to be raised to any power we choose.[11]

Admittedly, the passive 'being raised' clouds the all-important fact of human choice and commitment, but if we allow the word 'kinetic' to remind us of Bloom as 'kinetic poet,' active in the world, then the enlarged implication of man's relation to the universe carries over easily from the two previous answers. We should not be surprised, therefore, when a few pages later Bloom registers the sound of Stephen's departure as 'the double reverberation of retreating feet on the heavenborn earth' (p 704). We are faced once again with Bruno's divine nature: as McIntyre phrased the theme of *Cause, Principle and Unity*, it is 'the immanence or spirituality of all causation; the eternity of matter; its divinity as the potentiality of all life; its realisation, in the universe as a whole (as a "formed" thing); the infinite whole and the innumerable parts, as different aspects of the same' (McIntyre 38). These are sublime phrases, but what have they to do with Bloom's experience? In order to appreciate the relevance of squaring the circle, or of the finite reaching the level of infinity, we need to examine the end of 'Ithaca' and Bloom's final transformation.

In beginning, we must remember Joyce's belief in the integration of body and mind. Similarly, just as the kinetic is important in waking life, man also has need of passivity to enjoy his necessary sleeping life. On the last page of the episode, we find Bloom in bed, 'the childman weary, the manchild in the womb. Womb? Weary? He rests. He has traveled. With? Sinbad the Sailor and Tinbad the Tailor and...' (p 737). The list continues with another thirteen variations of the name. *Sinbad* had been mentioned earlier in the episode as a pantomime Bloom wanted to write a song for. Equally important, Sinbad is one of the names given by the narrator of 'Eumaeus' to Murphy the seaman. He is also called Ulysses, Rip Van Winkle, the Ancient Mariner, and so on. Since Stephen had compared Murphy to Shakespeare, claiming 'sounds are impostures ... What's in a name' (p 622), we may take Murphy as an appropriate figure to preside over Bloom's going to sleep; he will be safe in the arms of Murphy or Morpheus (pp 660, 639).

In any case, the list of variations on Sinbad's name leads to dreamland, where daylife associations fade away and nightlife images emerge; the final questions and answers of the episode illustrate this process of transformation.

When?

Going to a dark bed there was a square round Sinbad the Sailor roc's auk's egg in the night of the bed of all the auks of the rocs of Darkinbad the Brightdayler.

Where?

Stanley Sultan claims that the black dot represents the roc's egg connected with Sinbad. This seems to me a good interpretation, but it requires us to go beyond Sultan's further suggestion 'that Sinbad-Bloom in fact has the unattainable roc's egg' (p 414). I read the text to indicate not that Bloom *has* the egg but that he *becomes* the egg.[12] Literally impossible, this metamorphosis is made possible by the obvious regression of language which is intended to suggest Bloom's regressing to sleep. Joyce has already told us that he is the 'manchild in the womb' (an appropriate place for an egg). The list of variations on Sinbad's name is childish, as is the tone and content of the 'going to a dark bed' story. This reverse development, from maturity towards childhood, finally regresses back behind words in the last symbol of the episode, to the embryo as egg.

But a child's story is neither nonsense nor child's play to make out.[13] 'Darkinbad' for instance is the word 'Sinbad' transformed by its similarity to 'dark bed.' But 'the Brightdayler' is quite a different sort of transformation. On one level it is perhaps the self-reassurance of a child in a dark room (that when he opens his eyes after sleep it will be bright morning). On another level though, we come again to a main theme of Bloom's transformation cycle, the relation of darkness to light. Remembering the list of names in the obituary column (from Chapter 3), we can connect Darkinbad with Coleman and Sexton, and Brightdayler with Urbright and with Nurse Callan, who brings children out of the womb.

Sinbad is also connected with diamonds. Set by the roc in a 'valley of diamonds' (*Ulysses* 678, cf. Adams 79), Sinbad managed to escape with a large number of them. This idea of returning with something of value is intimated in the phrase, 'roc's auk's egg,' as we shall see presently. Certainly the diamond is connected with light and with Bloom. One appears on Bloom's hand during his fantasy triumph in 'Circe.' 'Bloom holds up his right hand on which sparkles the Koh-i-Noor diamond' (p 483). Its light-giving qualities are emphasized in other appearances of diamonds. Earlier on the strand Bloom thought, 'Jewels diamonds flash better. Light is a kind of reassuring' (p 376, cf. p 508). These are cut diamonds, of course. In 'Eumaeus,' that opaque character, the sailor Murphy, is appropriately called 'a rough diamond' (p 641). This might remind us that the diamond is an allotropic form of that strange transmutable element, carbon, which also appears as graphite, coal, and lampblack. As coal it can provide heat and light for man, or under great pressure turn into diamond. It suffers no death or life in these transformations, yet it does serve as a model for a natural cycle: in *Ulysses* Joyce adapted it to the most impenetrable of man's transformations, from life to death and back again. During 'Circe,' for instance, we saw Bloom at one point standing 'upright amid phoenix flames' and the next become 'mute, shrunken, carbonised' (pp 498-9). The large period that Bloom becomes at the end of 'Ithaca' can also be taken as a 'shrunken, carbonised' metamorphosis. Clive Hart, at least, sees this 'dot' as representing 'the microcosmic counterpart of the chapter's macrocosmic level. Bloom has literally been reduced to a tiny smudge of carbon. "Here is Bloom," says Joyce, in answer to our question. "Ultimately he is no more than printer's ink on my page." Thus, finally, is the Flesh made Word.'[14] Such a conclusion may seem overtaxed at first sight, but it is supported by a sentence I discussed in Chapter 3, Joyce's comment on the obituary list. 'Inked characters fast fading on the frayed breaking paper' (p 91). The pun on 'characters' alerts us to see the same process happening to the deceased in human memories as to the letters on the page. But we must equally emphasize the potential life in the particular black speck that Bloom has become. His retreat into sleep is a kind of death, but of his choosing, for the purpose of life. As Bruno characterized this process:

> By birth and growth the spirit-architect expands into this mass of which we consist, spreading outwards from the heart. Thither again it withdraws, winding up the threads of its web, retiring by the same path along which it advanced, passing out by the same gate through which it entered. Birth is expansion of the centre, life consistency of the sphere, death contraction to the centre. (*De Minimo*, translated by McIntyre 312)

And death is, as we have seen, an illusion from the cosmic point of view. More practically, the terms we are dealing with are sleeping and waking, but the same expansion-contraction process holds there too.

Several times in *Ulysses*, Joyce used a period or dot as a focal point. As Richard Madtes has documented, Joyce wrote the French printer of *Ulysses* that he wanted '*un point bien visible*' at the end of 'Ithaca.'[15] The word 'point' is of course commonly used in England for the North American 'period.' We may therefore take it that some of Joyce's uses of the word 'point' in Ulysses will have this overtone.[16] Thus Stephen without his glasses on the beach is startled when 'a point, live dog drew into sight running across the sweep of sand. Lord, is he going to attack me?' (p 45). Remembering that Dog can be properly understood as another form of God, I would take Stephen's use of 'Lord' here as unintentionally evocative. Life, animal or spiritual, materializes out of nowhere, a point in time and space, just as we have seen Bloom compressed to such a point.[17]

Bruno provides us with another way of approaching Joyce's intent here. He wrote often on the problem of boundaries: what is the smallest unit in the cosmos? how can it be circumscribed? These questions were explored and laid out by McIntyre. He noted that Bruno came to the same kind of conclusion here that he had in related problems: 'the minimum in each sphere of being contains implicitly in itself the whole reality of that sphere' (p 231). This seems to me exactly parallel to Bloom's 'nucleus ... containing succinctly the potentiality of being raised to the utmost ... power' (p 699). As Bruno put it in his Latin work, *De Mimimo*, 'The immeasurable universe is nothing but centre everywhere; eternity nothing but a moment always; immeasurable body but an atom; immeasurable plane a point; immeasurable space the receptacle of a point or atom.'[18] Bloom's reduction to a point is thus no contradiction of his cometary path or line, nor of the shape in which we are accustomed to 'know' the universal energy, the human body. As Bruno suggests in emphasizing that the universe is really undifferentiated: 'no part is greater and no part is lesser. ...You do not come any nearer to proportion, likeness, union, and identity with the infinite by being a man than by being an ant, by being a star than by being a man. And so in the infinite these things are indifferent' (McIntyre 136). Clearly in 'Ithaca' Joyce has lived up to Stephen's early dictum that the artist as creator should be indifferent. But the point of view Joyce adopted for 'Ithaca' was possible only after a prolonged immersion in the trials of Bloom. By the end of the day, Bloom himself is all but indifferent, his feelings about Molly's adultery being mainly abnegation and equanimity (p 733), a state justified finally by 'the apathy of the stars' (p 734).

But to leave it at apathy and indifference is to distort the philosophy of Bruno and the attitude of Joyce. In *Cause, Principle and Unity*, Bruno shows how lack of differentiation in the universe gives freedom and value to man: 'If point does not differ from body, centre from circumference, finite from infinite, maximum from minimum, we can securely declare that the universe is all centre, or that the Universe's centre is everywhere' (p 137). If the centre is everywhere, the divine is discoverable in nature; or to change the emphasis, as Bruno does in another Italian dialogue, 'It is not possible to understand supernatural things, except through their shining in natural things.'[19] We are returned again to the shining countenance of that dark man, Bloom (or Moses or Christus).

In thus summing up the universal themes of 'Ithaca,' we need to consider how Bloom's final transformation also represents the squaring of the circle. Sultan suggests that he achieves this feat by becoming a 'square round' egg. We might wonder how an elliptical egg can be square and round. It cannot, but if we step back from the passage, remembering the fuzzy associative development, we can see that Bloom is in bed (which, as a rectangle, is close to square) and that he is curling up as for the womb, regressing towards the egg state, as rendered in the final point (which, as a circle, is close to an egg ellipse). From this point of view, Bloom is successful through passivity.

From another point of view, Bloom succeeds in squaring the circle by being an active world traveler. Like the mariner Pseudangelos, Bloom has 'circumnavigated a bit,' and may be said to have 'boxed the compass on the strict q.t.' (pp 625, 626). When we apply these last two actions to a letter in which Joyce outlined his conception of Molly's soliloquy, we get more out of 'boxing the compass' than merely 'squaring the round.'

> There are eight sentences in the [Penelope] episode. It begins and ends with the female word *yes*. It turns like the huge earth ball slowly surely and evenly, round and round spinning, its 4 cardinal points being the female breasts, arse, womb and cunt expressed by the words *because, bottom* (in all uses bottom button, bottom of the class, bottom of the sea, bottom of his heart), *woman, yes*. (*J.J.* 516)

We may say of Bloom that, like all men, he has come from the womb, sucked on the breasts, and penetrated the cunt; he has for some time, Molly complains, been kissing her arse (p 739). The latter being the seat of dead matter (in contrast to the other three), Bloom's worship of Molly's buttocks indicates his having moved out of the life process, though not out of nature's cycle. Like the mariner Murphy, Bloom has touched bottom, the 'bottom of the sea' as the letter suggests, and can now return back to the womb as Darkinbad, to be reborn in the morning as the Brightdayler, fed by his wife-mother, later to penetrate her and, he hopes, beget himself a new sun.

Remembering that Molly is Gea as well as 'the huge earth ball,' we may connect Joyce's concern with Bruno's insistence on a similar metaphor in *The Infinite Universe*. Speaking of the unfolding of 'divine incorporeal perfection' through the 'corporeal mode,' Bruno pictures an animated cosmos: 'there must be innumerable individuals, those great animals, whereof one is our earth, the divine mother who hath given birth to us, doth nourish us and moreover will receive us back' (p 257). Bruno later pictures earth or heaven as a womb where nourishment, growth, and change can occur (pp 322-3, 361-2, cf. p 317). As cosmologist, Bruno tended to emphasize more the divinity in the animal; Joyce, coming from his strong early views of woman as animal, manages to blend it with the goddess image in 'Ithaca.'[20]

But we must still scrutinize what Bloom brings back from the bottom. His fortune is certainly figurative. Of returned adventures, Ulysses brought back gold, Sinbad, as we have seen, diamonds. Investigating Joyce's phrase, 'roc's auk's egg,' two scholars have found value or rarity attributed to the auk's egg.[21] During the library scene, for instance, after Mr Best makes a suggestion, we are told 'felicituously he ceased and held a meek head among them auk's egg, prize of their fray' (p 196). Earlier, a variation of this image had been applied to A.E. (George Russell). '– People do not know how dangerous lovesongs can be, the auric egg of Russell warned occulty' (p 186). In addition to the poet's pseudonym (A.E.) forming the anagram for the image, we might note that an auric (golden) egg is both materially and immaterially valuable. In view of the way Joyce associated Russell's occultism with Indian religions (pp 191-2), it is fair to turn to the most well-known exponent of the subject at the turn of the century. Expounding a Brahman creation myth, Madame Blavatsky wrote, 'At the beginning of each Mahamanvatara' Brahma lays 'a "Golden Egg." It typifies the great Circle of O, itself a symbol for the universe.'[22] The 'great Circle O' of the universe is parallel not only with Bloom as egg but with Joyce's explication of Molly's symbolism: 'the huge earth ball.' The more important parallel to Bloom's voyage becomes clear when we read Madame Blavatsky's evocation of the end of Brahma's cycle: 'Brahma merges back into Dayus, the Unrevealed God and, his task being accomplished, he falls asleep. Another day is passed, night sets in, and continues until the future dawn. And now again he re-enters the golden egg of His Thought, the germs of all that exist ... this Soul of all beings sleeps in complete repose till the day when it resumes its form, and awakes again from its primitive darkness' (I 376-7). In an early essay, Joyce himself referred to 'the ancient gods who ... die and come to life many times,' concluding that 'the miracle of light is renewed eternally in the imaginative soul' (*Critical Writings* 82-3). Regression leads to rebirth, dark to light, reduction to sublimation in a continually repeated cycle.

Similarly, excrement contains the seeds of life. Seen rightly, the deadest matter still contains the potential of life. One may, of course, choose to deny that life, and 'the miracle of light' within, as Stephen does when he reacts to the notion of his mother as beastly dead, or as Molly does when she acts as though sex were only a beastly life. Stephen is fascinated by the live dog inspecting the dog carcass on the strand, and thinks, 'moves to one great goal' (p 46). He means that the dog's life moves towards the goal of death. But he is using an earlier sententious comment by Deasy: 'All history moves towards one great goal, the manifestation of God' (p 34). Fearing God, Stephen connects him with death, either in the dog carcass or in the apocalypse he brings on himself in 'Circe.' But however Stephen twists it, whatever Deasy meant by his comment, it can still be understood in the Brunian sense which Joyce used throughout *Ulysses*.

The meaning of dog may be perverted until it stands for death or for life as a merely physical activity, but even a dog will still contain God, and a man will contain within the spark of the divine, an atom which is his centre, just as his physical body grew from a cell. Man finds himself in space which, as Bruno directly and Joyce indirectly affirm, is merely the receptacle of that atom; geographically this means that wherever man is located, that place contains the point on which he can focus, the point that then becomes the centre of the universe.

Bloom has energetically voyaged through space and time to the bed at the end of 'Ithaca,' where he can passively and confidently regress to a new point, a nucleus from which his life will be able to begin anew. His realism and his optimism, his receptivity and his insistence, his activity and passivity allow him this opportunity, but not because he is merely a common dog and certainly not because he is an intellectually superior human being. The opportunity comes because he can love and help another, because he has allowed his voyage to carry him to a confrontation with his own weaknesses and then to the discovery of a hidden self, the spark that was never smothered by the accidents of the world. 'The secret of the race' that was reflected in 'the light of inspiration' on Bloom's countenance earlier in 'Ithaca' includes a joke about his inadvertent tip on the horse race, a reference to his possible descent, as a Jew, from the Moses who originally passed on the divine light as a secret to his dark race, and a more general reference to the race of mankind which can find in literature (eg, Exodus) that affirmation of the human spirit to which Joyce devoted his artistic life. Stephen's insistence on this affirmation is correct but too narrow; Bloom's tacit dissent is also correct if it is based on scepticism of the word 'eternal' with which Stephen modifies 'affirmation.' Bloom knows what Stephen has not quite pulled together, that all forms pass, that an individual must experience the spirit within before he can affirm it, and that the spark may be found in all kinds of life, not just in a few superior artists.

But that affirmation finally has strength only if it faces the darkness of all that man has denied. That darkness will threaten the man who identifies it with death. On the other hand, it can solace the man who sees it as an opportunity. If man's knowledge can never penetrate darkness completely, then his will and energy become central, leaving him free to affirm his being. Despite all the conditioning he may have received from his particular environment, his vital spark is unconditioned; if he makes it the centre of his being, he may be reborn from that point of focus with full scope to use his faculties, with full confidence that the environment around will provide them with the material they need to bring everything into relation. Having come to this realization in the course of writing *Ulysses*, Joyce proceeded to act as though it were true (with the limitation discused in Chapter 8) and to fashion this conception into the even more thoroughly embodied vision of *Finnegans Wake*.

12 A great joker at the universe

In this chapter I propose to connect the thematic implications of 'Ithaca' first with the form in which Joyce cast that episode and then with his general artistic stance. Most critics have been willing to accept the question and answer form of 'Ithaca' as the balance Joyce sought between reduction and sublimation. Hayman suggests that despite Joyce's 'mask of perverse objectivity,' this episode is perhaps 'the warmest of them all' because we see 'Bloom and Stephen in conjunction' and are shown their 'similarities and differences in sharp, humorous, and human relief' (*Ulysses: The Mechanics of Meaning* 87). Although there is some truth in this position, we need to see the more straightforward effect of Joyce's technique, too. I argued in the last chapter that the universal perspective at once dwarfs man and shows him to have all the power of God. This suggestion needs further scrutiny.

From an aesthetic point of view it is as though Joyce in maturity decided to achieve via mundane naturalism what he had boasted of in his subjective, occult-yearning youth. In his university paper on 'Drama and Life' (1900), for instance, Joyce had insisted with theoretical coldness that 'drama has to do with the underlying laws first, in all their nakedness and divine severity, and only secondarily with the motley agents who bear them out' (*Critical Writing* 40). Unsympathetic though we may find this formulation, it does read like the premise on which 'Ithaca' is constructed, with the proviso that the later Joyce affirms the divine laws by indirection and the 'motley agents' through comedy. A similar early view is embodied in *Stephen Hero*, where Joyce criticizes his title character at university as a young and 'fantastic idealist.'[1] In a long and important peroration, he paraphrases the position of that cosmic seeker:

> The poet is the intense centre of the life of his age to which he stands in a relation than which none can be more vital. He alone is capable of absorbing in himself the life that

surrounds him and of flinging it abroad again amid planetary music. When the poetic phenomenon is signalled in the heavens, exclaimed this heaven-ascending essayist, it is time for the critics to verify their calculations in accordance with it. It is time for them to acknowledge that here the imagination has contemplated intensely the truth of the being of the visible world and that beauty, the splendour of truth, has been born. The age, though it bury itself fathoms deep in formulas and machinery, has need of these realities which alone give and sustain life and it must await from those chosen centres of vivification the force to live, the security for life which can come to it only from them. Thus the spirit of man makes a continual affirmation. (p 80)

The relevance of this passage to 'Ithaca' is indicated by Joyce's use of the last sentence above at the very beginning of the episode: 'Bloom dissented tacitly from Stephen's views on the eternal affirmation of the spirit of man in literature' (p 666). Bloom's reasons for dissent are not given and may be short-sighted, but he himself represents the necessary element to modify Stephen's views towards a less cosmic, more humane, and therefore more viable view of narrative art.

Stephen's phrase 'eternal affirmation' is a little grandiose, as was the 'heaven-ascending essayist's' insistence on 'the splendor of truth' in *Stephen Hero*. Neither truth nor affirmation is so easy to procure and purvey authentically as the young artist seems to think. It is not that Stephen's aspiration is wrong, any more than is the perception of Stephen Dedalus in *A Portrait of the Artist*.

The equation on the page of his scribbler began to spread out a widening tail, eyed and starred like a peacock's; and, when the eyes and stars of its indices had been eliminated, began slowly to fold itself together again. The indices appearing and disappearing were eyes opening and closing; the eyes opening and closing were stars being born and being quenched. The vast cycle of starry life bore his weary mind outward to its verge and inward to its centre. (pp 102-3)

This very Brunian vision of the 'vast cycle of starry life' is noble and figuratively true. The way in which maximum and minimum, macrocosm and microcosm become one is like Bloom's perception of stars, bloodstream, and numbers in 'Ithaca,' just as Bloom's going to sleep is anticipated in Stephen's 'weary mind' being born 'outward to its verge and inward to its centre.' But Stephen's linking of numbers, eyes, and stars is too subjective, too isolated, too lyric. His conception needs to be tested in contact with the actual – not the carnal knowledge of prostitutes but an emotional contact with a woman.

Joyce's point in *Ulysses* as a whole is that man must submerge himself in the darkness of the world, know its and his own vices and desires, and be purged before he can ascend to the light. And because it is a cyclic process, man can rest neither in light nor in darkness for long. In 'Ithaca' this submerging is aimed more directly at the reader than it was in 'Circe.' The reader is inundated with facts about water, its general properties and particular route to Dublin, about coal, about the books and knick-knacks, furniture and food in Bloom's home; then he is immersed in mathematical abstractions and projections about Bloom's age in relation to Stephen's, before being plunged into similar facts and figures about the constellations. From the latter there begins to emerge that 'truth of the being of the visible world,' about which the idealistic essayist was so sure; it emerges ambivalently, however, not from direct affirmation but tangentially from an almost crushing sense of isolation and minuteness. Joyce does offer us 'planetary music' in 'Ithaca,' but not in simple lyrics, rather in equivocal rhythms and meanings. A good example is the passage examined in the last chapter in which Bloom meditates on

> the universe of human serum constellated with red and white bodies, themselves universes of void space constellated with other bodies, each, in continuity, its universe of divisible component bodies of which each was again divisible in divisions of redivisible component bodies, dividends and divisors ever diminishing without actual division till, if the progress were carried far enough, nought nowhere was never reached. (p 699)

The universe is within, and the sub-universe turns out to be infinitely divisible, so that no matter how far we take it we never reach nothing. Joyce's verbal music is pronounced, in the elaborate syntax which carries the series on, in the repetition with variation which grows into an alliterative poetic pattern. Yet the basic language is abstract, almost completely removed from the concrete image we expect in a lyric or a novel.

Joyce's most poetic passage in 'Ithaca' is the lush description of Bloom's pleasure in kissing Molly's buttocks. This passage is introduced by another about the earth which contains more imagery than the cosmic passage given above. Bloom feels

> satisfaction at the ubiquity in eastern and western terrestrial hemispheres, in all habitable lands and islands explored or unexplored (the land of the midnight sun, the islands of the blessed, the isles of Greece, the land of promise) of adipose posterior female hemispheres, redolent of milk and honey and of excretory sanguine and seminal warmth, reminiscent of secular families of curves of amplitude, insusceptible of moods of impression or of contrarieties of expression, expressive of mute immutable mature animality. (p 734)

This music is less of the spheres and more of the solar system, with its heated nourishment. In a phrase like 'excretory sanguine and seminal warmth,' the abstract language insulates us from our civilized revulsion at the substances referred to, while the rhythm and the sound sequence lull us into a dreamy acceptance. The end of the sentence uses alliteration and assonance in a manner similar to the cosmic passage above.[2]

The next sentence is shorter and less covertly poetic. 'He kissed the plump mellow yellow smellow melons of her rump, on each plump melonous hemisphere, in their mellow yellow furrow, with obscure prolonged provocative melonsmelonous osculation' (pp 734-5). Rhyme, which was minimal in the previous sentence, is pronounced in this one. The increased abstraction of the language with which this sentence ends, like the other two, is mitigated by the onomatopoeia, which causes our mouths to imitate the action of Bloom's mouth. Some readers react to this vicarious sensuality with revulsion.[3]

On one level Bloom's appreciation of Molly's buttocks may be taken as his appreciation of the earth which sustains his natural body. By virtue of his commitment to her and it, and the energy he has poured into it, we could say he is engaged with the universe in a way Stephen is not. Bloom stands as a paradigm of the 'kinetic poet,' not as a direct model for Stephen as artist, but as an example of a man unconsciously engaged in the processes of the universe. If Stephen could give up his proud intellect and plunge into the various universes around him, he too would find a place in the natural and cosmic cycle. Rather than having to force circumstances to move his way, as Joyce did unsuccessfully for so long with the publication of *Dubliners*, he could focus on his commitment, on actualizing the artistic possible, and he would then find the universe bumping him up against the right circumstances, as Joyce did beginning with the publication of *A Portrait of the Artist* (cf. *J.J.* 360-5). Rationally, the universe is too large and complicated to be understood. Mysteriously, however, it offers the necessary power to him who commits himself. Aesthetically, it also offers the materials for beauty in the sense that Joyce early discerned, arising from pleasure gained in 'the activity of recognition' ('Pola Notebook,' *Workshop* 82).

In the two sentences describing Molly's bottom, Joyce offers the reader an opportunity to regress to infantile pleasure, not by robust comedy as in 'Circe,' but by a kind of humourous sublimation in which long latinate words are substituted for Anglo-Saxon monosyllables. The sensual pleasure of 'female hemispheres, redolent of milk and honey' reminds us of the mother's breasts, from which we were reluctantly weaned. When we register that these are 'posterior' hemispheres, we are taken into the actively forbidden territory of 'excretory sanguine and seminal warmth.' Wet warmth we can remember as Stephen experienced it by urinating in his bed at the beginning of *A Portrait of the Artist*. But the smells and texture associated with 'excretory sanguine and seminal' would (if rendered in images) take us into more powerful taboo areas than urine. So when Joyce renders the hothouse of the female anal cleft, instead of visual or olfactory images, he used repetitious sound patterns. The effect of the words is sensuous, with only one word, 'rump,' having a sensual meaning. The super-ego may thus not feel obliged to condemn our regression.

More clearly at the end of the episode, the regression of Bloom's mind towards sleep suffers no impediment from the super-ego because there is no taboo material present and because the stage is so obviously set for sleep, the one natural form of regression which we all allow ourselves. The child's nonsense variations on the formula 'Sinbad the Sailor' lead naturally to the little story already analysed: 'Going to a dark bed there was a square round Sinbad the Sailor roc's awk's egg in the night of the bed of all the auks of the rocs of Darkinbad the Brightdayler' (p 737). Sleep as darkness or unconsciousness calls us, and we give in knowing that the sun will rise, that light comes out of dark, that Bloom is really god because the divine spark lies at the centre of each man, ready if allowed to be 'raised to the utmost kinetic elaboration of any power of any of its powers' (p 699).

In both its ending and its general form, then, we could call the Ithaca episode a divine comedy. The effects of such comedy can be better appreciated by contrast with the animal impulses from which the comic springs. As Freud demonstrated, a smile signals hostility, although at the same time it replaces the acting out of a destructive impulse of which the smiler may be unaware. Similarly, what we call 'nervous laughter' releases the emotion of fear in disguised form. As Kris suggests, 'what was feared yesterday is fated to appear funny when seen today' (p 213). Society may agree that a previously fearful figure (the devil is Kris's example) is no longer to be considered so; then public licence must be given to what still remains a private fear. Previously potent and now dormant, the fear still exists (part of the Oedipal problem in Freud's scheme) as energy to be discharged.

This brings us to the highest form of laughter, as an accompaniment of insight, the actual shedding of a fear, the pleasure of relief in realizing that the seeming complexities of life are in fact quite simple, not to say absurd. As Freud recorded, when his patients were close to an insight about some unconscious mechanism, they were 'regularly in the habit of confirming the fact by a laugh' if he 'succeeded in giving a faithful picture' of it to them (*Jokes and Their Relation to the Unconscious* 170). When pressed to admit that it is a smile of recognition and release, such a person will often allow himself to feel it as such. Joyce clearly knew the phenomenon, since he has Stephen use the effect (laughter) in an attempt to achieve the cause (release): 'He laughed to free his mind from his mind's bondage' (p 212). Joyce himself, despite the bondage of his own mind, despite his troubles with his eyesight and his daughter, was able to keep in touch with the unattached self which sees unresolved complexities finally coalescing in a point, contraries coinciding in the simplest way.

This point of view, which Yeats celebrated as 'gaiety' in 'Lapis Lazuli,' which recently has been called absurd, can be found in most great works of art, from which one could argue that 'great' artists verify Keats's emphasis on negative capability. As I suggested in Chapter 7 the ability of the artist not to be fretfully striving after certainty, his ability not to be attached to what he records is aptly correlated by Frederick Crews with the unconditioned ego, or what I have called the self.

The humour of the Ithaca episode is clearly based on the absurd, on reducing all to nothing in a way that has caused one critic to suggest that *Ulysses* presents 'a hollow world.'[4] But we have already seen that the paradoxical effect of this reduction is to make possible a final affirmation. Similarly, Bloom as Noman is reduced at the end of the episode to almost nothing, a smudge of carbon which carries the crystalline potential of diamond in it. Our smile at the end of the episode implicitly includes not only pleasure in regression to sleep but a greater freedom in letting go all the daytime tension by which we hold on to our pride, our passions, our hates, and the other ego attachments.

Sleep is of course only a metaphor for the process of letting go. It could be argued that Bloom began to do so while still awake: as he lay in bed he finally faced his future with Molly. Since he had already in 'Circe' looked at his own complicity in her adultery, we could take his acceptance in 'Ithaca' not as weakness but as closer to the truth that jealousy is legitimately absurd. (Clinically, jealousy is a sexual feeling, a substitute for straightforward sexual desire.) Bloom's kissing Molly's buttocks could then be viewed as a triumph over the super-ego in an act of polymorphous perversity. To Joyce it may also have indicated Bloom's acceptance of the unity of body and mind. I must confess, however, that to me it appears a symptom of Bloom's continuing inability to act the biological role of the adult male. Since Bloom knows Molly has shortly before committed adultery, the act is all the more symptomatic. Whatever it is in itself, it is also, as I indicated in the last chapter, one stage in a cycle. When Bloom joins Sinbad the Sailor, he moves beyond the need to overcome resistance or lapse into carnal substitutes; he undertakes the deep voyage of discovery which can result in the finding and becoming of the treasure long lost.

Bloom's sublime reduction raises the end of the episode to a divine comedy. Whereas in a tragedy human pride is matched with a desire to suffer at the hands of stern-eyed gods, in a comedy man reduces himself to escape the ire of the gods. But in its most positive form, this reduction does more than disarm the threat: man is able to join in the laughter of the gods, releasing with impunity the sublime within. Insofar as the reader is with Bloom, his experience does approach the highest form of comedy. But insofar as the actual constructed form of 'Ithaca' is Joyce's, the reader is also subjected to another, not necessarily incompatible form of comedy.

A case could easily be made that in his way of ending 'Ithaca' Joyce makes sure that 'the artistic process is like the natural process' ('Paris Notebook,' *Workshop* 54). Such a case can also be made for 'Eumaeus' and 'Penelope.' But it cannot be made very easily for the bulk of 'Ithaca.' First of all, a catechism is a formal and, in this case, impersonal process. Second, the questions are often quite arbitrary and artificial, and the answers equally incongruous. We could say that Joyce has purposefully picked a rational human process and often intends to contrast it with the natural process. Without discounting some satiric intent, I prefer to follow another avenue for my final consideration of Joyce's art in this episode.

In Chapter 5 we looked at Bruno's distinction between two types of men inspired by the divine. One type, the divine fool, I compared to Bloom. Although he is 'void of any spirit and sense,' into this person 'as in a room which has been scoured, [can be] introduced a divine sense' (*Heroic Frenzies* 107). Reduction to nothing allows the divine to break through, a view equally applicable to Bloom's experience in this episode and to the reader's. As shown in Chapter 2, Dionysius would have provided Joyce with an appealing vision of that complete emptiness or openness which is one way of allowing the divine to enter.

> His incomprehensible presence ... plunges the true initiate into the Darkness of Unknowing wherein he renounces all the apprehensions of his understanding and is enwrapped in that which is wholly intangible and invisible ... being through the passive stillness of all his reasoning powers united by his highest faculty to Him that is wholly Unknowable, of whom thus by a rejection of all knowledge he possesses a knowledge that exceeds his understanding. (*Mystical Theology* 194)

Bloom's knowledge has substituted for his understanding in various parts of *Ulysses*, but towards the end of 'Ithaca' in 'passive stillness' he moves beyond mundane knowledge, the fool moving towards the divine.

The reminiscences of Jacques Mercanton contain several anecdotes which show Joyce taking on the role of fool or clown. For instance, just before speaking of the 'idiotic' nature of the universe, Joyce mimed with 'body lopsided, mouth open.' Then he asserted, 'I am nothing but an Irish clown ... a great joker at the universe' (p 728). This was in the thirties, but as I have insisted before, it is true of his view of himself as the creator of *Ulysses*. Kris would see such a stance connected with 'the comic as a mechanism of defense. ... the strongest incentive to playing the fool is exhibitionism' (p 215). The exhibitionism is defensive because it draws attention to the fool's harmlessness. Since, however, defensiveness and aggressiveness so often go together, we may anticipate the appearance of another side of this fool or clown. Beginning most obviously with 'Cyclops,' Joyce shows clearly as a joker or trickster, with his mocking asides which make fun of the narrator. This aggressive humour puzzles, befuddles, and irritates the reader; yet we have no choice but to suffer and enjoy the buffoonery and antics of this trickster demiurge. Joyce with his mouth hanging open may remind us, in fact, of the hydrocephalic Hobgoblin with the lipless face in 'Circe.' I would suggest there is a Freudian identity behind the seeming contrast between Joyce's loose, unthreatening mime and the tense destructiveness of the Hobgoblin.

Lee Byron Jennings, in his book on the grotesque, makes some helpful points about the effect on the reader of a creature like the Hobgoblin.

> The sight of a radically deformed person calls forth a peculiar kind of fear; it is not a rational fear inspired by the presence of a real danger, but something more profound and more primitive than the fear of wild beasts or strangers....
>
> But the sight of a deformed person also arouses another feeling, almost as primitive ... the feeling of amusement. ... The comic urge ... approaches the coarse laughter aroused by the vulgar, bestial, and cruel and the guilty pleasure with which morbid or obscene things may sometimes be regarded. (*The Ludicrous Demon* 11)

As Steig suggests, 'the comic ... lessens the threat of identification' with the threatening grotesque ('Defining the Grotesque' 259). But Jennings is correct in emphasizing that there is 'a basic interaction of' fear and amusement in many grotesque creatures. 'In the gargoyles of the Gothic cathedrals,' for instance, 'the great profusion of claws, beaks, horns, and so on, serves as much to diminish the elemental menace of the figure as to emphasize it, and the characteristic bestial leer of the face expresses idiotic clownishness as well as demonic malevolence' (p 14). The reader experiences a shifting focus or emphasis between these two in his response to Joyce's deaf mute at the beginning of 'Circe' and the Hobgoblin later in that episode. A similar shifting balance can be found in Joyce as artist. As we have already seen, the roles of clown and demon both attracted him. As clown, the artist seduces an audience; as demon, he frightens it. But both figures hint at the inadequacy of consciously accepted reason, laws, norms. Both suggest irrational forces which by threatening or cajoling demand recognition. Both figures exercise a power over the viewer or reader. The fool can amuse us by degrading himself or authority, but as clown he can also act as an authority and mock or degrade us, without our admitting it to ourselves, since it is all in fun and for the sake of laughter.

In the mock prayer that Joyce sent his brother in 1905, addressed to the 'Vague Something behind Everything' and complaining of his situation, he said, 'Whoever the hell you are, I inform you that this is a poor comedy you expect me to play and I'm damned to hell if I'll play it' (*Letters* II, 110). As I suggested in Chapter 8, Joyce must have seen that only by agreeing to play his part in the poor comedy of life could he turn his difficulties into success. The high-minded way of meeting the inevitable adversities of an imperfect universe lies in creating a more beautiful, more articulated universe. But that artistic creation can have depth only if it engages the hidden truths of the natural creation. The more he opens himself to that creative darkness, the more the artist realizes that his pride hides a perverseness, that the sins of temporal authority have common roots in the individual's own narrowness, that in fact it is the individual's blaming temporal restrictions that binds him in time and blinds him to universal light. Joyce, the rebel against institutions such as the church and marriage, contained within him an authority that desired to make others suffer as he had suffered from the restrictions of authority. The young boy who 'punished' his brothers and sisters by acting the role of the devil (*J.J.* 26) contained in embryo the artist who acts as an authority by making the reader go through his catechism in the Ithaca episode of *Ulysses*.

I am assuming here the presence of psychological ambivalence in Joyce. He fears the devil and imitates him (just as he feared thunder and made it the voice of God in both *Ulysses* and *Finnegans Wake*). He desires to free himself and his reader of these fears, but he believes that he risks destruction to do so. Even Leopold Bloom believes that 'catastrophic cataclysms have made terror the basis of human mentality' (p 697). In seeking to take on God's role to undo God's work and then to create anew, Joyce had to insulate himself against God's wrath towards all usurpers by acting like one who does not threaten, the fool or clown. But it takes a manipulating trickster to carry off this deception. He must therefore contain some of the duplicity and selfish desire that characterize the temporal authorities he also despises.

This ambivalence is more clearly visible in Joyce's pacifism. He moved to Zürich to escape the war, out of a hatred of violence. He admired Odysseus as 'a war dodger' (Budgen 16) and disliked the military, as we saw in Chapter 8. But the other side of this genuine pacifism was a fascination with military idioms which reveals an underlying tension. When critical reservations began to develop about the naturalness and accuracy of his rendering of the mind's stream of consciousness in *Ulysses*, Joyce commented, 'It hardly matters whether the technique is "veracious" or not; it has served me as a bridge over which to march my eighteen episodes, and, once I have got my troops across, the opposing forces can, for all I care, blow the bridge skyhigh.'[5] He applied the same motif of military pragmatism in a more sympathetic manner to his use of words. According to Budgen, Joyce believed 'they have a will and life of their own and are not to be put like lead soldiers, but to be energised and persuaded like soldiers of flesh and blood' (p 175). The implication is plain: Joyce's picture of himself as artist is of a general fighting a war against a hostile world.

Planning an English edition of *Ulysses* in 1934, Joyce wrote Harriet Weaver that pressure on the publisher had resulted in a promise to go ahead despite fears of legal prosecution. He concluded, 'I trust that the slow but steady advance of our depleted forces in this sector meets with Your Highness's approval' (*Letters* I, 349). Miss Weaver, as the good patron and undemanding empress of letters, enjoyed Joyce's allegiance and could command his life in a way no actual British monarch could. Stephen thinks of Queen Victoria as an ogre with yellow teeth (*Ulysses* 43); King Edward we saw masquerading as a peace-lover but emerging as bloodthirsty in 'Circe' (cf. Chapter 3); and King George's Zürich consul-general, Bennett, tried to force Joyce to enlist in 1918 (*J.J.* 455). When an English edition of *Ulysses* finally appeared in 1936, Joyce told one friend, 'I have been fighting for this for twenty years,' and said to another, 'Now the war between England and me is over, and I am the conquerer' (*J.J.* 705). As I suggested earlier, Joyce's pacifisim must have rested in part on an ego-defence against a very strong urge to violence.

This psychic ambivalence is evident in Joyce's choice of form for 'Ithaca.' To get an aesthetic perspective on that choice, we might note Ernst Kris's suggestion that in the arts, unlike the sciences, a given 'problem may be solved (and indeed, even formulated) in a wide variety of ways' (p 252). But there are artistic conventions too, and if they dominate a given art at a given time, rigid conventions will tend to carry it back

> from art to ritual. In ritual, form and content are strictly patterned, and repeated again and again with minimal deviation, on pain of losing the ritualistic efficacy. The ritualistic act is one of *participation* rather than creation: the response which the members of the group are required or expected to have is rigidly limited. (p 253)

The responses of the mass or to the catechism are examples of what Kris means. Joyce uses the latter in 'Ithaca,' though not for any mindless ritual purpose. It is ostensibly a scientific catechism which at the same time includes, as I have emphasized, the basis of a religious view of the universe. We might say that Joyce mocks catechisms by playing with the form. But my point would be that he *subjects* us to an interminable catechism. We both chafe at it and enjoy it. Joyce clearly enjoys setting us up, with short questions that have long answers, or with long questions that are answered in a monosyllable. But he is forcing us to follow his iron whim. Although he is ostensibly writing a novel, he keeps changing the rules – switching styles, inserting overtures and long asides, using dramatic form, and finally introducing an abstract catechism which is sometimes riddling, sometimes opaque, is in short perversely difficult. What makes us put up with this perversity? Both 'Eumaeus' and 'Ithaca' give us pleasure in their humour and in their suggestions of hidden truths that we can penetrate if we read the riddles right.

As Ernst Kris suggested, the riddle is intimately related to its obverse verbal form, wit; it also has a 'special position' at the centre of mythological thought (p 176, cf. Chapter 9). The latter point is explored by Johan Huizinga in *Homo Ludens: A Study of the Play Element in Culture*. Considering the riddle in Chapter 6, Huizinga concludes that it 'was originally a sacred game, and as such it cut clean across any possible distinction between play and seriousness.'[6] A riddle and a catechism share the question-and-answer format but differ, of course, in that the riddler wants to frustrate an answer while the catechist wants an already-agreed-on answer. But Joyce's catechism is often riddling, either question or answer being intended to dazzle or confuse us. Further, as I have suggested, Joyce's catechism in its religious aim is close not only to conventional catechism but to original riddles. Huizinga suggests that 'various hymns in the Rig-veda contain the direct poetical deposit' of questions that 'were primarily of a cosmogonic nature' (p 106). But Huizinga also reminds us of an implication of such questions besides the trickster's desire to amaze and confuse. 'The poet-priest is continually knocking at the door of the Unknowable, closed to him as to us' (p 107). Because man's intellect cannot penetrate the darkness, he creates the mystery of the void to tantalize his mind. The poet-priest takes the next step. Irrationally, he opens himself to feeling or mystery and gives voice to darkness. But when he stops speaking, he is no wiser than before. As Yeats insisted, man can embody truth, but he cannot know it. As Joyce himself put it, men 'are like deep-sea fish, swimming in water that is mysteriously irradiated with light from above the surface but unable to rise to the surface to see.'[7]

The poet-priest may embody truth in a riddle. Such a riddle may well not have a rational answer; like the Zen koan, it may exist to stimulate awareness rather than intellectual adeptness. Applying this possibility to Joyce, I would say that in 'Ithaca' (as in *Ulysses* as a whole) we see at work a trickster who wants to amuse us and to call attention to himself and his protean dexterity; but we also see a poet-priest who is above the sensory flow and wishes to make us aware of the mystery of the universe.

Francis Cornford pointed out that the tragic poet is stuck with a traditional story the important incidents of which he cannot alter, whereas the plots of comedy 'were freely invented' (*The Origins of Attic Comedy* 173). Taking his point a step further, we can theorize that the tragic poet adopts the fixed form of the establishment to reconcile us to the necessary loss of the hero; the comic writer on the other hand wishes to infuse us with 'the feeling of joy' ('The Paris Notebook,' *Workshop* 53), which means reconciling us to life rather than death. Although traditionally comic writers have been accused of being conservative, in this century that generalization will no longer suffice. Joyce believed and demonstrated that it is comedy that comes closest to the mystery of things. Riding the tide of his own desires and fears, the comic writer not only exposes our secret disregard of social rules and rational demands; he is also able to move beyond the world of man. By emptying himself of all conscious aims and all unconscious desires, by becoming the divine fool, the comic writer regresses to the primitive role of poet-priest, 'continually knocking at the door of the Unknowable, closed to him as to us.'

In 'Circe,' Joyce indulged Bloom in his worst fantasies of dominance and submission, and allowed his hero to be purged by them. He also faced Stephen with his worst internal threats; instead of accepting them in order to purge them, Stephen resists them and thus brings down violence on his head. Up until 'Eumaeus' and 'Ithaca,' Stephen has been too clever for his own good, as is most apparent in his disquisition on Shakespeare. He has tried to resolve the pain of his mind by relying on the tool of mind, intellectual analysis. If he were to try less hard, he could learn from Bloom's humility to open himself to the unity of which he is in *Ulysses* only a reluctant part. In the blackness of 'Eumaeus,' Stephen has a glimpse of the divine in Bloom. More convincingly rendered, however, is what happens to Bloom in 'Ithaca.'

Joyce provides his reader with involved descriptions of constellations, abstract, intricate, sublime; then he expands these to include sub-universes within humanity; and finally, in language which at once partakes of comedy and mystery, he leaves us standing at the perhaps-to-be-opened door of the unknowable: 'if the progress were carried far enough, nought nowhere was never reached' (p 699). If we stare hard enough at the dot which Bloom has become by the end of the episode, we can see in it an irreducible element which may become diamond bright; then we may realize in Bruno's words, that 'immeasurable body [is] but an atom,' while that eternity which we allow to dwarf us is really 'nothing but a moment always.'

In Chapter 11, I contended that Joyce celebrated what Swedenborg denied, space and time, memory and the senses. He created in Bloom a character who was physical and sensual, concerned with his own body processes; who remembered vividly his past with Molly; who endured a long day, moving through Dublin's streets and buildings. Joyce gave a sense of the time of day during which each incident occurs, what effect day or night, cool or heat, freshness or closeness have on his characters. More subtly, he provided another time sense, a legendary-mystical one, by the main clue of his title. It has been argued that the Homeric parallels are not very important to the average reader of the novel. The fact remains, however, that Joyce ensured the publication of extra-literary information which illuminates otherwise slight allusions, comments, and incidents within the novel. True to the portrait I have drawn of the artist as God-like creator and unobtrusive controller of his reader's reactions, Joyce did provide the basis for an understanding beyond intuition. In so doing he invited the reader, in Croce's words, to reconstruct 'the whole ideally, and thus know it with full and true knowledge' (*J.J.* 351). Finally, then he offered a view that approaches the timeless.

But this was no speciously easy invitation to abstraction. The sympathetic reader experiences the processes which Joyce made an integral part of the traversing of his work. Made aware of the relativity of form and the importance of point of view by this experience, the reader should by the end of 'Ithaca' be ready to move through the celebration of space and time to Joyce's perception and conviction that the universe and man's body are finally no more than an atom, and that the overshadowing mystery of eternity is really no more than a moment always. Focused on the moment, each individual can find all of the time, size, and energy that has ever existed. The life of the body-mind is worth celebrating, Joyce believed, because its mundane round contains the splendour of cosmic cycles. Its processes can be celebrated because in tracing them the artist releases the hidden light of dark words, through which can pulse the energy of natural transformation and mythical metamorphosis. This tracing is at the same time a recapturing, because the cycles Joyce puts the reader through are those integrating processes of emotion and transcendence which the conditioned ego has blocked off. Repressed by the mind in its pain and self-doubt, these processes will play themselves out for the individual or artist whose will demands truth. As a human being with physical ailments and psychic disharmony, Joyce was as far from autonomy as the rest of us. As an artist, however, he combined a craftsman's patience and dedication to language with an introspective truth-seeker's demand for emotional honesty. If his self-exposure has overtones of exhibitionism, it also has a core of authenticity, an insistence on uncovering the dark impulses which when hidden control the conscious mind, when exposed and felt offer an opportunity for freedom from the mind's bondage. In *Ulysses*, that uncovering and that opportunity were embodied in a fictional art detailed and enduring, an impressive illusory retracing of the physical and psychical processes that are humanity's most immediate and compelling world.

Notes

PROLOGUE

1 In his biography, *James Joyce* (New York: Oxford University Press 1959), Richard Ellmann printed a list of books sent Joyce by a bookseller between October 1913 and May 1914. The list includes *L'Evolution créatrice* 788.

2 *James Joyce* 124. The aesthetic is printed as 'The Paris Notebook' in *The Workshop of Daedalus* ed. Robert Scholes and Richard Kain (Evanston, Illinois: Northwestern University Press 1965) 52-5.

3 In a reading contrary to mine, Robert Klawitter, after stating Bergson's case against classical intellectual philosophy, contends that 'it is just these formal mechanical fictions of the intellect that characterize the world of *Ulysses* and *Finnegans Wake*' (in 'Henri Bergson and James Joyce,' *Comparative Literature Studies* [1966] 432). He argues that especially in *Finnegans Wake*, Joyce creates a completely determined world, a fictional world that 'is a parodic representation of unreality as Bergson describes it, a parody of the inevitable unreality of the human world' (p 435). Klawitter asserts the inevitability of this result once Joyce accepted Bergson's theory, since he would have realized that what he fixed in his fiction would not be flexible reality (p 436). In the best academic fashion, Mr Klawitter has used his intellect to prove the limitation of art. Joyce would have agreed with Galileo: *eppure se muove* (and yet it moves). As I shall be demonstrating, Bergson did not share Klawitter's pessimism about art. Neither did Joyce. Although the monstrous and arbitrary forms of Joyce's episodes do indicate his concern with artifice, they are also a flexible net in which to catch reality. Bergson believed that words are 'by nature transferable and free.' Although Joyce knew it was a little more difficult for the artist, he did believe words could embody the mystery of life.

4 *James Joyce and the Making of Ulysses* (Bloomington: Indiana University Press 1960) 327.
5 *Creative Evolution*, authorized translation by Arthur Mitchell (New York: Modern Library 1944) 343-4. All italics in subsequent quotations are in the original.
6 James Joyce, *Ulysses* (New York: Random House 1961) 37.
7 Jackson Cope argues persuasively that Joyce was preoccupied with the void, and that he used it positively 'as the foundation for the mystery of both Love and Creation.' He refers to the end of *Exiles* where Richard's self-induced doubt can be connected with a void on which his love rests ('The Rhythmic Gesture: Image and Aesthetic in Joyce's *Ulysses*' in *ELH* [1962] 76). I would agree with this reading of the play's end but would see Richard's masochism and manipulation of his wife there as throwing doubt on his choice of doubt. In other words, I believe Joyce and Bergson agreed that an insistence on the void is a mind game. Acknowledging its psychological reality simply makes it the point at which choice begins. Cope does establish, however, that Joyce was attracted by the mind game. I shall consider the matter further in Chapter 11, p 169.
8 *Letters of James Joyce*, edited by Stuart Gilbert (London: Faber & Faber 1957) 139. Hereafter cited as *Letters* I.
9 'Drama and Life,' printed by Ellsworth Mason and Richard Ellmann in *The Critical Writings of James Joyce* (New York: The Viking Press 1964) 41, 43.

PART I, INTRODUCTION

1 Stanislaus Joyce records his brother's reading of and admiration of Bruno; cf. *My Brother's Keeper* (London: Faber & Faber 1958) 132. Near the end of *A Portrait of the Artist as a Young Man*, Joyce has Stephen defend Bruno to someone at university named Ghezzi, the name of Joyce's Italian professor there. There are six of these Italian dialogues: *Cabal of the Cheval Pegasus*, *The Ash Wednesday Supper*, *The Expulsion of the Triumphant Beast*, *The Heroic Frenzies*, *Cause, Principle and Unity*, and *On the Infinite Universe and Worlds*. Only the first has not been translated into English.
2 Bruno called himself 'Il Nolano,' after the town near Naples in which he was raised. Anglicizing it, Joyce had an Irish-sounding name since 'the definite article before some old family names' is 'a courtesy title in Ireland' (*Brother's Keeper* 153).
3 As recorded by Richard Ellmann in his definitive biography, *James Joyce* (New York: Oxford University Press 1959) 656, 547, 549.
4 Herbert Gorman, *James Joyce* (New York: Rinehart 1939) 219. The inclination to see betrayal began early. Cf. 'The Holy Office' (1904) and a 1905 letter to his brother in *Letters of James Joyce* (New York: The Viking Press 1966) II, 110.

5 William York Tindall, *James Joyce: His way of Interpreting the Modern World* (New York: Scribners 1950) 72. Tindall had earlier made it clear that Joyce was only schooled by the Jesuits.

6 In *The Critical Writings of James Joyce* 69.

7 *The Expulsion of the Triumphant Beast*, translated and edited by Arthur D. Imerti (New Brunswick, NJ: Rutgers University Press 1964) 72.

8 The characters can also be seen as involved in a kind of Brunian dialectic, as Richard Ellmann demonstrates in *Ulysses on the Liffey* (New York: Oxford University Press 1972) *passim*.

9 *Ulysses* (New York: Random House 1961) 167.

10 *James Joyce* 370-2. Ellmann refers to a punning transformation of Ulysses' name in Greek. This pun, which has been discussed by Stanley Sultan, will be examined in Chapter 3. Future references to Ellmann's biography will henceforth be included in the text, using the abbreviation *J.J.*

CHAPTER 1: JOYCE AND BRUNO

1 *Stephen Hero* (New York: New Directions 1963) 177. Stephen is struck by Yeats's reference to Joachim, and the story, along with its companion 'The Adoration of the Magi,' generally strengthens his movement away from the Church (p 178).

2 'A Portrait of the Artist' in *The Workshop of Daedalus*, edited by Robert Scholes and Richard Kain (Evanston: Northwestern University Press 1965) 61. Hereafter cited in the text as *Workshop*.

3 From the *Ash Wednesday Night Supper*, quoted by Frances Yates in *Giordano Bruno and the Hermetic Tradition* (New York: Vintage 1969) 237. She points out (pp 239-40) how similar this passage is to one by Cornelius Agrippa, whom Joyce had also read. This passage and the next are more accurately translated by S.L. Jaki in *The Ash Wednesday Supper* (The Hague: Mouton 1975) 60-1.

4 The importance of the heroic role is apparent in the letter Joyce wrote Ibsen at the end of his third year at university. He admires Ibsen's 'lofty impersonal power' and his 'battles,' especially 'those that were fought and won' inside Ibsen's head, in short, his 'inward heroism' (*Letters* I, 52).

5 *Cause, Principle and Unity*, translated by Jack Lindsay (Essex: Daimon Press 1962) 79.

6 But Bruno was a Copernican; cf. *On the Infinite Universe and Worlds*, translated by Dorothy Singer in *Giordano Bruno: His Life and Thought* (New York: Henry Schuman 1950) 284, *passim*.

7 Michael Seidel suggests that Bruno's astrological allegory influenced Joyce's in *Ulysses*. Cf. *Epic Geography: James Joyce's Ulysses* (Princeton: Princeton University Press 1976) 55-6.

8 This is a mystical philosophic rendering of two of the famous gnomic utterances of Hermes Trismegistus in the Smaragdine Tablet: 'What is below is like that which is above, and what is above is similar to that which is below

to accomplish the wonders of one thing. ... Ascend with the greatest sagacity from the earth to heaven, and then descend again to earth, and unite together the power of things inferior and superior.' As quoted by H.P. Blavatsky in *Isis Unveiled* (Los Angeles: Theosophy Co. 1968) 507. This is a photographic reproduction of the 1877 edition, presumably the one Joyce knew. He mentions the book in *Ulysses* (p 191) and encouraged his friend Stuart Gilbert to use it as background in writing *James Joyce's 'Ulysses.'* Cf. Gilbert's preface and index.

9 *The Basic Works of Aristotle*, edited by Richard McKeon (New York: Random House 1941), footnote 3, Chapter 2, 877-8. He does go on to distinguish form from matter, as Bergson emphasizes, but contrary to Plato he believes form to be intimately connected with matter.

10 Translated from the Latin work, *De Immenso* by J. Lewis McIntyre, *Giordano Bruno* (London: Macmillan 1903) 196. In the *Cause*, Bruno says, 'He makes no mistake who declares that being, substance and essence are one being' (p 138).

11 This recent evidence of man's relation to the forces of the universe is usefully summarized by Marilyn Ferguson in Chapter 1 of *The Brain Revolution* (New York: Taplinger Publishing Co. 1973).

12 Frances Yates emphasizes the hermetic in Bruno (cf. n3), and Jack Lindsay justifies the dialectical, scientific side of Bruno in his introduction to *Cause, Principle and Unity*. Richard Ellmann, in his recent study of Joyce's novel, *Ulysses on the Liffey*, states that 'Joyce did not respond to the hermetic side of Bruno' (p 54). No one who reads 'A Portrait of the Artist' could agree with this statement. Ellmann cites Lindsay, and his version of Bruno is consonant with Lindsay's. He detects a Brunian dialectic quite Hegelian in his schema for *Ulysses*. Instead of Thesis-antithesis-synthesis, he offers Contraries-Coinciding by-Products for each episode in the novel.

13 She compares a long passage from the *Ash Wednesday Night Supper* with a dialogue between Hermes and Tat. The same hermetic dialogue also appears in Book 3 of Agrippa's *De Occulta Philosophia*. Agrippa's work was in the National Library during Joyce's years in Dublin; it is clear from *A Portrait of the Artist* 224, that Joyce had read Agrippa.

14 Phillip Herring, editor, *Joyce's 'Ulysses' Notesheets in the British Museum* (Charlottesville: University Press of Virginia 1972) 325.

15 Joyce later told a friend that he often thought of himself as a deer (*J.J.* 452).

16 *Joyce and Shakespeare* (New Haven: Yale University Press 1957) 100-4.

17 Norman Silverstein, 'Bruno's Particles of Reminiscence,' *James Joyce Quarterly* (1965) 271-80. He establishes an important allusion to Bruno's Circe in the Nighttown section. For another allusion to Bruno in that section, see Chapter 4, n4.

CHAPTER 2: MATERIAL UNIVERSE AND SPIRITUAL ACTIVITY

1 Quoted in Italian in the novel. For the translation and attribution, cf. Weldon Thornton, *Allusions in Ulysses* (Chapel Hill: University of North Carolina Press 1968). Since this book is organized serially, according to the page numbers in the 1961 edition of *Ulysses*, future citations (in the text as 'Thornton') will not include page numbers where I have provided a quotation from *Ulysses*.

2 The chart is given by Hugh Kenner in *Dublin's Joyce* (Boston: Beacon Press 1962) 226-7. If Aristotle is a rock, he is something on which Ulysses may be wrecked. Stephen, in giving up the dogma of Catholicism (founded on the rock of Peter) may well be substituting an equally rigid one in his allegiance to Aristotle. This is not to say that the mature Joyce rejected Aristotle; only that his allegiance was more temperate than the youthful Stephen's. As Robert Kellogg demonstrates, this opposition correlates with another, that between classicism and romanticism, in which Joyce also sought the mean (pp 154-5, *James Joyce's Ulysses Critical Essays*, ed. by Clive Hart and David Hayman [Berkeley: University of California Press 1974]).

3 *The Basic Works of Aristotle*, edited by Richard McKeon (New York: Random House 1941) 592, 595.

4 Cope includes this quotation and the following one in his essay (already cited in the Prologue, n7) 68, 78.

5 In *Dionysius the Areopagite*, translated by C.E. Rolt (London: Macmillan 1920) 189. Rolt translated from the original Greek; Joyce would probably have read the eighth-century Latin translation of John Scotus Erigina.

6 In the *Divine Names* (in the Rolt translation cited above) 157, Dionysius does mention 'the Void' as that upon which God founded the earth. In the Prologue, I quoted Bergson's disapproval of the void as a logical postulate of an ideal philosophy. Psychologically he saw it as a dis-ease of the intellect when faced with change. Dionysius' positive view of the void, and especially darkness, is compatible with Bergson's negative view if we understand that both advocate letting go of the fixed forms of an 'enlightened' intellect, to examine a reality that is more immediate. Cf. n7.

7 The conjunction of mysticism and scepticism in Joyce's mind is worth underlining, since it bears on Joyce's attitude to Bergson (cf. n6). Joyce included Bergson in a short list of 'Celtic philosophers' who were 'inclined towards incertitude or scepticism' in the notes he wrote for *Exiles* (New York: Viking Press 1951) 125. The list includes Hume with his scepticism of any cause and effect doctrine. Bergson's milder doubt of Aristotelian logic provides a base for his existential belief that 'we are creating ourselves continually' (p 9) and his 'mystical' belief that 'the Absolute is revealed very near us and, in a certain measure, in us' (p 324). (Cf. *Ulysses on the Liffey* 94.)

8 Frank Budgen, *James Joyce and the Making of Ulysses* 15-17 (hereafter cited in the text as 'Budgen'). Like Antisthenes, Joyce enjoyed putting Helen down (cf. *J.J.* 392). Although Joyce's view of Penelope is another matter, recently critics have come to realize that Joyce's Penelope (Molly Bloom) is not as unfaithful as the list (p 731) of her 'lovers' would indicate.

9 Robert Martin Adams, *Surface and Symbol* (New York: Oxford University Press 1967) 223. Joyce himself provides these identities in his notesheets for *Ulysses* (p 86).

10 How deliberate and how important this allusion was to Joyce is apparent in his way of ending a letter to Harriet Weaver in 1929. 'Having said which he laid his head on the table and lapsed into the arms of Murphy' (*Letters* I, 288, cf. 252).

11 Both before and after leaving the church, Joyce seems to have been drawn to the role of the devil. Cf. *J.J.* 26, 448, 703-5. The subject is discussed further in Chapter 7.

12 One of these was *The Secret Doctrine*; another was a work frequently cited there, C.W. King's *The Gnostics and Their Remains* (London 1887), a scholarly yet committed work that contains a summary of a genuine Gnostic document, the *Pistis Sophia*. The third was Charles Heckethorn, *The Secret Societies* (London 1875).

13 As Thornton records, this has reasonably been taken as a reference to Blake's character, Los, who uses a hammer to create.

14 Both these books were published in two volumes. *The Secret Doctrine: The Synthesis of Science, Religion, and Philosophy* (London: Theosophical Publishing Co. 1888). *Isis Unveiled: A Master-Key to the Mysteries of Ancient and Modern Science and Theology* (New York: Theosophical Publishing Co. 1887). For the latter I quote from a photographic facsimile published in Los Angeles in 1968. Other indications of the influence of Blavatsky and other writers on the occult are provided by Craig Carver in 'James Joyce and the Theory of Magic,' *James Joyce Quarterly* (1978) 15, 201-14.

15 On pp 185, 191, 301, 510.

16 His main appeal, in other words, is to Aristotle. On this question, cf. Joseph Duncan, 'The Modality of the Audible in Joyce's *Ulysses*,' *PMLA* (March 1957) 286-95; S.L. Goldberg, *The Classical Temper* (New York: Barnes & Noble Inc. 1961) Chap 2; John Killham, '"Ineluctable Modality" in Joyce's *Ulysses*,' *University of Toronto Quarterly* (1965) 269-89. I tend to agree with Killham's position, especially as put on p 283.

17 I suggested that Stephen is using Dionysius' doctrine of the primacy of darkness. Joyce would also have found this doctrine in Blavatsky and Heckethorn. She generalized the point: 'In all ancient cosmogonies, *Light* comes from *Darkness*' (*The Secret Doctrine* II, 485). Similarly, Heckethorn says, 'All light is born out of darkness, and must pass through the fire to arrive at light; there is no

other way but through darkness' (*The Secret Societies* 16).

18 He is thus committed, unlike any other Dubliner we meet, to accept Bloom without religious prejudice. He does retain intellectual prejudices, however, and we see him struggling to overcome these in the Eumaeus and Ithaca episodes. As already indicated, I believe he does admit Bloom's divinity in the former episode.

19 *J.J.* 238, 385. For Hunter's rescue of Joyce under conditions similar to Bloom's helping Stephen, cf. Richard Ellmann, *James Joyce's Tower* (Dublin: Eastern Regional Tourism Organisation Ltd 1969) 11, 12.

20 A. Walton Litz prints some of these in Appendix 3 to *The Art of James Joyce* (New York: Oxford University Press 1964) 132-41.

21 We may compare Mulligan with the well-fed prostitutes Stephen remembers in Paris: 'In Rodot's Yvonne and Madeleine remake their tumbled beauties, shattering with gold teeth *chaussons* of pastry, their mouths yellowed with the *pus* of *flan breton*' (p 42). Earlier, Mulligan 'filled his mouth with a crust thickly buttered on both sides' (p 15). Later he is twice similarly pictured with rich food in his mouth (pp 249, 580). The implication is clear that Mulligan, like the prostitutes, has bartered his soul for material comfort.

22 'James Joyce: Barnacle Goose and Lapwing,' *PMLA* (June 1956) 310.

23 Besides any more pious source, Joyce could have found this point in two volumes of the *Encyclopaedia Britannica* (Eleventh Edition), Vol. 3, p 367 or Vol. 26, p 284.

24 In the early Church, the fish was often eaten in a sacred meal. As a bishop in the second century wrote: 'Faith led the way, and set before me the fish from the fountain, mighty and stainless, whom a pure virgin grasped, and gave this to friends to eat always' (*Britannica*, Eleventh Edition, Vol. 9, p 871). Religious allegory and unconscious Freudian symbolism are nicely blended in this description.

25 Joyce's earlier reference to 'whales ... hobbling' (p 45) makes me suspect an allusion to Hobbes's *Leviathan*. In the Douai (Roman Catholic) Bible, Chapter 40 of the book of Job is titled, 'Of the power of God in the behemoth and the leviathan,' thus connecting rather than contrasting God and the whale (as leviathan is glossed in a footnote). The questions then put about leviathan, while assuming a negative answer, allow for the possibility of a whale's being eaten after being landed. As Chapter 41 makes clear, this monster while alive is to be feared as an instrument of God's wrath. Joyce's use of the dead whale fits leviathan into the pattern I have suggested of the dangerous-alive, edible-dead giant.

26 Just as Nora can be seen as Joyce's feather bed of comfort, so Molly as sensual object is connected with Dublin's Featherbed Mountain (cf. *Ulysses* 234-5).

CHAPTER 3: THE ROUND OF NATURE

1 Bruno includes *stone*, which is missing from Joyce's cycle, but not from the Lestrygonians episode. We might note that 'stoking an engine' implies coal, and indeed we shall encounter lumps of coal functioning as organic stones and thus part of the natural cycle in pp 45-7 of this chapter. But as Roy Arthur Swanson demonstrates, just plain rocks can be taken as the *prima materia* of the episode, appearing as house and road, as food, as teeth, as Christian substrate for living ('Edible Wandering Rocks,' *Genre* [1972] 387, 389, 396).

2 Bruno achieved this artistic aim effectively in the song sung by the nine formerly blind men at the end of *The Heroic Frenzies*; Bruno himself points this out to the reader in his introduction. They sing in turn,

> and that there may be no vacuum interposed among them, the end of one song coincides with the beginning of the other, and the end of the last song concurs with the beginning of the first as the circle is closed. For the most brilliant and the most obscure, the beginning and the end, the greatest light and the most profound darkness, infinite potency and infinite act coincide. (p 77)

This principle provides an obvious model for the beginning and ending of *Finnegans Wake*, but in *Ulysses* too a number of processes turn back on themselves to form a cycle.

3 That this equivalence was in Joyce's mind is indicated by a grotesque image in the Wandering Rocks episode: 'in fealty' to 'the representative of His Majesty' Edward VII, 'Poddle river hung out ... a tongue of liquid sewage' (p 252). This expulsive image connecting mouth and anus is matched by an intrusive image in Molly's mind: 'he can stick his tongue 7 miles up my hole as hes there my brown part' (p 780).

4 Sir James Frazer, *The Golden Bough*, Abridged Edition (London: Macmillan 1957) 652. On page 654, Frazer connects this secular aim with the allied religious one in the Eucharist.

5 The 'he' is Blazes Boylan, whose sexual relations with Molly will later confront Bloom directly in one of his Nighttown hallucinations.

6 Phillip Herring, *Joyce's 'Ulysses' Notesheets in the British Museum* (Charlottesville: University Press of Virginia 1972) 120.

7 Or as Joyce put it in the notes he took in medical school in 1902, 'alimentary canal – digestive canal from mouth to anus.' Reproduced by Avel Austin in 'Ulysses and the Human Body' (PHD dissertation, Columbia University 1963) 187.

8 'Lotuseaters,' *James Joyce's 'Ulysses': Critical Essays* (Berkeley: University of California Press 1974) 73.

9 As Clive Hart says of 'Wandering Rocks' and its 'organ,' the blood (stream), 'This is the same city as had

swallowed, and tried to digest, the Bloom of "Lestrygonians." There, however, we saw only its alimentary tract, whereas here we see the whole creature, whose lineaments are traced by the pattern of its veins and arteries' (*Critical Essays* 187). This view of the elephant seems as partial to me as that offered by any other episode.

10 The parallels with Fletcher's poem have been analysed by Austin in his dissertation (cf. n7).

11 As Swanson contends, 'God eats men through death and the blood of sacrifice; and men eat God (through the eucharist)' ('Edible Wandering Rocks' 390).

12 I am not sure what then corresponds to its passing them 'through the ordinary channel' (excretion), unless it is their bones coming to the surface.

13 Like Stephen, Joyce took pain personally and looked for someone to blame. In *Giacomo Joyce* he exclaims, 'O cruel wound! Libidinous God!' upon hearing that the young woman he loves has been operated on (London: Faber & Faber 1968) 11. Seeing her recuperating, he is unforgiving: 'A bird twittering after storm, happy that its little foolish life has fluttered out of reach of the clutching fingers of an epileptic lord and giver of life' (p 11).

14 P 673, my italics. Joyce's original note for this passage carries the emphasis I indicate: 'coal fossil trees sunlight' (Herring, *Notesheets* 454).

15 Cyclops is compared to a mountain in two of the translations of the *Odyssey* that Joyce would have known. In his *Adventures of Ulysses*, Charles Lamb has 'He looked more like a mountain crag than a man,' in *Life, Letters and Writings of Charles Lamb*, ed. Percy Fitzgerald (London: Moxon 1876) Vol. V, 146. Samuel Butler renders it, 'more like a peak standing out against the sky on some high mountain than a human being,' *Authoress of the Odyssey* (London: Cape 1922) 43-4. First published in 1897, this volume of theory and translation was in Joyce's collection when he died. Cf. Thomas Connolly, *The Personal Library of James Joyce* (Buffalo, NY: University of Buffalo Studies 1955) 10. For a discussion of which translations Joyce knew, cf. Hugh Kenner, 'Homer's Sticks and Stones,' *James Joyce Quarterly* (1965) 285-8.

16 Cf. Lady Gregory, *Gods and Fighting Men* (London 1904) 159-60. She refers to 'Slieve Bladhma,' which she identifies with Slieve Bloom in her notes, p 475.

17 As with *Finnegans Wake*, such a reconstruction of the story line distorts the overtones and ambivalences of the meanings we have seen for the names. To let one example stand for all: Call boy warns of death.

CHAPTER 4: ROADS PARALLEL AND ROADS CONTRARY

1 The same is true in 'Scylla and Charybdis,' as Stanley Sultan demonstrates in *The Argument of Ulysses* (Columbus: Ohio State University Press 1964) 166-80.

2 *J.J.* 351. This is Croce's attempt to restate part of Vico's theory of history. We know Joyce went on to use Vico as a main structural basis in *Finnegans Wake*. This quotation indicates the compatibility of Vico with Joyce's other main source, Bruno. Ellmann connects the Croce passage with *Ulysses* again, with commentary, in *Ulysses on the Liffey* 141-2.

3 The problem of the spiritual in the physical is also connected with women in 'Circe.' Stephen wants to visit Georgina Johnson (p 433), a prostitute he earlier remembered as 'a clergyman's daughter' (p 189). In the brothel, Stephen comments, 'and so Georgina Johnson is dead and married' (p 559). One of the whores tells him, 'It was a commercial traveller married her and took her away with him.' Another adds, 'Mr Lambe from London,' and Stephen responds, 'Lamb of London, who takest away the sins of our world' (p 560). As Thornton points out, this varies a refrain in the rites of communion, 'Lamb of God, which taketh away the sins of the world.' If Georgina has been saved by the Lamb of God, then she is like Mary Magdalene, and a reminder that man need not be what he has been. If this Lambe is a 'commercial traveller,' then Stephen may be able to see that the end of his earlier list of four characters ('God, the sun, Shakespeare, a commercial traveller') is in fact only the beginning of another cycle, since the last term (now seen as Christ) is a metamorphized version of the first (God). It also prepares Stephen to see Christ in Bloom while they are in the Cabman's shelter. Cf. Schutte 149-51, and C.H. Peake, *James Joyce: The Citizen and the Artist* (Stanford: Stanford University Press 1977) 275-6.

4 The relevance of Bruno is suggested by David Hayman in his short, valuable study, *Ulysses: The Mechanics of Meaning* (Englewood Cliffs, NJ: Prentice-Hall 1970) 65. He also points out, as others have, that 'Jewgreek is Greekjew' refers to Stephen's meeting with Bloom, and their subsequent blending in the mirror.

5 Another way of understanding Joyce's use of the octave is suggested by Joseph Campbell in his article, 'Contransmagnificantjewbantantiality,' *Studies in the Literary Imagination* (October 1970) 11. Cf. Peake 371-2, and Seidel in *Epic Geography* 50.

6 But the two can be interchangeable: Cosgrave's young woman, for instance, 'glanced at her lovely echo in the little mirror she carries' (p 416). The mirror can also be as revealing as Shakespeare's image already referred to. Joyce's concern with mirrors is indicated in the notesheets for *Ulysses* 320-1, 325, 330, 413, 425, 504, 511.

7 As Schutte points out (pp 151-2), Bloom in 'Ithaca' travels similarly on the cosmic level. He suggests also that Stephen and Bloom are themselves the fundamental and the dominant.

8 True to his love of puzzles, Joyce provided elsewhere in the novel information which can aid the reader who

wants to decipher this charade. (1) 'Rip' is connected with Molly's sexuality (p 89). (2) 'Breadvan' is connected with Bloom, Molly, food and keeping young (p 57). (3) 'Periwinkle' is associated by Bloom with oysters and Boylan's youthful virility (pp 174-5). Later Molly thinks of oysters as the source of Boylan's sustained sexuality (p 742). Like Rip Van Winkle, in other words, Bloom has 'been away from' his wife for over a decade. Like Rip Van Winkle's gun, Bloom's is 'rusty' (Joyce's phallic symbolism is overt on pp 542, 567).

9 The clown as buffoon intuitively strikes to the heart of Bloom. Having given up prestige, intellect, and conscience, he is able, as Bruno suggests, to break through to truth. A number of such breakthroughs occur in the last four episodes of the novel, as fatigue allows the characters to give up conscious control.

10 The meaning is discussed by Sultan 332-3.

CHAPTER 5: TRANSFORMATIONS OF THE CREATOR

1 For the aesthetic significance of this mass to Joyce, cf. Goldman 134-7. He was urging the importance of the 'solemn ceremonial of High Mass' to the Protestant Magee after becoming an apostate (*Workshop* 199).

2 The first two sentences are a paraphrase of the three tenets with which Yeats began his essay on 'Magic' (1901). Instead of 'universal mind,' Yeats referred to 'great memory,' a phrase that Joyce used in the same sense at the end of his 1902 essay on Mangan.

3 Although Joyce knew several translations of the *Odyssey*, the one he made notes from was by Butcher and Lang (Herring 50). I therefore use their edition (London: Macmillan 1921) 3rd ed., p 96.

4 *The Republic of Plato*, translated by Francis Cornford (New York: Oxford University Press 1945) 345.

5 I quote from *The Collected Poems* (New York: Macmillan 1951) 367. As the *Variorum Edition* indicates, the images I emphasize were present from the poem's first publication in 1892. This part of Yeats's poem left its mark in *Ulysses*. When the demon first appears, he is 'barking,' a likely influence on the protean dog that Stephen meets.

6 In his article 'Three Irish Allusions in *Ulysses*,' *James Joyce Quarterly* (1968) 301-3, Philip Marcus shows that the phrase 'Dark hidden father,' uttered by Mananaan, comes from A.E.'s poem 'The Children of Lir' (and ultimately from *The Secret Doctrine*).

7 Emblems of the head of Anna Liffey (or Livia) are on several bridges in Dublin. Joyce would also have seen the heads of various river gods carved in stone on what is now the custom house on the Liffey, and another on a building just off the O'Connell St bridge. Like several of those on the custom house, this one has sea creatures in its hair, including at least

one eel. (These heads also appear on the different denominations of pound notes of the Irish Republic.)

8 Other critics have also implicitly or explicitly disagreed with Goldman recently. Cf. Brook Thomas, 'The Counterfeit Style of "Eumaeus",' *James Joyce Quarterly* (1976) 14, 15-24; and Marilyn French, *The Book as World: James Joyce's Ulysses* (Cambridge, MA: Harvard University Press 1976) 208-19.

9 So was Stephen, as Joyce's notesheets make clear: 'Birth SD Acquarius' (*sic*) (p 297). We may thus put some weight on Stephen's significant deafness earlier in the day. Listening to a student read *Lycidas*, Stephen lets his thoughts cut him off from these lines (which do not appear in *Ulysses*):

> So sinks the day-star in the Ocean bed,
> And yet anon repairs his drooping head,
> And tricks his beams, and with new spangled Ore,
> Flames in the forehead of the morning sky:

As Edward Watson points out, Stephen does hear the lines before and after these ('Stoom – Bloom...' *University of Windsor Review* [Fall 1966] 18-19). What he suppresses is a pattern that promises hope, a pattern that we shall see Bloom following in the Ithaca episode (cf. Chapter 11).

10 Joyce had been aware of this sense of the word since 1904. Cf. *The Dublin Diaries of Stanislaus Joyce*, edited by George Healey (London: Faber & Faber 1962) 27-8. (I disagree with Healey's comment.) Bloom admires water in a page of praise (pp 671-2).

CHAPTER 6: THE COMIC VISION AND THE GROTESQUE

1 As Lee Byron Jennings suggests, the grotesque may be seen 'as a very basic, but pre-aesthetic form of expression not subject to the demands of beauty and artistic unity. ... This removal of emphasis from the aesthetic seems to call for greater concentration on psychological implications.' *The Ludicrous Demon Aspects of the Grotesque in German Post-Romantic Prose* (Berkeley: University of California Press 1963) 18. Richard Pearce suggests the relevance of the grotesque to the second half of *Ulysses* (especially 'Circe') in a short article, 'Experimenting with the Grotesque,' *Modern Fiction Studies* (1974) 20, 378-84.

2 'Forms of Folly in Joyce: A Study of Clowning in *Ulysses*,' *ELH* (1967) 260-83.

3 *Laughter* in the volume *Comedy*, edited by Wylie Sypher (New York: Doubleday, Anchor 1956) 84, 97.

4 Part Three, 'The Comic' of his *Psychoanalytic Explorations in Art* (New York: Schocken Books 1964) 178-9.

5 Many of these puzzles are explained by Don Gifford and Robert Seidman in *Notes for Joyce: An Annotation of James Joyce's 'Ulysses'* (New York: Dutton 1974). For a sampling, consult entries (301: 32) p 272; (303: 35) p 273; (307: 20-34) pp 275-6; (339: 21)

p 303; (339: 38) p 305. As Joyce said to a friend, of *Ulysses* as a whole, 'I've put in so many enigmas and puzzles that it will keep the professors busy for centuries arguing over what I mean, and that's the only way of insuring one's immortality' (*J.J.* 535).

6 Actually Joyce identified the nameless narrator as 'Noman' on his schema for the novel. He might also have admitted his own anonymous role as interpolator, the creative God-like shaper of the episode who appears as no man in it. But we are concerned here with Bloom's role as the Ulysses who has this double identity in the episode and the novel as a whole.

7 Translated by Ulrich Weisstein (New York: McGraw-Hill 1966) 21.

8 For an analysis of some of the weaknesses of Walpole's novel and some of the strengths of the Gothic novel, cf. Chapters 1 and 2 of my study of the irrational in the nineteenth-century English novel, *Imagination Indulged* (Montreal: McGill-Queen's University Press 1972).

9 Earlier in a comic grotesque vision, Stephen had imagined an auditory use of the same canal (top of p 38).

PART 2, INTRODUCTION

1 Cf. *The Interpretation of Dreams*, translated and edited by James Strachey (New York: Wiley 1961) 471. This edition, which Strachey calls 'in the nature of a "Variorum"' (p xx) dates all passages added by Freud in the course of the eight editions Freud published of this much revised classic.

2 In the appendix to *The Consciousness of Joyce* (London: Faber & Faber 1977).

3 Translated by A.A. Brill (New York: Mentor 1951) 14, my italics.

4 Translated and edited by James Strachey (New York: Norton 1960) 160, my italics.

5 Although Joyce owned the 1917 edition of the book, a Triestine student had talked with him about slips of the tongue as early as 1913 (*J.J.* 351). An extensive case for Joyce's knowledge of the book was made by Chester Anderson before Ellmann published evidence of Joyce's having owned it: 'Leopold Bloom as Dr Sigmund Freud' in *Mosaic* (1972) VI, 23-43. Although highly idiosyncratic, his analysis does include a number of examples of Freudian slips in one episode of *Ulysses*.

6 This passage was not included by Freud until 1919, but its assertion is implicit in several dreams analysed in earlier editions.

7 This point is eloquently made by Frederick Crews in his introductory essay, 'Anaesthetic Criticism,' *Psychoanalysis and Literary Process* (Cambridge, MA: Winthrop 1970).

8 This caution is given by Edward Brandabur in *A Scrupulous Meanness: A Study of Joyce's Early Work* (Urbana: University of Illinois Press 1971) 6.

CHAPTER 7: CONDITIONED EGO AND OBSERVING SELF

1 Richard Ellmann, 'Introduction,' *James Joyce Letters* II, li. But in his

biography, Ellmann quotes the view of Nora Joyce, confided to her sister: 'He's a weakling, Kathleen. I always have to be after his tail' (p 565).

2 James Joyce, *Exiles* (New York: Viking Press 1951) 118. The woman-killer remark is attributed to Nora in the Trieste Notebook (*Workshop* 103).

3 These epiphanies have been collected by Scholes and Kain in *The Workshop of Daedalus*; this one appears on p 11. It is only slightly reworked on p 8 of *A Portrait of the Artist* with the significant substitution of Dante for Mr Vance.

4 As Freud says in *The Interpretation of Dreams*, 'The blinding in the legend of Oedipus, as well as elsewhere, stands for castration' (New York: John Wiley and Sons 1961) 398. Cf. Robert Ryf, *A New Approach to Joyce* (Berkeley: University of California Press 1962) 113.

5 *Joyce in Nighttown: A Psychoanalytic Inquiry into 'Ulysses'* (Berkeley: University of California Press 1974) 89. The relevant letters are contained in *Selected Letters of James Joyce*, ed. Richard Ellmann (New York: The Viking Press 1975) 180-92.

6 P 354. The edition I am using (cited in n1 of the introduction to Part 2) is a reprint of the Standard Edition and contains indications of all Freud's revisions over the years.

7 Shortly before the umbrella statement, Stephen had been asked if he was suggesting that Shakespeare had been involved in 'misconduct with one of the brothers' (p 211). Shortly after, Stephen includes in a list of possible *alter egos*, 'brothers-in-love' (p 213). In the second episode of the novel, he had remembered the continental masseuse who rubbed 'male nakedness in the bath. ... Most licentious custom. Bath a most private thing. I wouldn't let my brother, not even my own brother, most lascivious thing' (p 43). This unconscious linking of the brother with massaging reinforces Stephen's comments in the library scene. Cf. Jean Kimball's comments on this relation in 'James Joyce and Otto Rank: The Incest Motif in *Ulysses*,' *James Joyce Quarterly* (1976) 13, 374.

8 The sense of impotence which is Stephen's main contention about Shakespeare appears in his image for one of the bard's lapses as potent creator: 'The other four acts of that play hang *limply* from that first' (p 211). Joyce's own interest in the problem is indicated in his using the modifier for Bloom's picture of himself in the bath, 'floating hair of the stream around the *limp* father of thousands' (p 86) Cf. Sultan's comment on p 97 of *The Argument of Ulysses*. The image of Prospero breaking his staff carries a similar concern (p 212, *Ulysses*).

9 Jean Kimball makes a case for Joyce's having read Rank's *Incest Motif in Poetry and Saga*. Cf. her article cited in n7.

10 'James Joyce: From Stephen to Bloom' in *Psychoanalysis and Literary Process* 150. Brivic was anticipated on this particular interpretation by Freud himself. In 1913, in *Totem and Taboo*, Freud referred to Adonis' death as

caused 'by the wrath of the father in the form of an animal' (New York: Norton [1950] 152). Whether Joyce had read this work is problematic. The brother of one of his best friends was a Freudian psychoanalyst. Joyce certainly talked about Freud's theories with the friend, Ottocaro Weiss, as he had earlier with friends in Trieste (*J.J.* 405, 411; 351, 486). If he had not read *Totem and Taboo*, he certainly wrote about Stephen's problem as though he knew much of its contents (especially the last half of the last chapter).

11 For the Freudian theory behind such a situation, cf. Brivic 129, 131.

12 Margaret Solomon also notices Brivic's error in 'Character as Linguistic Mode...' in *Ulysses cinquante ans après*, ed. Louis Bonnerot (Paris: Didier 1974) 114.

13 Since his book was published, Shechner has declared reservations about his use of the psychoanalytic approach. As guest editor of the 'Joyce and Modern Psychology' issue of the *James Joyce Quarterly*, XIII, 3 he discusses the disarray of psychoanalytic literary criticism in the seventies and includes an essay by Darcy O'Brien which uses Shechner's own book as a bad example of that approach.

14 In a subsequent and equally helpful and stimulating essay, Crews states unequivocally what he thinks criticism should aim at: not 'reduction to causes, but recognition of the inexhaustible and *irreduceable* vitality that somehow inheres in the works themselves'; 'Reductionism and Its Discontents' in *Out of My System* (New York: Oxford University Press 1975) 168.

15 C.G. Jung, *Aion: Researches into the Phenomenology of the Self*, or 'Two Essays on Analytical Psychology' (Part 2). See also Rollo May, *Existential Psychotherapy*, *Love and Will*, etc.; R.D. Laing, *The Divided Self*, *The Politics of Experience*, etc. Specifically, the views I hold are developed in *I AMness: The Discovery of the Self beyond the Ego* by Ian Kent and William Nicholls (New York: Bobbs-Merrill 1972). My debt to Dr Kent goes far beyond this book.

CHAPTER 8: THE IMAGE OF THE ARTIST: DESTRUCTION, PERVERSION, CREATION

1 Stekel is cited by Brandabur in his excellent analysis of *Exiles*, in *A Scrupulous Meanness* 138.

2 Mark Shechner argues convincingly that in Joyce's case, great creativity was also the response to a great sense of loss. He suggests that the death of Joyce's mother in August 1903 was a loss which her son tried to make good in the outburst of writing that followed (*Joyce in Nighttown* 238-9). I believe that a need to destroy and a sense of loss were both present in Joyce and were both associated with his mother.

3 Joyce's case is complicated since he might be violating not only his mother with his eyes but his daughter as well. He was superstitious about 13 December, 'the day of S. Lucia, the patron of eyes' (*Letters* I, 150). His

daughter's name was Lucia. Her madness became apparent in the later 1920s while his eyesight was steadily worsening.

4 Thornton finds another allusion in Stephen's phrase, to a couplet by Pope: 'There St John mingles with my friendly bowl. The feast of reason and the flow of soul.' This verse would have attracted Joyce by its possible application to Oliver *St John* Gogarty. (Joyce was careful in 'Oxen of the Sun' to refer to Buck as 'Malachi Roland *St John* Mulligan' 417, my italics). Both Stephen and Joyce interpret Mulligan's preoccupation with old men (pp 217, 411) as more than a joke.

5 Arnold Goldman also suggests Stephen's fascination with homosexuality, citing particularly his French pimp speech, 'Stephen's Parleyvoo,' *James Joyce Quarterly* (1971) 157-61. The possibility of sodomy is strongly implied in the Old Testament. Ham tells his two brothers of seeing the father naked. They drop a garment over him without looking: 'And Noah awoke from his wine, and knew what his younger son had done unto him' (Genesis: 10, 24, King James version). Merely seeing nakedness is hardly something 'done unto' nor does it warrant Noah's strong curse.

6 *The Works of Blake in Three Volumes*, edited by W.B. Yeats and Edwin Ellis. This edition of the poet's work has been in the National Library, Dublin, since it was published in 1893. As C.P. Curran records, Joyce 'read Blake closely in the Ellis-Yeats edition' (*James Joyce Remembered* 35). After my manuscript was typed, Anita Gandolfo investigated the parallel I am about to develop, in 'Whose Blake Did Joyce Know...,' *James Joyce Quarterly* (1978) 15, 215-21.

7 Stephen had earlier thought of a blasphemous book in which the paternity of Christ is ascribed to the Holy Ghost (p 41). A similar allegation is made by Joseph in the 'Cherry Tree Carol' (cf. Thornton for other analogues).

8 Like Claudius, Mulligan gives good advice when he urges Stephen-Hamlet to give up protracted mourning. But since Stephen also sees Mulligan as a Claudius-like usurper, he has trouble trusting his advice. Perhaps he has remembered that when Hamlet killed the usurper, it was at the cost of his own life.

9 Shechner makes a good case for an 'anal dialectic' (p 133) by applying Erikson's opposed modalities of anality to the development of Joyce's art. He treats it, however, as an unconscious battle, while my emphasis both in this chapter and in the last is on how conscious Joyce seems to have been of the anal overtones both of his characters' problems and of his own art.

10 Joyce saw himself as a miner also, while working on *Finnegans Wake*: 'It is like a mountain that I tunnel into from every direction, but I don't know what I will find' (*J.J.* 556; cf. also *Letters* I, 22). Erikson's portrait of Luther as wordmonger could pass as a

description of Joyce. He emphasizes 'Luther's immense gift for language: his receptivity for the written word; his memory for the significant phrase; and his range of verbal expression (lyrical, biblical, satirical, and vulgar) which in English is paralleled only by Shakespeare' (*Young Man Luther* 47).

CHAPTER 9: COMEDY IN 'CIRCE'

1 In *The Secret of Ulysses* (McHenry, Illinois: Compass Press 1953) 89-90.

2 The last sound contains an ambiguity which I have already noted, Bloom's experience at the beginning of 'Lestrygonians': 'Bloo ... Me? No. Blood of the Lamb' (p 151, Joyce's ellipsis).

3 Herring 101. This note was not lined out, an indication that it was probably not used directly in the novel.

4 On p 203 there is a somewhat illegible note. 'Joke: always make ?remd. to self no ?laughs 1st self to make up for...' (the question mark indicates 'remd.' and 'laughs' are dubious readings). This analytical comment on joking and laughing could refer to either or both of two points Freud made in *Jokes and Their Relation to the Unconscious*. (1) That the teller never laughs at his own joke (p 100) . (2) That a dirty joke is told by one male to another to make up for sexual refusal by a female (pp 99-100).

On p 429 of the *Notesheets* there is a possible allusion to one of Freud's sample jokes. 'MB in middle of fuck thought of jokes (German emporer)' (*sic*). In *Jokes*, Freud recorded the following: 'Serenissimus was making a tour through his provinces and noticed a man in the crowd who bore a striking resemblance to his own exalted person. He beckoned to him and asked: "Was your mother at one time in service in the Palace?" – "No, your Highness," was the reply, "but my father was"' (pp 68-9). James Strachey points out what Joyce would have known, that 'Serenissimus' was 'the name conventionally given to Royal Personages by comic periodicals under the German Empire' (p 68). Assuming Molly's thought comes to her during intercourse with Boylan, she may put her husband in the same position as the German emperor. She does think of Bloom as his highness (pp 738, 752).

5 'Forms of Folly in Joyce: A Study of Clowning in *Ulysses*,' *ELH* XXXIV (1967) 273.

6 This suggestion was first made by C.L. Barber in a footnote in 1951. Cf. 'The Saturnalian Pattern in Shakespeare's Comedy' in *Comedy Meaning and Form*, edited by Robert W. Corrigan (San Francisco: Chandler 1965).

7 Quoted by Sir James Frazer, *The Scapegoat* (London: Macmillan 1933) 332. This was the final volume of *The Golden Bough* in its second edition (1900). I am not arguing that Joyce had read Frazer. As John Vickery admits, (1) 'there is no mention of *The Golden Bough* in either his letters or critical essays'; (2) 'the Joyce-Frazer relationship' can be regarded as only 'a possible one.' *The Literary Impact of*

'The Golden Bough' (Princeton, NJ: Princeton University Press 1973) 326, 331. Nevertheless, Vickery writes three chapters on *Ulysses* and *The Golden Bough*, including one on Bloom as scapegoat.

8 In the third edition (1913) this chapter was placed as a note at the end of *The Scapegoat* volume. A footnote explains that it was moved out of the main body because of its speculative nature and because his 'views on this subject appear to have been strangely misunderstood' (p 412).

9 Cornford, edited (and rearranged) by Theodore Gaster (New York: Anchor 1961) 175.

10 Robert Adams gives even more information about Dublin pantomime in general and the 1892 production of *Sinbad the Sailor* in particular. Cf. *Surface and Symbol* 76-80. Cf. also Atherton's article, cited in n12.

11 Cf. E.K. Chambers, *The Medieval Stage* (London: Oxford University Press 1903) I, Chap. 2. Cf. also Enid Welsford, *The Fool: His Social and Literary History* (New York: Farrar and Rinehart 1935) Chaps 13, 14.

12 '*Finnegans Wake*: "The Gist of the Pantomime"' *Accent* (1955) 19.

13 As Atherton argues, in *Finnegan's Wake* this original sense of pantomime is taken to its logical conclusion.

14 Freud gives a brief but clear account of the relation of super-ego to id and ego in Chap. 5 of *The Question of Lay Analysis*. Cf. *Two Short Accounts of Psycho-Analysis* (Harmondsworth: Penguin 1962) 137.

CHAPTER 10:
THE GROTESQUE IN 'CIRCE'

1 The relevance of this disease to the episode is discussed by Norman Silverstein, 'Evolution of the Nighttown Setting' in *The Celtic Master* (Dublin: Dolmen Press 1969) 27-30; and by Mark Shechner in *Joyce in Nighttown* (pp 123-39).

2 Steig's article appeared in *The Journal of Aesthetics and Art Criticism* XXIX (1970) 258.

3 The relevance of Freud in connecting *ménage* and *menagerie* to 'menagerer' has been pointed out by Thelma Kintanar in her PHD dissertation, 'The Significance of the Comic in James Joyce's Ulysses' (Stanford University 1968) 161. She demonstrates the applicability of Freud's theories of dreams and jokes in her fifth chapter, '"Circe": The Unconscious, the Comic and the Grotesque.'

4 *The Writings of Irenaeus*, translated by A. Roberts (Edinburgh 1866) I, 22. This volume was in the National Library in Dublin from 1896.

CHAPTER 11: 'ITHACA':
REDUCTION AND SUBLIMATION

1 '"Nature it is": The Influence of Giordano Bruno on James Joyce's Molly Bloom,' *James Joyce Quarterly* 14 (1976) 40, 46.

2 *Ibid*. 47. Voelker depends entirely on McIntyre's book (and Joyce's review of it). He does not indicate that this passage is McIntyre's translation

of a part of Bruno's *De Immenso* (1591).

3 *Ibid*. 44.

4 *The Heroic Frenzies* 251. This is part of the original on which McIntyre based the paraphrase quoted on p 168.

5 Arnold Goldman takes up the relation of Bloom to Moses, pp 126-37. His conclusion is relevant to other connections I am trying to make: 'The association between Moses and Parnell and their typification of Christ thus formed an unbroken circle for Joyce' (p 136).

6 Phillip Herring, *Joyce's 'Ulysses' Notebooks in the British Museum* 455. This note and others were included by Richard Madtes in his PHD dissertation, 'A Textual and Critical Study of the "Ithaca" Episode of Ulysses' (Columbia University 1961). This study includes comment on the symbolism of two suns and Shakespeare, as well as on other light-dark symbolism in this episode.

7 Stanley Sultan provides a different, though not a contradictory, interpretation of the urination scene (p 399).

8 Sultan also comments on the infinity theme, suggesting Bloom and Stephen will meet in death (pp 372, 392). He also notes that they start the episode *united* (p 384).

9 Joyce's harmonizing in this episode of the artistic tendencies represented by Defoe and Blake is argued persuasively by A. Walton Litz in his excellent essay on 'Ithaca' in *James Joyce's 'Ulysses': Critical Essays*: especially pp 387-92.

10 Bloom has been justified as an artist by William Schutte in his article 'Leopold Bloom: A Touch of the Artist,' *James Joyce Quarterly* (Fall 1972) 118-31.

11 The word 'nebula' may contain a clue to the seriousness with which Joyce was using the microcosm-macrocosm analogy in this episode. In a letter of 1922 he spoke offhandedly of his further troubles with glaucoma: 'Dr Borsch told me the nebula had split at the top and was thinning slightly in the centre' (*Letters* I, 187).

12 Cf. Loehrich, *The Secret of Ulysses* 112.

13 Even on close inspection, this sentence remains dreamily incoherent, and neatly ambiguous. It may, for instance, be read with 'round' as an adverb: 'there was a square [a]round Sinbad the Sailor,' in which case 'Going to bed' becomes a dangling introductory modifier, and there is a pause denoting lack of continuity before 'roc's auk's egg.' It makes more sense to me to keep 'round' an adjective and take 'Sinbad the Sailor' as possessive – or better still to take 'roc's auk's egg' as being in apposition with 'Sinbad the Sailor.' Two early versions of this passage are recorded by Herring from the notesheets, pp 91, 469. Cf. C.H. Peake's comments on the passage in *James Joyce: The Citizen and the Artist* 296-7.

14 *Structure and Motif in Finnegans Wake* (London: Faber & Faber 1962) 113n.

15 Recorded by Madtes in his dissertation, p 196. Cf. n2 above.

16 Other synonyms for *period* are similarly used. Bloom regrets a bird of

paradise wing on Josie Powell's hat: 'it was a pity to kill it, you cruel creature, little mite of a thing with a heart the size of a fullstop' (p 449).

17 In Chapter 6 we looked at the scene in 'Oxen of the Sun' in which 'young Leopold' appears in the mirror of memory, until 'the mirror is 'breathed on and the young knight errant recedes, shrivels, to a tiny speck within the mist' (p 413).

18 Translated by McIntyre 238. These four clauses contain the basis for an understanding of what Joyce was trying to achieve thematically and artistically in *Finnegans Wake*.

19 Quoted by Frances Yates 260.

20 Joyce characterized Penelope (the episode, but also the woman) to Budgen as, 'perfectly sane full amoral fertisiable untrustworthy engaging shrewd limited prudent indifferent *Weib*' (*Letters* I, 170). I shall examine in the next chapter Joyce's sensuous-sensual evocation of Bloom's enjoyment of her hemispheric buttocks.

21 Sultan 414, 450; Thornton 180. For the theosophical doctrine of the auric egg, see Ralph Jenkins, 'Theosophy in "Scylla and Charybdis",' *Modern Fiction Studies* (1969) 15, 40-1.

22 *The Secret Doctrine* (London 1888) I, 359. As indicated earlier, this book was available in the National Library of Ireland before the turn of the century and would therefore have been available to Joyce during the period when he was reading Blavatsky.

CHAPTER 12: A GREAT JOKER AT THE UNIVERSE

1 This phrase is actually from the 1904 'Portrait' essay (*Workshop* 61), where the same irony was evident.

2 Although a woman's buttocks are 'insusceptible of moods of impression,' we know from 'Penelope' that Molly's mind is susceptible. More important, by their ignorance of 'contrarieties of expression,' the buttocks constitute a low version of that Brunian principle which the high-minded young Joyce admired; in the divine there are no contraries; all coincides.

3 On a more sublime level, it could be argued that Bloom is really trying to get back to the womb, that once he gets to 'the land of the midnight sun' he will find out about 'the hidden life of Christ' before being reborn. But on a Freudian level, it has to be objected that Bloom was presumably purged by Bello in 'Circe' of being an 'adorer of the adulterous rump' (p 530). From the perspective of 'Ithaca' that charge reads like prophecy. Furthermore, it carries with it the additional implication of homosexuality: presumably it is the afternoon's adultery that causes Molly's cleft to have '*seminal* warmth' (though she claims to have 'washed out' herself, pp 742, 763). The answer to the problem seems to me still to lie in Bloom's dual nature (active-passive, masculine-feminine). As I emphasized earlier, the dominant result is that Bloom becomes more assertive, but we

find this out only in Molly's section of the novel.

4 Robert M. Adams, *James Joyce: Common Sense and Beyond* (New York: Random House 1966) 171. In the sentence before, Adams said the 'cosmos' of *Ulysses* may well prove to be 'inexhaustible.'

5 *J.J.* 543. (Cf. p 191, *Ulysses on the Liffey*, 1972, or p 192 in the corrected 1973 edition.)

6 (Boston: Beacon Press 1955) 110.

7 Quoted by Jackson Cope in his essay on 'Sirens' in *James Joyce's 'Ulysses': Critical Essays* 223.

Index

absurd, the: Joyce's use of 7, 86, 191
Acteon 15, 16
Adam 119
Adams, R.M. 27, 75; *Surface and Symbol* 125
A.E. *See* Russell, George W.
Aeolus 42
Agrippa, Cornelius 14
alienation: Joyce's use of 86, 89, 125, 154, 155, 161, 166
anastomosis: concept of 89
animal, the: Joyce's use of viii, 11, 21, 28, 31, 32, 35-6, 39, 58, 65, 77, 86, 98-9, 146, 150-1, 153, 155-6, 159-61, 181, 183, 188; ape 90, 156-7; bull 84-5 (cow 160); dog 17, 27-8, 31, 33, 98, 125, 126, 151, 181, 184; lamb 43, 82, 159; panther 28, 156; pig 124, 156, 160; stag 16-17, 28
Aquinas, Thomas xi, xviii, 8, 23, 24, 32, 107
Aristotle vii, xi-xii, xviii, 12, 15, 19, 20-3, 26, 31, 52, 56, 62, 67, 90, 169, 176; *Metaphysica* 12, 21, 22, 52; *Physics* 12, 176; *Poetics* vii; *Psychology* 21
artist, the: Joyce's conception of xv, 11, 18, 29, 36, 62, 64, 65, 76, 108, 111, 113-14, 116, 117, 119-20, 121, 123, 136, 176-7, 186-7, 191, 193, 194, 198
Athena 51, 68, 69
Atherton, J.S. 150-1
Augustine, St 30, 36, 88
Austin, Avel 41

Beebe, Maurice 35
Bennett, Percy 128, 195
Bennett, Sgt Maj. (Circe episode) 128, 129
Bergson, Henri xi-xix, 20, 22, 60, 78, 81, 88, 96-7, 137, 169, 175; *Creative Evolution* xi-xix, 96; *Laughter* 81
Black Mass: in *Ulysses* 27, 31, 124-5, 162
Blake, William 24, 124, 128-9, 173, 175
Blavatsky, Helene 29, 32, 36, 61, 183; *Isis Unveiled* 29; *The Secret Doctrine* 29, 32, 36, 61
Bloom, Leopold: and blood 42-3; and cannibalism 39-40, 43, 48; and the circle 57, 182; and death 45-7, 172; and eating 38-9, 41, 43, 48; and excrement 38-9, 47, 140-1, 143, 182; and freedom 26, 60; and Molly 37, 47, 51, 59, 80, 108, 110, 151-2, 159, 181, 182, 188-9, 191, 197; and obituary column 45-9, and the past 54, 56-7, 59,

90-1; and Rudy 150; and sex 40-1, 47, 55, 143, 144, 159-60; and sleep 179-80, 187, 191; and Stephen (*see* Dedalus, Stephen); as animal 7, 83, 150-1, 158, 159-62, 184; as carbon/diamond 151, 180, 191, 197; as comic 78, 79, 82, 140-1, 143-4, 145, 148; as divine 26-7, 66-7, 75, 79, 81-3, 145, 148, 149, 169, 171, 182, 184, 190, 192, 197; as dark crusader 170-1; as masochist 56, 109, 111, 138, 142, 145-6, 151, 158, 160-1, 166; as Noman 45, 47-8, 172; as Odysseus xi, xv, 7, 48, 51, 73, 82, 170, 176; as poet 177; purging of 19, 66, 167, 197; thought process of 5-6, 179. *See also* Bella Cohen, jewishness, scapegoat

Bloom, Molly: and Bloom (*see* Bloom, Leopold); and Stephen Dedalus 109, 174; as earth 22, 37, 177, 183, 188-9; as Nature 168, 170; as vital being 169; form of her monologue xvi-xvii, 182

Bloom, Rudy 150, 173

Boylan, Blazes 110, 149, 152, 159

Brivic, Sheldon 100, 108-10, 111, 113

Browne, Sir Thomas 90, 91

Bruno, Giordano: biography 3-4; influence on the form of *Ulysses* 4-5; on the animal vii-viii, 11-12, 28, 99, 183; on Aristotle 12, 15, 20; on becoming exalted 16, 17; on Circe 18, 19, 68; on the coincidence of contraries 13, 51, 53, 181, 197; on the divine xv, 11-12, 14, 16, 23, 24, 26-7, 53, 66, 73, 100-1, 168, 183, 192; on form and matter 40, 168, 180; on freeing the mind xix, 10; on the limitations of intellect 14-15, 67, 169-70; on the monad nature 16, 18, 168; on the transformation process vii, 4-5, 22-3, 38; on the unity of all things 11-12, 13-14, 52, 59, 178

Budgen, Frank: Joyce's statements to, on Bloom's homosexuality 110; on 'Circe' 32, 51, 157; on Dublin in *Ulysses* 121; on ideas xii; on 'Ithaca' 172; on mind and body 40, 42; on 'Oxen of the Sun' 65; on 'Penelope' 22; on the protean animal 28, 153; on psychoanalysis 106; on Ulysses xv, 194; on words 45; on Yeats's doctrine of magic 62-3

Callan, Nurse (Oxen of the Sun episode) 46, 49, 179

Carlyle, Thomas 84, 91

Carr, Pvt 43, 53, 55, 121, 124, 125, 127-30, 132, 138, 152

castration: as motif in *Ulysses* 104, 108, 110-11, 117, 158-60

catechism: influence of on Joyce 192, 194, 195

catholicism, Roman: Joyce and viii, xi, 3-4, 11, 24, 27, 62, 88, 96, 104-5, 124-5, 157

Circe 18, 19, 47, 50, 51, 55, 68

Circe episode, the xvi, 7, 17, 26, 28, 31, 32, 37, 43, 49, 50-6, 63-6, 71-3, 83, 88-9, 91, 99, 106, 111, 115, 123, 126-8, 137-41, 142-51, 153-60, 163-6, 167, 169, 173, 180, 189, 191, 193, 195, 197

citizen, the (Cyclops episode) 43, 48, 81, 125, 129, 169

Cohen, Bella (Bello) 19, 47, 55-6, 59, 109, 126, 142, 144, 146, 151, 158, 160, 162

coincidence: Joyce and 50, 63, 67, 74, 116-17

coincidence of contraries, the: in Joyce 12-13, 42, 53, 59-60, 63, 89, 168, 191

Coleman (Hades episode) 45-6, 49, 179

comic, the: Joyce and vii, 77-8, 81-3, 86, 87, 91, 101, 121, 125, 135, 136, 137-40, 142, 145, 146, 148, 149, 151, 155, 157-8,

161, 162, 163, 164-7, 186, 190-1, 193, 194, 196, 197
consciousness: of characters in *Ulysses* xiv, xvi-xvii, xviii, 39, 64, 175, 194
Conway, Dante 105, 119, 120, 122
Cope, Jackson 22
Cornford, Francis: *The Origins of Attic Comedy* 149, 196
creation: Joyce and 120-1, 122-3, 125, 135-6, 165, 194, 198
Crews, Frederick 106, 113-14, 119-20, 191; 'Anesthetic Criticism' 113
Critical Writings of James Joyce, The. See James Joyce
Croce, Benedetto 52, 60, 198
Crow, the Reverend Carrion 131-2
Cyclops episode, the xiv, 38, 42-3, 48, 64, 73, 79-83, 129-30, 137, 141, 159, 169, 193

Daedalus 30, 63, 126
Darwin, Charles xix, 88, 90, 96, 98
Deasy, Garrett 30, 34, 53, 184
Dedalus, May 31, 44, 110, 123-4, 131
Dedalus, Simon 19, 74, 75, 126-7, 142
Dedalus, Stephen: and the animal world 31, 126; and his brother 107; and conflict between fixity and change xi-xv, xvi, 16, 22-3, 27, 30, 32, 34, 169, 189; and creation 88-90; and darkness 30, 132; and death 31, 34, 36, 44, 69, 88-90, 124, 125, 128, 131-2, 184; and father figures 71, 108, 126, 195; and freedom 10-11; and Leopold Bloom 50-1, 59, 63, 66, 111, 150, 173; and Molly Bloom (*see* Bloom, Molly); and the nature of the world xiv, 29, 53, 165, 169; and the void xiii, xiv; and women 108; and words 62, 133; anger of 123; as limited 16-18, 26, 53, 55, 67, 75, 78, 98, 126-7, 128-9, 131, 190, 197; as poet 54-5, 176, 187, 189; as younger Joyce 20, 25-6, 32-3, 36, 64, 100, 104, 113; fears of 118, 120-1, 123, 184. *See also* God (Catholic and hangman) and homosexuality
Demiurge, the: Joyce's use of 28, 32, 36, 61, 118, 120, 122, 157, 163, 165
destruction: and connection with creation in *Ulysses* 121-2, 125, 135, 161-2, 165, 190
Diana (goddess) 15-16, 18-19
Dickens, Charles 8, 84, 91
Dignam, Paddy (Hades episode) 38, 40, 45-6, 49, 83, 144
Dionysius the Areopagite 3, 15, 18, 19, 20, 27, 67, 100; *De Mystica Theologia* 24, 30, 66, 192; *The Divine Names* 24, 25
divine, the: Joyce and 10, 12, 14-15, 16, 23, 24, 27, 53, 66, 70, 120, 163, 166, 168, 169, 171, 175, 182, 186, 190, 191, 192, 197
Doyle, Conan 27, 74-5
dream: role of in *Ulysses* 86, 95, 97, 98, 99, 137, 165, 166

Edward VII (king) 42-3, 127, 195
ego, the: Joyce and 100, 114-15, 118-20, 136, 139, 142, 145, 151-2, 154, 161, 166, 191, 195, 198
Ellmann, Richard 7, 52, 63, 99, 109, 133, 135; *The Consciousness of Joyce* 15; *James Joyce* xii, 9, 22, 29, 33, 34, 62-3, 68-70, 78, 95, 102, 103, 116, 119, 121-2, 128, 133, 136, 153, 182, 189, 194; *Ulysses on the Liffey* 42, 44, 60, 127
Erikson, Erik 134
estrangement. *See* alienation
Eumaeus episode xvi, 26, 51-2, 62, 66, 73-6, 167, 180, 192, 196-7

Eve 88-9, 119
evolution: Joyce's conception of xvi, xvii, xviii, 62, 65, 85, 88, 97, 133, 165

fantastic, the: Joyce and 86, 87, 157-8, 161, 164, 186. *See also* the grotesque
Fawcett (Hades episode) 42, 47, 49
Ferenczi, Sandor 98, 99
Finnegans Wake. See James Joyce
Flaubert, Gustave: *Madame Bovary* 131; *The Temptation of St Anthony* xi
form: Joyce and xvi-xvii, 5, 12, 34, 62, 76, 165, 167, 184, 198
Frazer, Sir James 40; *The Golden Bough* 148; *The Scapegoat* 147
French, Marilyn: *The Book as World* 169
Freud, Sigmund vii-viii, xviii-xix, 91, 97-101, 137-8, 145, 151, 153, 166, 175; *A Childhood Memory of Leonardo da Vinci* 95; *The Interpretation of Dreams* 97, 98, 107, 113, 135, 137, 142; *Jokes and Their Relation to the Unconscious* 97, 137, 139, 141-2, 190; *Psychopathology in Everyday Life* xviii, 95, 97, 98

Gifford, Don 90
Gilbert, Stuart xi, 35, 176
glaucoma: Joyce and 68, 69
Glaucus 28, 69-70, 72, 75, 97
Gnosticism 29, 30, 61, 163
God: *abba* 48, 83; ape as curse of 90; as almighty 127; as creator 23, 52, 55, 98, 111, 117, 120, 132, 194; as dark 25, 171, 192; as destroyer 105, 110, 117-18, 121, 123, 127, 132, 194; as dog 31, 125, 181, 184; as eternal perfect animal 21-2, 31; as fish 36, 82; as the goal of history 184; as hangman (*dio boia*) 43, 53, 55, 98, 120, 127; as intellect 14; as Jew 82-3; as light 171; as mystery 149; as shout in the street 53; as sodomite 127-8, 129; as something behind everything 135, 194; as trinity 130; as unknowable 66, 192; as unrevealed 183; as very existence 25; Catholic xviii, 105, 123; honoured by silence 15; in the individual soul viii, 186, 190; in nature 11-12, 44, 52, 73, 82; in the sun 12, 84, 101; Jove (Jupiter) 11, 26, 31; loves everybody 80; man can unite with 24, 53; Zeus 48, 82. *See also* Aeolus, the Demiurge, Glaucus, Hermes, Mercury, Saturnalia
gods, the 11-12, 14, 22, 26, 32, 43, 66, 120, 164
Goldman, Arnold 63, 72-3, 75, 176
Gorman, Herbert xi, 20-1, 22, 29, 99, 102-3
Gregory, Lady Augusta 9; *Gods and Fighting Men* 71
grotesque, the: Joyce and viii, 44, 77, 85, 86-91, 101, 125, 139, 146, 153-8, 161-4, 167, 193. *See also* the fantastic
Gummy Granny (Circe episode) 124, 125, 130-1

Hart, Clive 180
Hayman, David 59, 78, 146, 149-50; *Ulysses: The Mechanics of Meaning* 186
Hermes 28, 50, 51, 60. *See also* Mercury
Hermes Trismegistus 14, 164
Hermetic position, the: Joyce and 12, 14, 16
Herring, Phillip 151; *The Notesheets for Ulysses* 31, 41, 68
Hobgoblin, the (Circe episode) 165-7, 193
Holmes, Sherlock 74-5
Homer 7, 50, 67, 68-9, 96; *The Odyssey* 31, 34, 39, 48, 51, 62, 65, 68, 69
homosexuality: Joyce and 103-4, 106-7, 108-10, 125-8, 129-30, 132, 153, 174

Howth, Ben 47-8, 59, 63, 141
Hugo, Victor: *L'Homme Qui Rit* 163
Huizinga, Johan: *Homo Ludens* 196
Hyde, Douglas: *Literary History of Ireland* 71

Iago 55, 193
Ibsen, Henrik xix, 8, 20, 31
Icarus 54, 120
id, the: Joyce and 100, 136, 139, 145, 151, 158, 166
imagination, the: Joyce and xii, 7, 23, 58, 64, 65, 118, 133, 183, 187
intellect, the: Joyce and xv, 26, 30, 32, 64, 66, 67, 95-7, 123-4, 127, 140, 169-70, 176, 196-7
Ireneous 29, 163
Irving, Washington: 'Rip Van Winkle' 56
Ithaca episode, the xiii, xvi, 47, 49, 51, 57, 91, 115, 149, 151, 167, 168, 169-71, 172-84, 186, 188-92, 195-8

Jennings, Lee Byron: *The Ludicrous Demon* 193
Jesus Christ 26-7, 28, 35-6, 41, 43, 74-5, 82, 83, 105, 130, 135, 148, 157, 169, 171, 182
Jewishness: Joyce and 30, 32, 95, 105, 148, 157, 169, 171, 184
Joachim of Floris 10
John of the Cross, St 30
joke, the: Joyce and 28, 81-2, 112, 136, 137-8, 140-1, 142, 144, 165, 184, 192-3
Jones, Ernest 95, 107; *The Problem of Hamlet and the Oedipus Conflict* 96
Joyce, Eva 33
Joyce, James: biographical information on xi, 3-4, 8-10, 23-4, 64, 68, 75, 102-6, 116-17, 119, 122, 128-9, 133-4, 135-6, 194-5. *See also* entries relating to Joyce's concepts and attitudes
WORKS
– *Critical Writings of James Joyce, The* 9, 17, 22, 23, 24, 32, 77, 79, 133, 173, 175, 183, 192
– 'Day of the Rabblement, The' 4
– 'Drama and Life' xviii, 79, 186
– *Dubliners*: 'A Painful Case' 106; 'The Sisters' 62
– *Exiles* 103, 109
– *Finnegans Wake* xii, 27, 31, 36, 42, 61, 89, 118, 121, 133, 139, 168, 185, 194
– 'Holy Office, The' 9, 16, 133-4
– letters xvii, 37, 51, 65, 116, 135, 172, 194, 195
– 'Paris Notebook' viii, 62, 192
– 'Portrait of the Artist' 9-10, 16, 22, 121
– *Portrait of the Artist as a Young Man, A* xiv, 9, 16-17, 23, 25, 32-3, 35, 64, 67, 81, 112, 118, 133, 176, 187, 189
– *Ulysses*: conception and composition of xi, 5, 27-9, 31-3, 40-2, 44, 50-2, 54-5, 58, 60-5, 68-72, 84, 88, 96, 98, 106-7, 121-2, 128, 132-6, 141-2, 149-51, 154, 157, 161, 164-7, 172-3, 175, 186-8, 192-3, 194-8; episodes: Aeolus 25, 51; Hades 38, 44; Lestrygonians xiv, 38, 39, 41, 42; Nausicaa xiv, 5, 47; Penelope xvi, xvii, 167-70, 182, 192; Scylla and Charybdis xi, xii-xiii, 20, 107, 112; Sirens xiv, 5, 68, 139; Telemachus 50; Wandering Rocks 120. *See also* Circe, Cyclops, Eumaeus, Ithaca, Oxen of the Sun, Proteus episodes
– *Workshop of Dedalus, The* 16, 22, 30, 31, 62, 121, 189, 192, 197
Joyce, John 105, 106
Joyce, Mary 103-4, 105, 106

Joyce, Nora Barnacle 33, 34-5, 99, 102-3, 108, 113
Joyce, Stanislaus 33, 103, 110, 119, 135; *Dublin Diary* 105-6; *My Brother's Keeper* 62, 104, 105, 106, 122
Jung, C.G. 114

Kayser, Wolfgang 87, 88, 153, 155, 161, 162; *The Grotesque in Art and Literature* 86, 154
Keats, John 114, 191
Kenner, Hugh 41, 74-5; *Dublin's Joyce* 41, 74
kinetic response, the: Joyce and 176-8
Krafft-Ebing, Richard von 108
Kris, Ernst 78-9, 118, 120-2, 135, 144, 158, 165, 190, 196; *Psychoanalytic Explorations in Art* 117, 161

Lawrence, D.H. 100
Loerisch, Rolf 139
Lowry (Hades episode) 45-6, 49
Lucifer. *See* Satan
Luther, Martin 134
Lynch, Vincent 32-3, 44, 53, 55, 125

McIntyre, Lewis 52, 59, 66-7, 168, 178, 180-1; *Giordano Bruno* 23-4
Maclir, Mananaan 70-2, 164-5
Madtes, Richard 181
magic: Joyce and 12, 62-4, 116-18
magus, the: as conceived by Joyce and Bruno 10-11
Malory, Sir Thomas 84, 88
Mary, the Virgin 88-9, 130, 157
Menelaus 31, 70
Mercanton, Jacques 58, 61-2, 64, 102, 192
Mercury 26, 28, 50-1. *See also* Hermes
metamorphosis: in *Ulysses* 7, 28, 35, 85, 90, 150-1, 154, 165, 179, 198. *See also* transformation
Momus: in Bruno's *The Expulsion of the Triumphant Beast* 11, 28
Morpheus 27-8, 75, 179
Moses 58, 63, 171, 182, 184
Mulligan, Buck 31, 33-4, 50-1, 107, 131-3, 145
mummery: Joyce and 28, 31, 147, 151
Murphy (Eumaeus episode) 27, 73-5, 179, 180, 182
mysticism: Joyce and 10, 20, 24, 173, 198

nature: 5, 16, 18, 21-3, 29, 38, 44-5, 62, 125, 165, 168-9, 170, 182
Naumann (Hades episode) 45, 47-8, 49
Nicholas of Cusa: *Of Learned Ignorance* 15
Nighttown scene, the 7, 19, 50, 78, 91, 128, 154, 166. *See also* Circe episode
Noah 126, 127

Odysseus xi, 18, 26, 32, 39, 48, 51, 63, 68-9, 73, 82, 84-5, 151, 168, 170, 174, 194
Oedipus complex, the: Joyce and 107, 110-11, 120
O'Molloy, J.J. 58, 63, 144, 171
Ormand Bar, the 5, 19, 60
Ovid 5-6, 38, 72, 96, 126; *Metamorphoses* 3, 6, 14, 69
Oxen of the Sun episode, the xvi, 44, 65, 73, 84-91, 125, 127, 131, 135, 171

pantomime: Joyce and 149-51, 163, 179
parody: Joyce and 65, 79, 84, 87, 90, 130, 135, 163
Parnell, Charles 117
pastiche: Joyce's use of 65, 84, 87, 91, 135
Pater, Walter: 91; *The Renaissance* xii
Peake (Hades episode) 45, 47-9, 63

perversity: Joyce and 111, 118, 123, 138, 143, 145, 151, 154, 189, 192-3, 194

Plato xi, xii, 20-1; and the Platonic 4, 12, 24-5, 67; *The Republic* 12, 70; *The Symposium* 126

poet, the: Joyce's conception of xvi, 16, 177, 196-7. *See also* the artist

Portrait of the Artist as a Young Man, A. See James Joyce

Prometheus 117

protean, the: Joyce and 28, 31-2, 35-6, 68, 71-2, 73, 97, 196

Proteus episode, the xiv, 27, 29, 31-2, 33, 44, 61, 67, 117, 120, 125

psychoanalysis. *See* Brivic, Crews, Erikson, Freud, Jones, Jung, Kris, Loerisch, Shechner, Steig

punishment: Joyce and 55, 104-5, 117-20, 122-3, 129-30, 131, 147-8, 151. *See also* sado-masochism

Purefoy, Mrs Mina (Oxen of the Sun and Circe episodes) 46, 124-5

Pythagoras 14, 15, 38

rebus: in *Ulysses* 11-12, 31, 73-4. *See also* riddle

reduction: as literary device in *Ulysses* 157, 172, 180, 183, 186, 191, 192

regression: Joyce and 97, 118, 135, 139-41, 146, 152, 155, 159, 165, 179, 183, 189, 190

return motif, the: in *Ulysses* 52, 54, 56, 57, 59-60

riddle, the: in *Ulysses* 51, 144, 174, 196. *See rebus*

Rowan, Bertha 109-10

Rowan, Richard 109-10, 174

Russell, George W. (A.E.) 9, 29, 71-2, 164-5, 183

Sacher-Masoch, Leopold von: *Venus in Furs* 108

sado-masochism: Joyce and 108-9, 119, 120, 129-30, 138, 142, 146, 151, 160, 166. *See also* punishment

Satan 30, 118, 119, 120, 122-3

Saturnalia 147, 161

scapegoat, the: in *Ulysses* 146, 147-8, 158, 162-3. *See also* victim

Schutte, William 55, 120; *Joyce and Shakespeare* 107

sex: Joyce and 40-1, 47, 59, 81, 84, 100, 103, 106, 107-13, 122-3, 127-8, 130, 134, 138-9, 142-5, 156, 159-61, 167, 184, 191

Sexton (Hades episode) 45-6, 49, 179

Sinbad 75, 151, 179-80, 190, 191

Shakespeare, William 5, 7, 17, 22, 27, 52-3, 59, 76, 163, 173, 179, 197; *Cymbeline* 55; *Hamlet* 5-6, 56, 61, 107, 112, 131; *King Lear* 71; *Othello* 55; *The Taming of the Shrew* 112; *The Tempest* 69; *Venus and Adonis* 108

Shaw, G.B. 8

Shechner, Mark 100, 106, 111-13

Shelley, P.B. 23, 133

Socrates 53, 126

spiritual, the: Joyce and vii, xix, 10-11, 23, 36, 40, 49, 88, 100, 133, 165, 175, 178, 181, 184, 187

Steig, Michael 157-8, 161, 166, 193; 'Defining the Grotesque ...' 157

Stekel, Wilhelm 119

Stephens, James (author) 116-17, 122; *Dierdre* 117

Stephens, James (Fenian) 116-17

sublimation: Joyce and 172, 175, 183, 186, 189, 191, 197

Sultan, Stanley 48, 53, 82, 108-9, 111, 120, 179, 182

super-ego, the: Joyce and 100, 123, 135, 136, 138, 142, 144-5, 151, 158, 161, 166, 190. *See also* punishment
Swedenborg, Emanuel 173, 175, 197
Swift, Jonathan 87; *A Tale of a Tub* 84
Synge, J.M. 87; *Riders to the Sea* 131; *In the Shadow of the Glen* 131
Sypher, Wylie 81

theosophy: Joyce and 29, 164-5
Thornton, Weldon 28, 29, 48, 50, 52, 70, 71, 83, 117, 120, 130-1, 148, 163, 164; *Allusions in Ulysses* 126
Tindall, W.Y. 4, 140; *A Reader's Guide to James Joyce* 141
tragedy: Joyce and viii, 77, 78, 101, 135, 163, 191, 196-7
transformation:
– cycles, in *Ulysses* 5, 34, 35-6, 38-9, 42-3, 44-5, 45-9, 52, 57, 64, 82, 90, 101, 115, 179, 180, 183, 187, 189, 198
– process, in *Ulysses* vii, 4-7, 25, 28, 34-6, 40-2, 51-2, 62, 64-5, 69-70, 72, 85, 91, 96, 114, 162. *See also* metamorphosis

Ulysses, the character. *See* Odysseus
Ulysses. See James Joyce
unconscious, the: Joyce and xviii, 39, 97, 105, 108, 113, 123, 139, 151, 153, 161-2, 174, 189, 190, 197
unmasking, the, of Bloom 141, 144, 146
Urbright (Hades episode) 45, 48, 49, 179

Vance, Eileen 119
Vance, Mr (character in epiphany by Joyce) 103-4
Vico, Giambattista xii, 60, 96
victim, the: Joyce and 125, 127, 148-9, 151, 161. *See also* scapegoat
Virag, Lipoti 28, 59, 66, 155-7
Voelker, Joseph 168, 170
void, the: Joyce and xiii-xiv, 169, 175, 188, 192

Walpole, Horace: *The Castle of Otranto* 87
Weaver, Harriet 65, 116, 195
will, the: Joyce and xvi-xix 7, 56
Winkle, Rip Van 56, 170, 179
words: Joyce and xvi-xvii, 45, 62-3, 133-4, 139-40, 151, 172, 178, 189, 198
Workshop of Dedalus, The. See James Joyce

Yates, Frances 10, 14
Yeats, W.B. xii, 62, 71-2, 128, 196; 'Lapis Lazuli' 191; 'The Tables of the Law' 9; *The Wanderings of Oisin* 71

zodiac, the: Joyce and 11, 22
Zoe (prostitute in Circe episode) 109, 144, 146